*Beyond the Rainbow* tells the spiritual journey of Aubrey Rose, son of immigrants, who became adviser to governments and Prime Ministers.

Honoured with OBE, CBE and honorary doctorate, the writer held significant public, communal and international offices, worked enthusiastically as environmentalist, lawyer, author, interfaith leader, human rights activist, gardener, humorist and seeker into the world of the spirit.

For more details visit *www.aubreyrose.org.uk*

Previous books by Aubrey Rose
*Journey Into Immortality*
*Judaism and Ecology*
*Brief Encounters of a Legal Kind*
*Letters To My Wife*
*The Rainbow Never Ends*
*Sea Olympics*
*Jewish Communities of the Commonwealth*
*Arieh Handler – Modest Jewish Hero*

Edited by Aubrey Rose
*Vera* (Life of Vera Chesno)
*From Bitter Came Sweet* (Life of Ruth Grant)

## DEDICATION

To all who have helped me with their thoughts and hopes, here and beyond, and particularly to David.

Our birth is but a sleep and a forgetting:
The Soul that rises with us, our life's Star,
Hath had elsewhere its setting,
And cometh from afar:
Not in entire forgetfulness,
And not in utter nakedness,
But trailing clouds of glory do we come
From God, who is our home:
Heaven lies about us in our infancy!

Our Souls have sight of that immortal sea
Which brought us hither,
Can in a moment travel thither,
And see the Children sport upon the shore,
And hear the mighty waters rolling evermore.

**William Wordsworth (1770-1850)**
*Ode: Intimations of Immortality*
*from Recollections of Early Childhood*

Man has no Body distinct from his soul:
For that call'd Body is a portion of the
Soul discern'd by the five Senses, the
chief inlets of Soul in this age.
Energy is the only life, and is from the
Body; and Reason is the bound or
outward circumference of Energy.
Energy is Eternal Delight.

**William Blake (1757-1827)**
*The Marriage of Heaven and Hell*

I am not sorry to have lived, since the course of my life has encouraged me to believe that I have lived to some purpose. But what nature gave us is a place to dwell in temporarily, not to make one's own. When I leave life, therefore, I shall feel as if I am leaving a hostel rather than a home. What a great day it will be when I set out to join that divine assemblage and concourse of souls and depart from the confusion and corruption of this world!
I shall be going to meet not only all those of whom I have spoken, but also my own son. No better, no more devoted man, was ever born.
He should have cremated my body but I had to cremate his.
Yet, his soul has not gone from me, but looks back and fastens upon me its regard, and the destination to which that soul has departed is surely the place where it knew that I too must come.
To the world I have seemed to bear my loss bravely.
That does not mean that I found it easy to bear, but I comforted myself with the belief that our parting and separation would be of short duration.

**Cicero (106-43 BC)**
*On Old Age*

*To Mike
With many many
thanks.
June 2016   Aubrey*

# BEYOND THE RAINBOW

## The spiritual autobiography of
## AUBREY ROSE

'My heart leaps up when I behold a rainbow in the sky'

William Wordsworth

Companion book to
*The Rainbow Never Ends*

*Lennard Publishing*

Published in 2015 by
Lennard Publishing
a division of
Lennard Associates Ltd
Mackerye End, Harpenden
Herts AL5 5DR

©Aubrey Rose 2015

The right of Aubrey Rose to be identified as the author of this work has been asserted in accordance with the Copyright Designs and Patents Act 1988.

All rights reserved. No part of this publication may be reproduced, stored in a retrieval system, or transmitted, in any form or by any means, without the prior permission in writing of the publisher, nor be otherwise circulated in any form of binding or cover other than that in which it is published without similar condition including this condition being imposed on the subsequent purchaser.

A catalogue entry is available from the British Library.

ISBN 978-1-85291-159-1

Cover design by www.designbycaroline.co.uk

## ACKNOWLEDGEMENTS

My grateful thanks to my publisher Adrian Stephenson for his understanding and courage, and also to Chris Smith, Caroline Sloneem, Steve Sharpe, Harry Luck, Mike Sellar, Heather Allan, Mike Cowan, Georgina Oliver, Kirsty Ennever, Howard Cooke and Ray Branch for all their helpful advice and suggestions.

My grateful thanks also to all those who have given permission to quote from their copyright material, including *Two Worlds*, Tony Ortzen, Alan Ross and Ross Publications. Every effort has been made to obtain other permissions.

Printed in Great Britain by CMP (UK) Ltd, Poole, Dorset

# Contents

| | |
|---|---|
| Foreword | 9 |
| Guide to *Beyond the Rainbow* | 10 |

**PART I**

| | |
|---|---|
| Introduction | 11 |
| Voices | 15 |

**PART II**

| | |
|---|---|
| Introduction | 19 |
| The World of Leslie Flint | 20 |
| Strike a Happy Medium | 27 |
| Physician, Heal Thyself ... | 29 |
| Virène – Mother and Daughter | 34 |
| Sai Ram – Sai Baba | 38 |
| Knight and Ray – or Oliver and Raymond | 42 |
| Rescue – Michael Evans | 45 |
| The Chinese Dimension | 48 |
| Brief Encounters | 51 |
| Four Legs, Two Legs | 55 |
| Faith and Hope Eternal | 59 |
| Sir Arthur Conan Doyle | 61 |
| Jesus | 63 |
| Sacks and Dawkins | 66 |

**PART III**

| | |
|---|---|
| Introduction | 71 |
| The Creative Spirit – Whence Does It Come? | 72 |
| Cancer – A Theory | 90 |
| The Habirus of Outer Space | 100 |
| Jesus the Jew | 109 |
| Articles from *Two Worlds* | 112 |
|    Leading Lawyer Backs Case for Afterlife | 112 |
|    Suicide Bombers and the Beyond | 115 |
|    It Could Happen to You | 117 |

|  |  |
|---|---|
| The Mission – A Metaphysical Fantasy | 121 |
| The Dunblane Tragedy | 140 |
| Articles by Michael Evans | 142 |
|     What Have Spiritualists Done for Society? | 142 |
|     Alfred Russel Wallace: Scientist and Spiritualist | 146 |
|     The Scientist's Dilemma | 150 |

## PART IV

|  |  |
|---|---|
| More Voices | 153 |
| The World of Leslie Flint | 154 |
| Sir Oliver Lodge and Raymond Smith | 156 |
| Sir Arthur Conan Doyle | 161 |
| Sai Baba | 169 |
| Douglas Conacher | 173 |
| Virène – Mother and Daughter | 177 |
| Jesus | 181 |

## PART V

|  |  |
|---|---|
| Religious Rituals: What They Do and Don't Do | 185 |
| The Failure of Religion | 188 |
| Scientific Recognition: The Key to Spiritual Progress | 192 |

## A FINAL WORD    197

## APPENDICES

|  |  |
|---|---|
| Author's Postscript | 201 |
| My Religious Experiences | 202 |
| Author's Postscript (continued) | 216 |
| List of Books | 220 |

## INDEX    224

# Foreword

I pen these words with great pleasure. Aubrey has set out his innermost thoughts, feelings and experiences in the world of the spirit and he has done so with rare clarity and honesty.

It will not be easy for everyone to accept his conclusions but, having myself spent many decades in the world of spiritual healing, I can confirm the truth of his words. There is so much more to reality than we think.

I congratulate him on this new Rainbow book. May its manifold colours bring to readers a deeper perception of the worlds around us and within us.

**Ramus Branch**

*Ramus (Ray) Branch, with his wife Jo, has spent much of his life assisting the famous healer Harry Edwards, whose biography he has written.*

## GUIDE TO *BEYOND THE RAINBOW*

I do believe the book to be all of a piece – at least I hope so – even though it contains five separate sections. May I give you a brief guide to each:

### Part I
Really a kind of introduction, though it comments on the views of those antagonistic to religion, usually scientists, and those who just think that religion is irrelevant, usually Humanists. Included too are relevant quotations from the great and the good.

### Part II
Describes my own experiences in the world of communication with those who have departed this earthly life as well as the extraordinary story of spiritual healing.

### Part III
Is a modest exercise in immodesty. The section includes speeches and articles of mine, and of others, that I believe are relevant, autobiographical, and descriptive of the evolutionary growth of experience. I am still learning. There is so much I don't know.

### Part IV
Harks back to Part II, providing the actual words of the remarkable beings referred to in that section. Some of the expressions are quite wonderful.

### Part V
Looks at patterns within religions, the failure of religion, and offers a challenge to the men and women of science.

I wish you well as you delve into what follows.

# PART I

## INTRODUCTION

I recall a particular incident in my career. As a lawyer for a Commonwealth government, I was invited to a small dinner at the Foreign Office in honour of a departing High Commissioner. I don't know if this practice is still followed with fifty-three Commonwealth countries now. I doubt it. We were about a dozen guests enjoying the bounty of Her Majesty's Government. The conversation entered into the realms of philosophy. One luminary held forth: 'Nothing is absolute. Everything is relative. There is nothing absolute in the world, in society, in mankind. All is relative.'

We shuffled in our seats. Why disturb a pleasant meal with ideas unrelated to the event? The fellow was going on and on so I thought I would redeem the situation somewhat. Innocently, I asked him: 'Are you absolutely sure?' A look of complete bewilderment; he sank back into his seat, quietly, and dinner proceeded happily.

In a way, that's what this book is all about. Is there anything absolute, permanent, eternal, or is everything transient, changing, relative? I have enjoyed a busy career as a London lawyer, representing the great and the good, the less great and the less good. Alongside this I have been caught up in all manner of local, communal, national and international organisations, described in my previous book *The Rainbow Never Ends*. Many thought it worth reading. You may do too.

And yet, with all this physical and professional activity, I was at the same time engaged in a search for truth, for reality, even from my teens. My Jewish parents had come to England from East Europe, father in 1897, mother in 1902, to escape the poverty, persecution and pogroms committed in the name of another Jew. I grew up in a kind of London East End ghetto, full of the fasts, feasts, festivals, age-old rituals and beliefs of that religion. Yet I always looked beyond one single faith. My father was an upright, hard-working, and supremely honest tailor. My mother, ever-cherished for being loving and totally non-possessive, used to teach me that, 'no one is superior to you and no one inferior'. No wonder I got involved later in race and community relations.

I was eager to know about other faiths. Aged sixteen I used to wander down to Conway Hall in Holborn where on Sunday mornings the South Place Ethical Society held its Humanist services. No God was involved, unlike my own tradition which is God-obsessed.

At school my friends and I were full of Jeans and Eddington, astronomers and scientists, fascinated by the former's allusion to the universe as a 'great idea'. A few of us wandered the streets until late at night pondering on what was true or false. The others went on to have scientific careers. At the age of seventeen I sat down and wrote a small book entitled My Religious Experiences. Heaven knows what experiences I could have had at such an age!

Some attractive girls in our class invited me along to a local Church of England church. They were struck by the dynamic young vicar: I was more struck by the girls. However, I imbibed quite a lot of the Christian ritual and hymns and became an advocate of the cause of Jesus. My mother said he was a good man who suffered because of orthodoxy. Maybe she was right. My mother was usually right.

There followed a period in the Army, which dampened any religious enthusiasm I might have had. My legal apprenticeship finished in the City of London, not far from St Paul's Cathedral. Little did I suspect then that in later years my friend, Wilfred Wood, would become the first black bishop in the Church of England. He invited me to attend the ceremony in the Cathedral, adjuring me to keep an eye on a special guest of his, the son of Martin Luther King.

And so it went on throughout my strange life: I always seemed to touch religion of all kinds in one way or another, and yet also non-religions. For example, in 1979 I was invited to a ceremony in Paris, to receive a certificate as an 'Ambassador for Islam'; at about that time I also created, with a leading Hindu, an Indian-Jewish Association; and I became Patron, with the Archbishop of Canterbury, of over 200,000 Christians in Britain in The New Assembly of Churches.

As a Commissioner for Oaths, people swore legitimately in front of me. (They probably also swore behind me.) I got paid, pitifully, for this service. One day I had to administer an oath to the Council of the Humanist Society, so in my innocence I took along copies of the Old and New Testaments, usually used in the process. The enlightened and learned group, professors included, looked at me askance. 'We don't need any of those books, we will affirm', they said, and affirm they did. I later studied Humanist literature in some depth, all very sensible indeed but without the need for anything beyond ourselves. Such a view was a long way from my own upbringing.

Even further away from it is the prevailing mood in this new millennium that excludes God completely, as being irrelevant to reality. An erudite, brilliant, sincere professor called Richard Dawkins has expounded the view that belief in God was 'a delusion'. There was no God. I read his book, which performed a service in that it provoked much thought amongst religions. Then I read all the counter-arguments, especially those of the religious, but even the opinions of scientists, too. During this process I turned to a favourite tome of mine, *100 Famous Scientists*. I was fascinated by the number amongst them who actually support both the reality of God and the value of religion.

But Richard Dawkins, and even more so, brave but afflicted Stephen Hawking, had set the world thinking – at least the free, open-minded world, in which I include myself. However, alongside my busy, practical life of profession and organisations, decade after decade, I had come face-to-face with unusual experiences that did not accord with the conclusions of Dawkins, the Humanists or the atheists.

But the question remained. Who would believe me if I set out these experiences in yet another book? I had already touched, albeit briefly, on those experiences in two previous books, *Journey Into Immortality* and *The Rainbow Never Ends*. I am no scientist, yet my career has been based on the strength of evidence, the sine qua non of scientific analysis. Scientists of all kinds have achieved wonders for the world, but their work has always been based on empirical study. They have transformed society, as religion had done in former times. Would they, could they, possibly accept my own claims at face value? Was the challenge to their training, their assumptions, their mindset, too much for them to accept?

Yet I recalled that the theory of evolution by natural selection was made public in 1858 by two great men, Charles Darwin, unhappy about religious claims, and Alfred Russel Wallace, a man who believed without doubt in the reality of the world of the spirit. Incidentally, I loved Disraeli's comment: 'We are now asked whether we came from the apes or the angels. For myself, I am on the side of the angels.' One can almost hear Gladstone grinding his teeth.

When someone handed me a copy of the Universal Declaration of Human Rights, I noted particularly its declaration that 'Everyone has the right to freedom of thought, conscience and religion and the right to change his religion or belief.' With this in mind, I launched myself into the world of books. I have one room at home in which desks and bookcases stagger and groan under the weight of books that I have read and consulted. (A list of some of them is appended at the end of this volume.)

What struck me forcibly is the limited role reason plays in human affairs. The scientists and the humanists sought reason in support of their views, but reason plays little part in the affairs of the world. A glance at past and current history confirms the intense power of emotion, of ritual, of belief, of ambition, of material gain – all of far greater influence than weak reason. Get a (literally) reasonable man like Socrates, and he is despatched. The same applies to Bruno, extinguished by the church who also persecuted the great Galileo. Even profound Spinoza was excluded from his community.

In maintaining world peace, religion has been a failure, as I will describe later. Yet religion survives because it satisfies needs, the need for an explanation of how and why we are here, for a sense of security, and of identity, for companionship, for moral teachings and an outlet for promoting moral causes, for rituals, for music and the creative arts. One should never underestimate the immense and powerful hold religions, and their rituals and rules, exert on the mind of adherents.

Whatever the underlying truth or myth may be, these thoughts led me to put pen to paper to produce the book you are now reading, and which I hope you continue to read. For indeed, I believe you may find things within its pages that you never thought possible. Once you have read it all you may still shake your head in disbelief, and wonder what kind of a fellow I am. But I wish you good luck, and patience, as you read on. Do please read on. It is not a big book and is divided into separate parts for ease of assimilation. You will come across some of the most extraordinary individuals in modern history, of whom you may never even have heard. I am now in your hands.

## Voices

Before putting before you particular evidence as to matters of the spirit based on my experiences and the many books I have read, I thought it might be useful to note a few thoughts of some of the great figures of history and of science.

I actually waded through an entire book on quantum theory. As I wandered through waves, particles, electrons, photons, certainty, uncertainty, I came across the following statement. Make of it what you will.

'In spite of local appearance of phenomena, our world is actually supported by an invisible reality which is unmediated and allows communication faster than light, even instantaneously.'

I hope to present to you with much evidence in support of that assertion. Now for the quotations.

> The love of truth is not entertaining any proposition with greater assurance than the proof it is built upon will warrant.
> *John Locke*

> Humanism is the belief of those who insist on the right to test their doubts, who want to be informed of the choices open to them and to choose freely for themselves.
> *Kit Mouat*

> My religion is to do good.
> *Thomas Paine*

> If there were no God it would be necessary to invent him.
> *Voltaire*

> Fix reason firmly in her seat, and call to her tribunal every fact, every opinion. Question with boldness even the existence of God.
> *Thomas Jefferson*

> Humanism in all its simplicity is the only genuine spirituality.
> *Albert Schweitzer*

It is important that no supernatural reasons are needed to make men kind and to prove that only through kindness can the human race achieve happiness.
*Bertrand Russell*

There is no absolute knowledge. All information is imperfect. We have to treat it with humility. That is the human condition, and that is what Quantum Physics says. I mean that literally. The world cannot be separated from our perception of it. No events can be described with certainty. All knowledge is limited. Every judgment in science stands on the edge of error.
*Dr Jacob Bronowski*

My karma has run over my dogma.
*Graffiti on a London wall*

God does not play dice with the Universe.
*Albert Einstein*
To which *Niels Bohr* is reputed to have responded:
'Stop telling God what to do!'

In other words, a man's ethical behaviour should be based on sympathy, education and social ties. No religious basis is necessary.

*Einstein* adds:
A knowledge of something we cannot penetrate, of the manifestations of the profoundest reason and the most radiant beauty which are only accessible to our reason in their most elementary forms. It is this knowledge and this emotion that constitute the truly religious attitude. In this sense, and in this alone, I am a deeply religious man.

He also added:
Imagination is more important than knowledge.

I believe in one God and no more and I hope for happiness beyond this life.
*Thomas Paine*

I may say that the impossibility of conceiving that this grand and wondrous universe, with our conscious selves, arose through chance, seems to me the chief argument for the existence of God but whether this is an argument of real value I have never been able to decide. The safest conclusion seems to be that the whole subject is beyond the scope of man's intellect though the theory of evolution is quite compatible with the belief in a God.
*Charles Darwin*

By setting mankind apart from the rest of creating, Western Humanism has deprived it of a safeguard. The moment man knows no limit to his power, he sets about destroying himself.
*Claude Levi-Strauss*

All organised religion is institutionalised delusion, shared muddle and derisive savage tribalism.
*Lynn Margulis*
(biologist)

My views are in head-on contradiction to the religious beliefs of billions of human beings alive today.
*Francis Crick*
(co-discoverer of the structure of the DNA molecule)

This marvellous world could not possibly be a stage so that God can watch human beings struggle for good and evil which is the view that religion has. The stage is too big for the drama.
*Richard Feynman*

Incidentally, J.J. Thomson, discoverer of the electron, was a devout Anglican who prayed daily.

The idea of a universal mind would be a fairly plausible inference from the present state of scientific theory. Science cannot tell whether the world spirit is good or evil.
*Sir Arthur Eddington*

In the eighth century BC, in the heart of a world of idolatrous polytheists, the Hebrew prophets put forth a conception of religion which appears to be as wonderful an inspiration of genius as the art of Pheidias or the science of Aristotle.
*Thomas Henry Huxley*

You don't write melodies. You find them.
*Hoagy Carmichael*

# PART II

## INTRODUCTION

Scientists sometimes talk about parallel universes. I know what they mean. I have lived in such a state for years. At the same time as helping to establish the National Lottery, defending a capital case in the Old Bailey or appearing as an advocate at the famous Scarman Inquiry into the 1980 Brixton riots, I was also deeply enmeshed in the phenomena of communication between two worlds or the seeming miracles of spiritual healing. Some of the latter I did in my office. I was the senior partner. I would lock my door, and my gifted partners never had an inkling of what was going on behind it.

As time progressed, my experiences, legal and spiritual, widened, from the late 1970s until the present day. On 7th June 2011, I received a glorious looking certificate from the President of The Law Society, congratulating me for being on the Roll of Solicitors for sixty years! Strange, I don't feel very different even now from the enthusiastic young lawyer of 1951, but my body brings me up sharp and reminds me of what I can and cannot do. Yet during the last thirty years significant things have happened to me, people have entered and left and extraordinary events have occurred, some delightful, others sad: all of this makes up that strange mixture we call life. What this part of the book tries to do is to reflect my contact with unusual and remarkable people who enriched my experiences and my perception. You don't have to believe all you read but I do assure you that I am an honest reporter and tell it like it is, or was. So here goes.

AUBREY ROSE

## THE WORLD OF LESLIE FLINT

Leslie Flint came of good working-class stock. His family had little, worked hard, and shared the problems of the 'have-nots' during the years between the two World Wars of the twentieth century. To that extent Leslie and I shared a similar background, both of us living in the London area, and not the best parts. I had one big advantage – the educational drive that pervaded the Jewish world into which I was born, as well as the absence of any class consciousness in our community.

Yet, despite coming from a disadvantaged background, Leslie achieved international fame. People came to him from all over the world, though he himself never quite got over his lack of formal education. That did not matter. Strangely, for one born into a family that had to scrimp and save to scrape a living, he had no real idea of the value of money. Perhaps that was just as well, as his special gifts took others into realms far beyond the material. The question is, how did I ever make contact with such a man? I had long been ensconced in the English world, while my parents, immigrants from Eastern Europe, came from a vastly different tradition and history.

So how did we meet? Well we met because our son, David, died on 5th July 1978, aged twenty-one. He was our eldest child, full of creative gifts, mature beyond his years, sensitive to reality, full of friendship and good humour, with a future glowing with promise.

Like other parents, especially more recently those whose offspring have been suddenly taken from them by hate-filled terrorists, my wife, Sheila, and I were devastated by our loss, yet strangely inspired by David's steadiness in the face of an inoperable cancer.

A month after David's departure I was in the home of a friend, a remarkable woman, whose voice could be heard in some of the James Bond films emanating from the silent lips of the beautiful leading ladies. This voice-over actress was studying law, as was her friend who was helping with the washing-up. The friend casually mentioned a relative of hers who happened to have a tape-recording of the voice of the famous English judge, the late Lord Birkett, a noted public lecturer. I expressed an interest in hearing this, in view of my legal background. Not long afterwards, I went to the relative's house in Kingston, a Thameside town in Surrey, where I sat and listened as the uncle, a pleasant, retired civil servant, played a tape in which the judge expressed his views with that distinctive clarity for which he was famous: 'When I was on your side I supported the death penalty, but now that I am here I am against such an act'.

'Now that I am here'! What did he mean? Where was he?

The uncle explained that physical death was just that, death of the body, but not the end of the essential being, the real person. There was an element within us that survives the death of the body. I was not unaware of this idea from my knowledge of various religions, but only in general terms. Survival of the soul was mentioned often, and it seemed a possibility but, like the world in general, I just nodded and hoped all would be well. I had no particular experience. But then Leslie Flint came into my life.

The Kingston relative went on to explain that there was this man Flint who sat in darkness with small groups of people, perhaps eight or ten, and suddenly out of thin air, came voices which all present could hear. I was invited to attend one of these gatherings. Some time later, as I sat in an old house in Bayswater, West London, in complete silence and bereft of light, I was amazed to hear voices, talking naturally, both men and women, addressing those present.

The voices stated who they were and their relationship to the various members of the assembled group, as well as dealing with the concerns of those of us who sat there in a conventional manner, totally without any sense of religious holiness. Clearly the speakers were still much the same as they had been before death but with a wider vision.

I was quite entranced by what was happening. Then, out of the blue, came a voice: 'I am David, I am well, I am all right.' It sounded so natural, so right. That was all that emerged for me, but Leslie, and his assistant friend Bram Rogers, were happy that I had received a message from our son. This was the beginning of an extraordinary set of experiences and relationships that continued over many years.

After this first contact with David, I rushed home. My wife, immensely practical, could not believe that what had occurred was genuine. There had to be another explanation. Why did we sit in the dark? What prior knowledge did Leslie have of me? And so on. However, loving soul that she was, she agreed to join me at another sitting. As the lights were turned off, and the voices came, she gripped my hand tightly, and sat tensely. David spoke, a few more words on this occasion. We were told not to worry, he was well, somehow he had known his time with us was up, and that he had met many family members we had not previously mentioned to him.

Back home, in the brightness of broad daylight, my wife pondered on our strange experience. Sheila's mother was a strong character, who spoke her mind clearly, a woman with a large personality, and a love of material things, but also one who had a deep love for David, her first grandchild. In no way could she accept the truth, the reality, of what we related to her. There just had to be some other explanation. Reluctantly, though, she agreed to join us on our next visit to Leslie Flint.

So again with a small group, we sat and waited. Grandma, as she was known to all, but sometimes also as 'The Duchess' in view of her imperial presence, heard voice after voice describing in detail, almost prosaically, what was taking place in the lives of those present. It was uncanny, yet there was no gainsaying the reality of what took place.

When the lights went on, we just sat and talked. This was a group who sat regularly together. Grandma was completely nonplussed. They all seemed sensible people, with their feet on the ground. There was no financial gain to Leslie. We paid but a nominal sum and a few pounds for the cost of the tape-recording later sent or given to us. Grandma had lost her gifted husband, Barney, a year earlier, yet, on this occasion, neither Barney nor David had spoken.

Determined character that she was, Sheila's mother engaged in a lengthy conversation with Leslie. Both were strong, extrovert characters, who said things as they were, never beating about the bush, and as a result the two of them became firm friends. Grandma, despite herself, knew at once that Leslie was genuine, was not the type who would be party to any pretence, and, especially, was a man who had no financial stake in what he was doing. He simply felt that he had a gift that could be of service to those who grieved over a personal loss. He could bring comfort to the bereaved.

Thus, as 1978 drew to a close, we, the three of us, began a relationship, a friendship, with Leslie that lasted until his final days in Hove, on the south coast, in 1992. During those years, we sat regularly with Leslie and a group of people, including Jim Ellis, a Canadian, and an expert in the field of mediumship. Occasionally other mediums such as Jessie Nason sat with us, and also some noted healers. Sometimes voices came from the past, including a soldier in Cromwell's day, sometimes there were strange, even ancient languages, often there was humour. Sometimes I sang to encourage links, other times we all sang along with 'deceased' famous artiste Marie Lloyd.

The parade of people, of vastly different backgrounds, was so revealing and fascinating that we knew this was something true and real and that it could never be falsely concocted. Why, anyway, should anyone, particularly Leslie, want to deceive others? There was nothing to be gained from so doing.

In all these sittings there was a link, a kind of compère, on the other side. He was known as Mickey, a cheerful soul, who had died in London in 1919 aged eleven as the result of a motor accident, yet he had, in his world, developed to maturity, as all do, whether young or even stillborn. This aspect particularly intrigued me as my mother had had two stillborn children. I often wondered about them. My mother, incidentally, who had passed on in 1967, told me from her new abode how excited she was to make contact with me, but there was no contact from either my father or my sister.

I am not a man of science. I wish I were, but a very detailed explanation exists of this phenomenon of direct voice mediumship. Thought is at the heart of communication. The thoughts of the communicators are directed into an ectoplasmic voice box emanating from Leslie's throat. Helpers were able to keep the voice box steady and thought was converted into sound, whilst the thinkers/speakers were always aware of our thoughts and our voices. Indeed, they knew our thoughts before we gave voice to them.

There is considerable detail about this method of communicating but few scientists have taken the trouble to analyse the process properly. Such a complaint is often levelled against those scientists who naturally believe in the vital importance of evidence, yet who rarely take the trouble to examine all the evidence of direct voice mediumship: a most unscientific attitude.

Meanwhile, the evidence of the content of our sittings piled up: the tapes, hundreds and hundreds of them, piled up. As the sittings continued, people came from all over the world to participate in them. Jim Ellis deposited a vast library of tapes with a Canadian university. Others collected recordings of messages from famous people – Mahatma Gandhi, Winston Churchill, Ellen Terry – as well as ancient figures from the past. If correct and true, and I had no reason to doubt their veracity or genuineness, these contacts showed another world or worlds, in dimensions which we could not clearly understand, but which might one day make sense to the most advanced and open-minded of modern scientists. There is talk nowadays of many dimensions, of the infinitely big and the infinitely small, where a pocket-sized mobile phone can put us in touch with all parts of our planet, both verbally and visually, and where the march of science seems endless.

Leslie rarely held sittings outside his own house, but on one occasion we gathered in the dining-room of our house on Hadley Green, a suburb at the northern edge of London. The house, a few centuries old, had a quality that lent itself to ease of communication. Believe it or not, my down-to-earth mother-in-law told me that she had seen eighteenth century ladies walking up and down the stairs, in crinolines! At our sitting there came through (the usual expression) one Jasha, a doctor, who had sat with us many times and had only recently passed on; he talked to his voiceless wife, smitten by motor neurone disease, a dreadful illness, that sent her to join him shortly thereafter. We could feel the pain of the sympathetic husband and the deep frustration of his wife, Stella.

However there was also humour. A lady who had lived in Derby years ago came through, and on being asked whether she was a suffragette who had tied herself to railings, she replied, 'No, it was bad enough being tied to my husband'! I gather the ties of marriage beyond here remain only if there was true love between husband and wife – or, as I suppose today, we may also refer to the love between partners.

We sat with Leslie month after month, year after year. I had been privileged to learn of the world next to ours, alongside ours, intimately concerned with and about ours, but respectful of the free will we enjoyed, always emphasising the force of thought and the power of love. The former I refer to later in the world of eminent scientist Sir Oliver Lodge, whilst the latter arises in connection with the statements said to emanate from Jesus of Nazareth.

The history of modern mediumship began in the mid-nineteenth century in the United States and blossomed thereafter until recently. Even Abraham Lincoln was involved, while Queen Victoria's friendship with John Smith derived from the latter's ability to put her in touch with her beloved husband, Albert. Many prominent public figures, including a Prime Minister of Canada, testified to the result of spiritual communication, but others kept quiet about their contacts for political reasons.

One man and his wife who kept in touch through Leslie, in a loving and revealing way, not anyone well-known, was a London book publisher named Douglas Conacher, and his wife Eira. They married late in life, had no children, but loved each other very much. Eira sat by herself with Leslie in the 1960s, as a result of which two books were published, entitled *There is Life after Death* and *Chapters of Experience*. These volumes record clearly what Douglas, formerly a dedicated Church of England man, discovered in his new abode, to which I refer later.

Whilst I have set out in some detail my experiences with Leslie in the book about David, *Journey into Immortality*, I believe some quotations from the words of Douglas would be useful. He was a person of complete integrity, and he records honestly how his views had changed as a result of his experience beyond the veil of death. Some of his words appear later on.

In due course, a group of us formed the Leslie Flint Educational Trust, which republished his autobiography, to which I wrote the Introduction. Leslie was a devoted film lover and put on film shows. His great interest was Rudolph Valentino, the noted screen lover. Leslie actually held a sitting once in Valentino's Hollywood home. Whilst in America he was tested in detail by Columbia University who could find no evidence that contradicted the genuine nature of his mediumship. It is difficult to know why Leslie was chosen for this role, but I noted that a wholesomeness of feeling rather than any intellectual quality was the mark of Leslie and others like him.

As noted earlier, he moved eventually to live in Hove. His work declined. He declined, deeply affected by the loss of his friend, Bram, and others, although an 'Ian' emerged to look after him. When he passed, many people attended his funeral. *The Times* produced an expanded full-page obituary. I had the honour of giving the main address at a memorial meeting. And so this servant of the spirit passed on, to join those who had preceded him and to whom he had given a voice. Part of my address was as follows:

*We have gathered today, to remember Leslie and his achievements and his service, for he served us all.*

*As an independent direct voice medium, he was the finely-tuned instrument who opened up for us the pathway to a wider perception, a window on the world next to ours. For over fifty years he sat in the darkness of his room bringing light through his mediumship, knowledge to the eager, comfort to the distressed, joy and laughter to his friends. People of every rank and degree shared his sittings, but I believe he was especially fond of those who inhabited the creative worlds of theatre and of films, of music and of ballet. Many famous people, household names, will miss him.*

*How incredible that many were so deeply concerned about this one individual, who was unlettered, who held no degree, who had achieved nothing of note in the arts or in business, who was sometimes obstinate, occasionally dogmatic, and who held strongly to his beliefs and his opinions. One of those beliefs, expressed increasingly in recent years, was that the gift of mediumship, in whatever form, should not be used for material or commercial purposes, but only for truly spiritual objectives.*

*He was a rare soul, who served us well. May he have the peace and joy he so richly deserves.*

As I have already mentioned, my life throughout this time was a strange one. I was a partner in an important firm of London lawyers, representing governments, prime ministers, banks, insurance companies, and so on. In addition I was involved actively in communal and public bodies (described in *The Rainbow Never Ends*), yet I had to balance the practical with the spiritual. Each element was like a different gear in a car. One changed naturally from one gear to another and then back again. In addition, one set of colleagues usually had no idea of my transactions with the other set. It all made for a stimulating life, each part refreshing the other.

## Strike a Happy Medium

Well, not really: they are far too nice. Leslie was pre-eminent, but he was not alone. The Spiritualist world is explored in prominent journals such as *Psychic News*, *Two Worlds*, and others. Around the country are spread a host of Spiritualist churches, each with their own range of mediums, healers, singers and speakers, in a way parallel to the established churches. Some do continue a link with the Christian tradition though the majority do not but still have hymns and readings. Notable figures involved at the same time as Leslie included journalists like Maurice Barbanell and Hannen Swaffer.

Arthur Findlay had been a successful businessman yet held a passionate view as to the basic truth of Spiritualism, which he set out in a series of books of notable quality and erudition. His analysis of traditional dogmas was penetrating, even merciless, in its logicality. Eventually he donated his mansion and estate to the movement, now known as Arthur Findlay College in Essex, still a major training and residential centre.

He was not alone either, nor was his college. In Kensington stands the long-established College of Psychic Studies, founded in the 1880s by eminent persons including Sir Oliver Lodge and Sir Arthur Conan Doyle. It has a comprehensive library and offers extensive training programmes. Associated with it have been people like Paul Beard and Brenda Marshall, both of whom prominent and active in their support.

One day I was invited to lecture there. My subject was 'The Creative Spirit – Where Does It Come From?', with particular reference to David's remarkable poems, produced from the age of seven until his mystical words when aged nineteen. I was amazed at the diversity and size of the audience: the hall was packed. After the lecture many people came up to talk to me – young people, professors, bank managers, a complete cross-section of the population.

It was on this occasion that I met the famous novelist, Rosamond Lehmann, a tall, statuesque figure. She had lost a daughter and presented me with a copy of the moving, graphic book she had written about that young woman. I remained in touch with her until she, too, passed on but a year later.

Belgrave Square boasts an elegant collection of fine, nineteenth century houses surrounding a garden of lawns and trees, in one of the most expensive and fashionable parts of London, if not of Great Britain. To it have gravitated a host of foreign embassies. In my work for overseas governments I had been involved in the purchase of two of those grand properties. For years I spent hours and hours in them, at meetings, receptions and various events. Another of the buildings had the letters 'SAGB' on its nameplate, alongside the words 'Spiritualist Association of Great Britain'. Here were to be found resident mediums of high quality. In later years I had fascinating sessions with Alan Acton and others, but of course there was no one truly comparable with Leslie.

Yet there were two mediums who particularly deserve mention. One is Albert Best, who came from Glasgow. I think he was a postman, a modest man. Much has been written about him. We sat together and David spoke, no direct voice, but Albert simply repeated the words that came to him. I was struck by one phrase from David, 'I am only a thought away'. Again, the emphasis was on thought and its power and effect, which I had read about in detail in a book called *Thought Forces* published in 1911.

This raises the issue of the nature of thought. From where does it emanate – the brain, the mind? Can it have an effect on people, on plants? Can its effect circle the globe in an instant? What did David mean exactly? I am sure many scientific studies have peered into the problem.

Nan McKenzie smiled into her hundredth birthday. This former nurse was a wonder, at least to me. I met her at The London Spiritual Mission in Notting Hill, West London, an important church. She was a delight to talk to, unaffected and joyous. We celebrated her hundredth year while she spoke to us. She was a natural and gave me sound advice not only from her lifetime experiences but also from the words that flowed into her and through her.

There were other mediums, some described later, but for some reason, the quality of mediumship has not improved or even equalled the great figures of the past. The churches still hold their meetings, new names arise. There was once Gordon Higginson, later came Gordon Smith, but for reasons which I do not understand there are no more Leslie Flints. Is the world sinking deeper into a materialistic, technological morass? Did those in the world ahead object to some mediums using their gifts for material ends, sometimes appearing like a variety artist in huge theatres?

Mediumship, I feel, should be a personal matter, not a public performance for gain. It should be (and be seen to be) a form of service, particularly to those who are bereaved. Perhaps we are at a low-water mark, a psychic rather than a spiritual level in this intangible field; or perhaps we are close to some new development of a nature yet unknown.

Whatever the answers to all these questions, I have been so lucky to have had a wealth of experiences from my contact with mediums and I am grateful to all of them for creating such a potent link between here and there.

## Physician, Heal Thyself ...

But also, keep healing others. The advance of medical science in the last two centuries has been phenomenal. We owe so much to the doctors and scientists who have prolonged life, eased pain, cured diseases. That is one reason why, for the last decade or so, I have been happy to be part of a medical education trust that seeks to find ways of teaching those in less advanced or fortunate countries. Among the trustees I was almost the only one without a medical qualification, yet they continued to put up with me. I learned a lot from these leading experts, all of them bent on helping the disadvantaged in underdeveloped countries.

For some strange reason the nursing profession also made advances to me. The first organisation of nurses in the world saw light in Britain in 1887, no doubt inspired by the great Florence Nightingale, and proudly bearing a Royal Charter. When the presidency of their body fell vacant in 2009, I was utterly amazed to find myself elected as their president. What an honour! Put me among the nurses!

Thus I have had the rare privilege of close, regular contact with both medical and nursing practitioners. But I had contact, too, with these worlds in my profession as a lawyer. One of my first cases required me to read a volume on orthopaedics. A famous abortion case took me into other fields. Medical reports flowed around my desk in accident claims cases. When David was laid low with cancer I made a study of the problem and, as a non-expert, even had the chutzpah to engage in debate with the leading lights of the Imperial Cancer Research Fund, as it was then designated. I learned much about epidemiology, whilst they learned from me the significance of diet, a subject they had previously appeared to ignore.

The advance of medical science has not always been plain sailing. Penicillin seems to have been discovered by accident. After Fleming came Ernst Chain. Poor Dr Semmelweis died in misery when doctors laughed at his injunction that they wash their hands properly before operating. And, dear me, even the famous Louis Pasteur was reviled by his colleagues for his ideas about bacteria. Thus there is also an unscientific strain in the medical world, simply because doctors and scientists are also fallible human beings, treating other fallible human beings. A later chapter tells the story of the fight against TB, tuberculosis, as well as new methods of detecting illnesses remote from traditional medical diagnosis.

And so I come to the subject of healing – spiritual healing. It is real, it works, it has been tested and verified, and has been a blessing to vast numbers of people. Doctors, busily engaged with a heavy list, in surgery or hospital, haven't really got time for non-material treatment, partly because of their training, partly because of pharmaceutical pressure, and partly because they don't want to be sued. So they stick to the straight and narrow path, and who can blame them? And yet, alongside their discipline, exists the quite remarkable world of the healer. May I illustrate their work with two brief personal stories?

As an irresponsible father, I used to take my daughter Esther tree-climbing. We climbed a vast number of trees. She survived and grew to glowing womanhood and motherhood uninjured. Her father though, in the 1990s, at a more advanced age, was ascending a eucalyptus tree when he slipped and fell to the ground. Serves him right.

The consequence? Back trouble. Doctors, osteopaths, chiropractors, all tried their best but it was not good enough. So, one day, breathing hard, I found myself in a Chelmsford waiting room with about fifty souls, mainly of Indian background; on the walls were displayed signs with the consoling words of Sai Baba inscribed on them. Here practised a psychic surgeon. There were a few in Brazil and the Philippines, but no others as far as I knew in Britain. When it was my turn, this gentleman laid me on my face, made a cut (no anaesthetic) in my back and withdrew from my inner body an offending piece of bone that had been the cause of all the trouble. I felt no pain, no blood flowed, and it was all over in under ten minutes. I got up, paid a modest bill, and walked away. I made a further visit the following week for him to check that all was well and I never had a moment's problem thereafter.

Now this story makes no sense at all to experienced surgeons and scientists. They would find it hard to believe. It contradicts their experiences. They would, understandably, seek other explanations, or just shake their heads in disbelief. I don't blame them. Yet what the man did goes to the heart of what a human being is and the forces that exist in life. It could be that recent advances in keyhole and other forms of surgery may just lead to new conclusions.

The second story is even more personal. In my professional life I had a wonderful mixture of clients, from ambassadors to street cleaners, and the most varied ethnic and religious mix imaginable (many of them are described in my book *Brief Encounters of a Legal Kind*). For instance, in the 1960s I was fascinated to watch the growth of Carnaby Street in London's West End as a world centre of new designs of men's clothes: in my capacity as a lawyer I was intimately involved with the development of that street.

Further westwards, in fashionable Knightsbridge, a ladies' hairdresser plied his creative trade. One day he came to my home to discuss practical matters, and in the course of our conversation observed sadly that he would soon have to cease work. When I asked him why, he showed me that some of the fingers on one hand seemed locked into a permanent arch, meaning that he could no longer hold a comb or scissors comfortably. His medical advisers seemed to have no answer to this problem, he told me. Feeling sorry for him, I took his hand in mine and stroked the offending fingers. I had no idea why I did this and he did not object. Soon afterwards he left for home.

On the following day a very excited hairdresser rang me, demanding to know what I had done to him. Apparently, overnight, the offending fingers had returned to normal functioning. He was thrilled: and so was I. That was in 1981. He continued to work normally for years. I pondered what had happened, and launched into a study of healing, spiritual healing. I knew, of course, of the Biblical stories of Elijah, Elisha and Jesus. There were similar examples in other cultures. I discovered that Britain was actually the home of great healers. I read the books of and about Harry Edwards, perhaps the greatest healer of modern times, possibly the greatest healer since Jesus. Thousands were in touch with him and thousands were healed by him. Later in life I had the great pleasure of friendship with Ray and Joan Branch, his associates for many years.

As with Leslie Flint, people came from all over the world to see Harry Edwards and to be healed of serious conditions that had defied conventional medicine. He demonstrated his gift at mass meetings in the Royal Albert Hall and people who had arrived as cripples left the platform walking normally. Now what would a materialist, a scientist, make of this phenomenon? This type of healing was not due to the kind of hypnosis founded by Anton Mesmer and developed by Richet in France. Neither was it linked to the diagnosis and treatment prescribed by a sleeping Edgar Cayce in America, remarkable though that was.

Again, we are back to the nature of man, his very essence, as with mediumship. Are we purely an aggregation of material parts, evolved over countless years to adapt to our environment, naturally selected to survive where other species have declined and disappeared? Edwards thought otherwise. He believed there was a non-physical element in man that could respond to a special kind of force that emanated from the world of the spirit. Some receive this force and use it for healing. Again, we are remote from the doctor's surgery and the operating theatre, but the evidence is there, in case study after case study, in the thousands of grateful letters he received from all over the world, but, just as there is a degree of acceptance in many, so in others there is an enhanced degree of scepticism and mental rejection of any of the fruits of the spirit that I describe. No blame or criticism attaches. It is just the way we are made.

I continued to pursue my studies. This included meetings with celebrated healers such as George Chapman and Ted Fricker, from whom I learned of guides in the world beyond. Many of these had been here on this earth, as conventional medical experts. Again, please excuse me: I have no interest in increasing the book's circulation, but these encounters are described more fully in *Journey into Immortality*.

There was nothing particularly striking about any of the healers whom I studied. Some were housewives. George Chapman was a fireman. Edgar Cayce, over in America, had been a photographer. But what was significant about these people was that the heart seemed to take precedence over the brain. For example, a friend and healer, Ruth, restored a principal ballerina to the stage when broken wrists seemed logically to indicate the end of her career. A few churches did suddenly realise that healing was at the heart of Jesus's teachings, healing not rituals, and, to their credit, conducted healing sessions.

I also learned of healers abroad, notably in India, but, as usual, some unusual experiences occurred in my own backyard. The hairdresser used to visit me at my office, ostensibly on some minor legal matter, but really for me to heal a bad back or a headache. I always locked my office door whilst healing. Similarly, a woman came with her husband and I healed her shoulder. A woman in our office came in bent and left upright. The pain from a whiplash injury in a secretary was much reduced. A cleaner's cracked wrist, to her amazement, afterwards showed no crack at all on an X-ray. A builder's arm and our son Jon's knee responded to the healing process. And so it went on. None of my distinguished legal partners had the slightest idea of what I was up to: and this went on for years.

But there is yet another quite remarkable aspect of healing – absent or distance healing. Amazingly, it works. How on earth can you heal someone miles away, whom you never see? Harry Edwards explained the phenomenon in detail. It is a form of mental visualisation combined with healing wishes transmitted by thought forces, in an instant, across continents, faster than the speed of light. Doesn't sound possible, does it, but it happens. It happened to me. I cured a frozen shoulder on a woman 7,000 miles away. Often in this process I tried to transmit healing colours.

Again, cynics, detractors, doubters, should examine impartially the claims made. The evidence, and, as a lawyer, evidence was central to my work, is all there. It just needs people to rise to a different level and to consider the evidence as they would for anything else. Harry Edwards believed absent healing was even more significant than hands-on healing. So there we have touched on two elements of the human scene – mediumship and spiritual healing – but there are many more personal experiences to relate.

## Virène – Mother and Daughter

These two women were so close, their lives so intertwined, that Vera, the mother, and Irène, her daughter, could be naturally conjoined into Virène. Vera passed away in 1985 aged ninety-six. Irène expired in 2005 aged seventy-five.

I first saw Irène, clothed all in white, standing at her front door in Hove, a south coast resort, in 1995. That was the last time I ever saw her outside her home and probably the last time she ever ventured into the fresh air – fresh to us, but fatal to her. She was one of the few people in Britain who suffered from MCS, or Multiple Chemical Sensitivity syndrome. The 60,000 chemicals in our 'fresh' air could have killed her. I had never come across anyone in such a situation before. How had this come to pass?

To explain, we have to consider the pre-1939 worlds of Riga, St Petersburg, Odessa, Marseilles, Paris, London, as well as the hills of Switzerland and the Holocaust camps. Both mother and daughter were enormously talented, gifted in many different ways. When in her nineties Vera wrote the story of her life, and Irène, whom I had met quite accidentally, asked me to edit it. This I did, and more than edit: it took me three months. Eventually the book was published under the simple title *Vera*. Spielberg, you will not film a more phenomenal story than this, combining as it does elements of both James Bond and Elie Wiesel. Barbra Streisand, you would be perfect to play mother or daughter.

Let me sketch you a brief outline of the qualities of these two people. Vera was a musical prodigy, outstanding as a pianist from the age of twelve, holder of the Royal Academy Gold Medal, and a playing colleague of Vladimir Horowitz and Nathan Milstein; she continued to play and compose into her nineties. She was also a linguist, had studied at the Sorbonne, and could count herself a friend of the leading artists of Paris during the 1930s. The story of her survival from 1940 to 1945 in Vichy France offers all the drama and breathtaking qualities of a wartime thriller. Her husband and almost all of her family were murdered in the Nazi Holocaust.

Vera was born in Riga, Latvia in 1890, at a time when the parks had notices that read 'No Jews, no dogs'. She, her parents, brothers and sisters escaped to St Petersburg, experienced the Russian Revolution, somehow reached Odessa, and then a British ship took them to Marseilles. Eventually Vera settled in Paris. She was not then short of money, coming from a family background of famous Jewish religious leaders, but after 1940 she lost everything. Somehow, though, she and her cherished daughter survived.

That daughter, Irène, an only child, was born in 1929, and had been invited to travel to Hollywood in September 1939 to become a second Shirley Temple in the film world, but World War II erupted and ended all her hopes. By the skin of their teeth the two of them, mother and daughter, escaped the Nazis in Paris, and then evaded too the equally determined pursuit of the Vichyites for almost five years. The pair had to hide constantly, travelling from village to village, living from hand to mouth, until 1945, when the Allied victory found them living in Grenoble.

However years of malnutrition gave rise to tuberculosis in Irène, who spent the four immediate post-war years on her back in Swiss clinics. There her mother taught her languages, history, and indeed a whole educational programme. Irène became fluent in six languages, which, after a period at the noted Geneva School of Linguists, enabled her to have a career as a simultaneous interpreter. But the devastation of her immune system through wartime hardship brought on in the early 1990s the MCS syndrome already mentioned.

Both mother and daughter were survivors. Both, until their dying days, were victims of Nazi Germany's sub-human fury. Yet both overcame adversity of the severest kind, which somehow heightened the latent and patent qualities inherent in them. It is difficult to summarise briefly, let alone adequately, the extraordinary lives of these two women. I strongly recommend that you read the book *Vera*, not because I was involved in it, but because it describes such an outstanding example of sheer, unadulterated courage.

Why, you may ask, do I bring their story into my experiences in the world of the spirit? I could so easily expand on Vera's music, on Irène's singing. Indeed the latter, in the last year of her life, made a CD, singing six love songs in six languages! There is something so inspirational about these people, who were ever-creative, despite the worst the world could do to them.

Whenever I visited Irène at her home on the Sussex coast, I had to remove every vestige of my normal clothing and don special garments made only of natural materials. Likewise there were in the house no plastic or artificial objects: all was steel, wood, wool, all natural products. Irène's diet was also very restricted. Yoghurt, for example, came from a special Kent farm. At one time the supply was threatened by the possibility of a mobile phone mast being installed, which would have adversely affected the cows and their yield. I managed to get the mast project rejected.

Similarly, the failure to clear chemicals from a Hove development site near Irène's house could have ended her life. Again, fortunately, I managed to push the local council and developer into removing all the chemicals. It was useful being a lawyer sometimes.

So back to my question, though, about the importance of these two women in the context of the spirit world. The answer is that they were both outstanding examples of healing and mediumship. Their spiritual perception was greatly enhanced by the immense tribulations that they had suffered. They had been tested to a high degree of intensity, and somehow, by overcoming such adversity, they had developed rare spiritual antennae.

Both mother and daughter displayed remarkable healing abilities, especially with animals. Irène also became a noted teacher of healing, a member of county, national and international healing federations. She was a member of the Jewish Association of Spiritual Healers of which I, alongside Ray and Joan Branch of Harry Edwards fame, became one of the three Patrons. Irène developed, too, as a clinical ecologist, offering a range of perceptive treatments that somehow worked. She was expert, too, as a radionics practitioner, analysing on her machine physical problems based not on examining the person but on the vibrational evidence provided by a photograph, a single hair or a drop of blood.

I was indeed amazed at the accuracy of her conclusions. She reminded me of Agatha Christie's detective, Poirot, who found conclusive evidence in the most unlikely of objects. In this way Irène solved problems that baffled conventional analysis of the evidence. Indeed, doctors were among her patients.

But there were occasions during my association with Virène which these doctors, and others, would find bizarre. Again, this is a reflection of the nature of a human being and his or her relationship to the world of the spirit.

Being involved in communal activities I was invited to speak to various organisations. On one occasion I spoke to members of an Essex synagogue congregation, dealing with various issues of concern to them. My words, based on a limited sectional approach, seemed to satisfy the audience.

After the tea interval I again spoke, but I knew that it was not me speaking at all. Someone else was speaking through me. I had not the faintest idea of what I was about to say or was actually saying, but it transpired, and my practical wife confirmed, that my words were universal in content, but contradicted everything I had said before the interval! The audience, absolutely shocked, was silent. I was never invited back to that mystified community.

There was an echo of this experience with Irène. Sitting with her one day I realised that she was looking at me very carefully. Suddenly she announced that my features had changed. Apparently I had become a celebrated eighteenth century rabbi. This was a startling example of what is called 'overshadowing', though I had felt nothing. Similarly, on being greeted by Irène one day, in her mother's Paris dress, I knew that I was in fact being greeted not by Irène but by her long-deceased mother, Vera. It was an extraordinary sensation, confirmed by the daughter later.

But an even more remarkable link was one I was told by Vera, from the world of the spirit, not to mention at the time. For about a year I was in regular and direct touch with Vera. This contact was not via a direct voice, but occurred during a telephone conversation with Irène (who was a medium); she went into trance and I heard the voice of Vera. This was not a one-off event but continued week after week, month after month. I made a full note of every conversation, which was usually about maintaining good health and not doing too much (my permanent problem), whilst other souls, some of medical background from a previous century, added their advice.

The extraordinary thing is that it all seemed so natural. The strength of character and vivacity of Vera was reflected in her voice, her words. When Irène came out of her trance, she confirmed that she had not the faintest idea of what had been said or what had taken place.

I had never met the corporeal Vera during her life, but I met her very frequently after her time here had expired. When Irène joined her mother on 8th October 2005 I organised a memorial meeting at which many tributes were paid to them both. In October 2010, five years later, I arranged an Irène Noah Day in Brighton, at which we paid tribute to 'Virène', this devoted duo, and at which we listened to the love songs CD made by Irène. One of the songs was called, appropriately, 'The Nearness of You'.

## Sai Ram – Sai Baba

The great religions of the world attempt to define man's relationship with God, that indefinable power or force, behind all creation. Many words are used to describe that power: God, Lord, Almighty, Allah, Father, in fact a host of appellations. Personally I like the Hebrew word 'the Place', whilst Spiritualists often refer to the Great Spirit. But I also do believe some of the main religions are dominated by ideas of sex, male and female, Adam and Eve. Examples abound.

The Bible is full of sex, the obtaining of wives, polygamy, adultery, so much so that the Ten Commandments, a tremendous advance, clearly enjoined marital fidelity, 'Thou shalt not commit adultery'. Adulterers, particularly women, were then stoned to death, a barbaric act that occurs, amazingly, even today. Story after story, for example those featuring Joseph and David, had a sexual element. The account of Jesus and the woman taken in adultery serves to illustrate a higher morality.

But faiths continue with their sexual overtones. Moslem men were allowed four wives, no doubt more for sexual than other reasons. They even created women-only harems, no doubt for the same reason.

Early Biblical Judaism seems to have adopted similar beliefs. For generations polygamy existed in parts of the Jewish world, whilst the practice of self-immolation, *sati*, by those recently widowed, darkened Hinduism. Buddhists had different ideas, whilst Christians, so often equating sex with sin, developed one stream where a class of men and women were even forbidden to marry, an injunction leading to terrible child abuse.

Of course, all these patterns of behaviour were devised and directed by men. Women had little say in the matter, though Sikhism tried its best. In a strange way the absence of sexual contact became part of Christianity, with its single sex convents and monasteries and ideas of a virgin birth. There are elements of this in Buddhism too. Even in China and Japan women suffered disadvantages. It has only been in the last hundred years or so, and then only in Western-type democratic societies, that the fresh winds of sexual equality have blown. We have various declarations of human rights, conventions, and so forth, but complete equality of male and female is far from universal in belief or practice. Until that day dawns it is doubtful whether peace will settle on our planet. The masculine instinct remains too violent, too intense. The feminine element makes for creative peace.

This is but a brief note to introduce the sudden emergence into my Monkenholt home of a dozen or more Sai Baba devotees. I had never heard of this religious leader or of his followers. My pharmacist's sister, a fellow lawyer, had asked whether she could bring them and I agreed. Why me, I do not know, but perhaps she thought they would be of interest – and they certainly were.

So, in they came to my house, both men and women, of mixed background but all united by their devotion to an avatar in India, namely Sri Sathya Sai Baba, a man who I was fascinated to learn was born in the same month and year as myself. India is an amazing, ancient civilisation, possibly the oldest of all. I have always thought of the Jewish and Indian traditions as the true basis of world religion. One produced or begat Judaism, Christianity and Islam, whilst from the other came Hinduism, Buddhism, Jainism and partly Sikhism.

My interest was particularly aroused by the influx of Indians into Britain, perhaps a million or more, an upwardly mobile, peaceful minority with a strong family tradition and a love of learning. In the context of my communal activities, I felt a link between the Jewish and Indian communities would be beneficial for both them and wider society.

Within the group of guests, I was fortunate to meet a man called Pranlal Sheth, an Indian from Kenya, who had achieved considerable business prominence. We took to each other at once, as we had a common approach to life. He had been Deputy Chairman of the Commission for Racial Equality, the UK's main body seeking good relations between ethnic groups, an office I subsequently held. Pran and I organised private meetings and seminars between the leaders of the two communities and set up the Indian Jewish Association UK to bring British Jews and British Indians into closer contact. (This body still exists today.) Among the functions that took place was our visit to the fabulous Hindu temple erected at Neasden in north-west London. It is a building that seems to come out of fairyland. As I explored its statues and studied similar erections in India I could not help but notice the explicit sexual elements, voluptuous women and virile men, with sexual features all agog. This added to the impression of an emphasis on sex that I had observed in other faiths.

I had known of a few other emanations in the UK of Indian religions. I had taken part in gatherings of Brahma Kumaris, a worldwide organisation largely run by women, which offers a positive spiritual approach to life. Also a legal case I had concerned an Indian charity aimed at helping children. In addition I had lectured at the Nehru Centre in Central London, had read journals like *India Today* and *New World*, which described the emergence of India as a new world power, alongside personal stories of individuals and businesses. Like most people, I was inspired by the lives of Gandhi and Tagore as well as the gurus of the land. I had even visited Bhaktivedanta Manor, the Hare Krishna centre at Aldenham, north of London. There seemed to be a healthy attitude to the body and soul, though coming from my own tradition, I caught my breath at some of the statues involved in services.

But, here at home on the occasion I mention above, I discussed with my visitors the nature of Sai Baba. They seemed to regard him as a kind of semi-god in human form, a creator of minds. They gave me books to read. I read them all. Learned folk from all parts of the world gravitated to his ashram, happy to derive benefit just by being in his presence, or being blessed by him, or, at its highest level, meeting him. These were not gullible people. They were educationalists, psychologists, doctors, leading Indian scientists, even a Prime Minister of India. They analysed his power and described his influence case after case.

Like Harry Edwards, Sai Baba had cured the incurable. The cripple walked, cancer was eradicated, even at a distance, and special healing ash, *vibhuti*, appeared suddenly thousands of miles away. Fruit suddenly appeared on trees; from his hands came rugs, ornaments, where before there had been nothing. My friend Ruth wears and cherishes a gold ring he produced out of thin air. These are not magicians' tricks. These are emanations from something within the man himself. But what was it that was there in him, in Edwards, in Flint, in those who seemed to defy the natural order of things? The wonders of Sai Baba have been described in prosaic terms, often by scientists, but few Western scientists have studied the evidence. Are these events a challenge to the basis of modern science as it has been taught or is it better not to try to explain them at all?

I myself have no explanation other than that the power of thought forces acts on the physical world, often forces emanating from other worlds. The facts are incontrovertible but the explanations vary. There is the religious explanation of miracles, but how often do the main personalities state that there are no such things as miracles, only something we cannot explain?

So here, with Sai Baba, and the millions worldwide who follow him, we see healing, messages, the creation of something out of nothing ('nothing comes from nothing' said William Shakespeare), the conquest of both time and distance in results achieved. One can ignore all this, try to explain it away, but the facts remain. Perhaps there are more things in heaven and earth, and in man, than are understood in our philosophy.

Sai Baba passed on aged eighty-four on 4th April 2011 but his influence remains powerful and his teachings elevated, and amazingly, the *vibhuti* ash continues to come.

## Knight and Ray – or Oliver and Raymond

More correctly, Sir Oliver Lodge and Mr Raymond Smith. The co-operation between these two dissimilar characters represents one of the outstanding stories of mediumship and is, in my view, of notable significance. I cannot recall how I first met Raymond or why, but it was during the last decade of his life. He passed in 2009 aged 78. He was not a well-known public figure, except in those few specialist areas in which he worked.

Oliver Lodge, on the other hand, was a scientist, inventor, and educationalist of considerable fame. Some of his inventions are still at the heart of our motor car, radio, and television industries. He was born in 1850, died in 1940, and he and his wife, with a kind of mathematical equality, produced five sons and five daughters.

Both men illustrated a feature of British life that has always intrigued me: the fame and acclaim of some alongside public ignorance of others who yet had made a sterling contribution in their fields. Britain has an outstanding record in producing great figures, in science and other disciplines. Within fifty miles of Birmingham in the British Midlands were born three figures of world significance, William Shakespeare in Stratford-on-Avon, Charles Darwin in Shrewsbury and Isaac Newton near Grantham. Is there any similar area on earth that can compare? I doubt it.

Similarly, in science and medicine, Britain can reel off a story of great achievers. Priestley, Maxwell, Davy, Faraday, Lister, Rutherford, J.J. Thomson, Graham Bell, alongside those involved in jet engines, radar, television and other discoveries. Lodge's name would not be out of place in such a list. On the other hand the name of Alfred Russel Wallace is far less known than that of Charles Darwin, yet they both produced publicly, at the same time, the theory of evolution by natural selection. That applies, too, to the origin and development of the computer. The name Babbage is not so widely known. Recently I wrote a book about the life of one Arieh Handler, who may have saved more souls from the Nazi madness than the celebrated Schindler – the latter widely known because of a book and a subsequent film, but the former hardly heard of in the world.

Oliver Lodge had a glowing career, as Professor of Physics in Liverpool, Principal of Birmingham University, a man of considerable public stature, in a way a pillar of conventional society. This contrasts with Raymond Smith, who came from a Lancashire family of no great distinction, but who by his natural ability and enquiring mind became proficient as a teacher, musician, yachtsman and a student of science. Both he and his healer wife June lived for some years in La Linea, a town in Southern Spain close to Gibraltar.

On the surface the backgrounds and lives of these two men would not have naturally brought them together, yet they developed a powerful, regular and almost daily relationship. That was after Lodge had passed from this world of ours in 1950.

I first met Raymond and June in 2007. It was in a miserable room in a distinctly unpretentious King's Cross establishment called, somewhat undeservedly, a hotel. Ray and June made the best of a bad job. They were due to meet various spiritual circles in the north of the country. He was short, compact, clear-eyed. She was warm-hearted, outgoing. Both were easy to get on with.

Who would have thought that Raymond sat in a trance and dictated to June the words that came to him from Oliver Lodge? This was not a rare occurrence, but almost a daily event. This prolific communication resulted in three remarkable books, namely *Nobody Wants To Listen – And Yet*, *For Those Who Are Willing To Listen*, and *The Truth, The Whole Truth And Nothing But The Truth*.

I have read these books again and again. They contain so much wisdom and so many explanations, as well as words often in poetical form from Oliver's son, also a Raymond, who was killed in World War I, but also fascinating insights from Lodge's colleagues in the world beyond, also men of science. Additional messages came from a lady who had been in a religious order, as well as from Raymond's uneducated father who had taken his own life and who enjoined others never to do likewise.

Just as my experience with Vera had brought to me the voices of medical experts of earlier days, so Oliver brought, through Raymond, the words of notable figures.

On a later visit I took Raymond and June to meet a woman in London who was sorely afflicted by MS, multiple sclerosis. She was brave in her affliction and, despite it, she had helped many others. Her efforts had been recognised by a public honour. One can cope with the occasional illness but one that is permanent can destroy the will to live, yet this widow was buoyant in spirit and in mind. I had brought Raymond to her, in the hope that Oliver and his medical colleagues could pass on information that might encourage her in her affliction. I believe that he tried to do this in a sympathetic and understanding manner. Raymond, of course, had no idea what was being said at the time, sitting there quite still with eyes closed.

It is useful to compare the activities of two men in the world of advancement of spiritual knowledge in more detail. As I have said, Oliver Lodge was well-known and a public figure. With Sir William Crookes, another notable scientist, and others, he founded organisations and initiated research in the last decades of the nineteenth century and beyond. This coincided with the work in the same field of another knight, Sir Arthur Conan Doyle. This was the heyday of the Spiritualist movement.

Here were scientists of note, presenting the gospel, or good news, of the survival of the individual human spirit or consciousness, and of communication between the two worlds. Indeed, it was in the 1880s that the magazine *Two Worlds* was founded, which publicised these advances in matters of Spiritualism. The magazine continues to this day, and I was delighted to become a director of the parent company a few years ago.

Raymond also had a role to play. He spoke on the radio, organised meetings in Gibraltar, brought leading mediums there, and generally expanded local knowledge of the subject. He mentioned that even devout Catholics attended his gatherings. He and June went on tour to America and Canada, as well as to Britain. Yet daily he sat and Oliver spoke to and through him.

I was so sorry to hear from June in 2009 that Raymond had succumbed to an illness and left this world to join Oliver and his friends beyond. In due course June, also bearing an affliction bravely, left La Linea to settle in Gibraltar, where she and her husband had done so much.

I have read again and again the words of Oliver. I doubt whether many scientists, indeed many people, have read these three books, yet they contain the accumulated wisdom of a man of science whose vision was expanded by his higher experiences both here and in the world he now inhabits.

## Rescue – Michael Evans

Exeter is a fine city on England's south coast. Not far away are the cliffs of Devon and Dorset, a special World Heritage Site, the ancient cliffs of the Jurassic Coast. Also nearby is the River Exe and the town of Exmouth, as well as the beautifully preserved and charming seaside resort of Sidmouth. There, my wife and I used to take our children, to spend many happy summer holidays. There too took place the International Folk Dancing Festival, which we watched with much enjoyment.

Exeter itself has a splendid cathedral, one of those vast and impressive stone tributes of medieval times to the Christian church. One day a man who lived in the city contacted me, or I contacted him, I cannot really recall: anyway, he invited me to his house. He was Michael Evans, formerly an officer in the Royal Air Force, a magistrate, a carefully-spoken, upright man.

Sadly, he had been a widower for some years. Sadly, too, a local lady had been a widow for some years. Gradually the two of them got to know each other, made closer contact, and, lo and behold, they got married. This happens frequently now in a society where people live longer, at least the widows and widowers do. I remember how my wife arranged for two friends, a widow and a widower, to be seated together on the same table, side by side, at our son Jon's wedding to Caroline. The two found much in common. Sheila and I were delighted to attend their subsequent wedding. They have been happy together ever since, as I am sure was the case with Michael and his wife.

Why did I travel all the way from London to Exeter? Not to see the cathedral or the coast, but to have an entirely new experience in the world of the spirit. Michael was a very practical man. He understood modern technology, whilst I try in vain to understand the hieroglyphics that adorn modern machines. I booked into a local hotel for a couple of nights and on two occasions sat in his living-room with half a dozen people, two or more of them mediums. No direct voice, no trance, but voices certainly.

To understand what happened one must accept certain propositions. First is acceptance that physical death is not the end of the person. What is buried in cemeteries is only corpses, bones and flesh, that have no life in them. When I once proposed buying and erecting a tombstone over our David's grave, he said, via Leslie, 'Don't waste your money, I am up here not down there'. Maybe, but people like to do something, lay flowers or erect stones, in memory of the departed. Understandable. So, as I say, you have first to accept that the individual spirit, the essence of a person, survives.

What you have then to accept is that normally the spirit, in his or her new environment, gravitates to the level created by the level reached by the person when here on earth. As Rabbi Nachman once said, 'There is level above level'. Where the spirit goes to depends on the moral and spiritual growth attained here on earth, this testing ground, often referred to by Lodge as a 'nursery'. Most spirits are met by family and friends. Those whose passing was grievous or violent have special care. Those who have lived wicked lives may find themselves in a dark, dark, low level, similar to earth conditions, but they have a chance to progress to levels of greater light.

The third aspect you have to accept, and it is not easy to do so, is that some souls, on passing, are so confused, often unaware of physical death, that they live in an unhinged condition between here and there. I remember the soldier who had been in Cromwell's seventeenth century army and who was still unable to find a resting place. I suppose he was in a kind of purgatory, but much more than that. This is often the basis of ghosts and haunted houses. Michael told me how he had often been to such houses to encourage the ghostly occupier to understand what had happened and to leave the house. Usually he succeeded but then Michael accepted the reality of spirits who were suspended between heaven and earth. (This brings to mind the evocative story of Jacob's Ladder.)

The final thing one has to accept is that, through mediums, it is possible for us here to speak to those sad souls, explain their predicament, and encourage them to go forward. These four points are quite a lot for most people to accept, and would of course be treated with contempt by secular humanists, Marxists, materialists, and closed-minded adherents of many religions. The former would regard it all as a kind of charade, self-delusion, flights of imagination – while the latter would regard such contact as the work of the devil, literally. The latter really do believe there is such a being as a devil, an actual Satan. I can assure those believers that we have many more examples of Satanic characters in physical form down here than up there.

So in Michael and Lily's house, we sat together, not in darkness, but in comfort and expectancy. This was a Rescue Circle, who came together every week, whose purpose was to rescue confused souls. This they did regularly over the years. They were not alone. There were similar Rescue Circles up and down the country. Lord Dowding, Royal Air Force Air Chief Marshal and victor of the 1940 Battle of Britain, has described the process in a subsequent book.

I listened intently during the dialogue between Michael and the smitten spirits. There was no condemnation, no judging, only a careful process of suggesting a step-by-step approach, encouraging the spirit to understand what had happened. I heard half a dozen such conversations, feeling much admiration for the healthy approach of the circle members.

Perhaps most significant was the case of the suicide bomber, who had blown himself up and many others. Clearly he had been mentally and emotionally hypnotised and indoctrinated by evil teachers that his act would be holy and for the advancement of himself in the faith. What had such an effect on this being was the failure to find all he had been promised. There was no reward, no available virgins, no honour, indeed no paradise the holy book had suggested there would be. He told us exactly what he had been promised if he carried out his act. Those promises never materialised and so he was in a state of confusion. He thought he was a martyr, but he learned that a martyr is not one who takes the life of others.

Bit by bit, Michael took him along the path he had travelled and explained the changes necessary in what he believed so that he could take his place in the appropriate part of the world of the spirit. This redemption, this change of belief, would not suddenly take place as a result of the circle's efforts, but would continue after he left us.

What a lesson this would be to all suicide bombers and even more to the evil men who encourage and teach such inhuman, anti-human acts. We have seen this self-immolatory practice among Japanese pilots in World War II, among Tamil Tigers in Sri Lanka, and especially from within elements in the Muslim world.

I attended two sessions with Michael's circle and was fascinated and encouraged by him and his colleagues, and the vital work they were doing, work unknown to the vast majority of their countrymen. *Vivat* Exeter and all who live in her!

## The Chinese Dimension

These various chapters of experience contain but the barest and briefest elements of the episodes described, the bare bones of the experiences encountered. Each chapter could, by more detailed illustrations and examples, be expanded into a book, but I have purposely limited myself to a mere summary with only a few examples, in order to highlight the range of experiences but not to test the reader's patience.

However, later in the book I do include details of relevant further reading and pertinent quotations of teachings and messages. I thought this format would be sensible and acceptable. There are so many other names I could mention in this field. I have referred already to the editor and medium Maurice Barbanell, to famous journalist Hannen Swaffer, and to Air Chief Marshal Lord Dowding, apart from Doris Collins, Doris Stokes, and the extensive teachings of White Eagle and Silver Birch, great souls of an advanced nature.

Similarly (again not wishing to over-burden you), despite my Indian experiences, I have not touched on reincarnation, a belief widely accepted in that sub-continent, or the influence of past lives on present behaviour and sentiments.

My hope is that you, the reader, may feel that there is something in the claims made by Spiritualists, even if you are not attracted to them or their institutions. The literature on the subject is vast and not all the practitioners are of the same quality. In fact, care is needed and doubt valuable when first embarking on a study of this scene. There are fraudsters and confidence tricksters in every sphere.

Let me take you now to China, not literally, but to the Chinese world of the twelfth century of the current era. My journey there is via two individuals, John Podmore and Mary Absolum.

Often I found myself invited to speak at organisations in different parts of the country. Once I found myself in Lincoln Cathedral as a participant in a seminar on the environment. A similar invitation had been issued to me some years earlier in Canterbury, all due to a book I had written on the subject. But then in the early 1990s a group I had never heard of, beholden to faith and hope, asked me to address a weekend seminar in Oxford. There I spoke, even sang, on aspects of my particular Jewish background. But I also watched as another speaker produced the most evocative and artistic photographs of nature, alongside music and words.

This man was a photographer of great ability, indeed president of the Leica Photographic Society, a committed Leica devotee. We took to each other, though dissimilar in family and form. John Podmore was a big man, tall, substantial in chest and stomach, with a big head, a big laugh, and a big heart. Looking into his estate car I could see he was one of the untidiest of men, but that didn't matter.

John came from a Jersey family. His wife, whom I met later, was a complete contrast, being diminutive, self-contained, unemotional. Subsequently, the couple stayed with us in Monkenholt, especially when I tried to help John during the financial disaster that afflicted him, and countless others, as a 'name' at Lloyd's. Later, after his wife passed on, John entered into a wonderfully positive relationship with a woman of nursing background, much closer to him in spirit. I often visited them in Sutton Coldfield in the Midlands.

John introduced me to Mary Absolum. I had never heard of her. We went to her home close to the Thames in East London. She was a lively, pleasant woman, easy to talk to. She had been married and had a grown-up son. There seemed nothing unusual about her. We sat for a while, she, John and me. Soon her features began to change, her movements changed, her voice changed. She became more of a man than a woman. Even her pattern of speech changed. What had happened to me in that Essex congregation, and with Irène, happened to her.

Her real being was in abeyance, whilst through her spoke a twelfth century Chinese man of distinction, who answered to the name of Mandarin. Hearing his words in this way was an uncanny experience. I had read some of the words of Lao-tzu and especially of Chang-tzu. I had a little knowledge of the extraordinary Chinese culture, and of course, knew of the words of Confucius. But here was someone from that civilisation, possibly the greatest of all civilisations and certainly one of the oldest in human history.

For almost an hour Mandarin spoke to us. He was particularly interested in colour, referring to colours around me, linking them to vibrations. He told me much about myself. I particularly liked his expression 'we are a being not a doing'. I spoke about my book on David. He encouraged me, saying 'it is part of the fulfilment of yourself'. He also spoke about his own son, and his life.

When I asked him if I could put one last question to him, he agreed, indicating that he had nothing but time! He stated that 'man must experience God, he is not taught'. He felt very much that the heart, to which he pointed in an elaborate gesture, was more significant than the head. He referred again to the colours that emerged from words, making their way to the heart of another. He advised, too, that 'one should open doors where you can for those against whom doors are closed'. He actually used the expression 'death has no ultimate meaning at all'.

But Mandarin was also a very practical man. He had, as a local ruler, experimented with minerals and vitamins and had some specific advice: 'take potassium for the hormone system', and also advised the eating of bananas, mushrooms, avocados, to help a particular emotional problem. I was fascinated by his reference to animals, how dogs heard a certain 'hum' in people. He mentioned that in his day he sometimes kept a dog in his wide sleeves.

Yet, looking at a wider perspective, he felt that the earth had moved on its axis at a certain rate and the planet had changed slightly because of explosions at the centre of the earth. We were still, in his view, a learning planet. Optimistically he thought that man would ultimately absorb a higher vibration.

I mention but a few phrases from our sessions in Mary's home. Here was this woman who was totally overshadowed by this Chinese Mandarin. The exterior form was Mary, but everything else came from the being who had taken temporary possession of her. I learned more and more about his own life as a prominent figure in his time.

When John said 'Hello Mandarin, how nice to see you again', the reply from Mandarin to the substantially-built Podmore was: 'How extremely nice to see you with some diminution of form.' We all had a good laugh. Thank heaven, there is still humour in the world of the spirit.

## Brief Encounters

I know there is a famous film by that name. The book I wrote which contained an account of some of my law cases was called *Brief Encounters of a Legal Kind*, a title surprisingly supplied to me by my Inspector of Taxes! That is quite true. The circumstances were so strange, as if heaven-sent, that I dedicated the book not only to my wife and mother-in-law, but also to my tax inspector. Get it out of the library or, better still, buy a copy. You will see.

Now I want to introduce you to desperate folk who never knew one another but whom I came across, some personally, some in print, but all a reflection in some form of this strange world of the spirit I have inhabited. Most remarkable was the person who had a vision of me from far across the ocean.

I was standing by the window in an upper room of a Harley Street medical specialist. He had just told me that my son David's cancer was inoperable. My heart sank. I stood there, overwhelmed with sadness, completely transfixed. But apparently a woman in Vancouver, on the far west coast of Canada, told me that she actually saw me at that moment. She was not a friend. I had merely helped her with a transaction and she had visited my office a couple of times. After she emigrated I never thought I would hear from her again.

To digress for a moment, her own history is of interest. She had been brought up in a Moslem family in Trinidad. She became a nurse but then suffered from a seemingly intractable illness. At night she prayed devotedly to Jesus. She awoke on the following day, completely cured, and she became a fervent Christian. She developed the gift of seeing the aura that surrounds every person, whose colours indicate the nature of that individual. Some closed spiritual doors had opened for her. This release took her to many countries, where she stood up before large audiences, opened her mouth and talked, leaving the words to whoever was inspiring her.

When David passed on in July 1978, she wrote me the most beautiful letters, describing him as a gift from God. But the written word was not enough for her. She and her husband came several times from Canada to see me. On each occasion we sat in our Monkenholt home in a small circle, holding hands and praying – at least, she led the prayers with enormous devotion. This pattern continued through the decades, even after her husband had died. She came again in 2010. She had a particular love for the Bible, Israel, and an especially deep feeling for Jesus.

What a change in her life and what a support was her faith. That she really did see me looking forlorn in that upper room I have never doubted. Her description was far too accurate. Just as healing can take place from miles away, I have no reason to doubt the veracity of this woman's vision from a faraway land.

There are many accounts of how a person has sat at a piano and played or composed music quite beyond his or her ability or capability. This even happened to Irène Noah, a non-pianist who played only when inspired by her mother Vera. There is also the phenomenon of automatic writing when the writer just writes, though the words come from above.

I sat once in the somewhat cavernous Belgrave Square SAGB (Spiritualist Association of Great Britain) premises and watched a woman draw a portrait of someone who had passed on but who was related to one of the people who sat there.

This ability was the special gift of the psychic artist, Coral Polge. She drew many portraits of people whom she had never seen or known and who were no longer alive here. She did this for forty years. In her book *Living Images* can be seen side by side her drawings of those in the world ahead and photographs of them when in this world. The resemblance is uncanny.

When asked 'How do you know what to draw?', she replied: 'When linking with a spirit communication, a complete change of personality seems to take place within me, and having "become" that person, I attempt to portray my character. Actual features are incidental and somehow just follow on, after the expression.'

She even acknowledged that she was helped by artists of past centuries, such as Giovanni Masaccio from the fifteenth century, Maurice de la Tour from the eighteenth century. She found help too from Frank Leah, another famous psychic artist, who had drawn so accurately the face of Douglas Conacher – he who had conversed with his wife, Eira, in sittings with my old friend Leslie Flint. (Speaking of Leslie, I omitted to mention earlier that he was kind enough to give me his grand piano, later much used in our family.)

Coral Polge described one unusual episode. 'I found myself drawing a gentleman in the spirit world, but my heart lifted with excitement when my lady sitter suddenly announced: "That's my father. It's the living image of him!" We had done it at last. There was my first portrait of a recognisable relative taking shape on paper. Delighted, I carried on with the drawing, but my elation was short-lived because my sitter immediately went on to add: "He's the last person I want, I hated the sight of him!" ' Which only goes to show…

Coral Polge had many experiences with leading mediums, including materialisation of relatives in a session with Helen Duncan, whilst she also lists mediums she knew including Nora Blackwood, Ronald Heath and Doris Collins. Perhaps, as her fame spread, she was particularly happy when a letter arrived one day at her home, simply addressed to 'Coral Polge, London, England'.

My own contact with people all over the world continued. There was Anne, the gifted poetess and author in Sri Lanka; Jack, the psychologist in Arizona; from which state delightful Professor Louis Grossman used to sign his letters 'Grossly, Louis', alongside his devoted wife; Jim Ellis, who had hundreds of tapes of sittings with Leslie; the woman healer in Ilford, Gladys Hayter, who first encouraged my healing efforts in her clinic; as well as lively medium Avril Price and my friends in the London Spiritual Mission in west London. Oh, so many people, including even a former Attorney General of India, all interested in aspects of what I had written, the practical daily world alongside the world of the spirit.

There was also dear Billie Hart in the Midlands, who always took Sheila and myself to lunch at her golf club. She adored her late husband and could not join him soon enough. Oh, the power of love, deep love, the greatest power in the universe! How that word is misused. Billie plied me with books including Paul Brunton's *Search in Secret India*.

That brave man wandered throughout India seeking true spirituality. He searched and searched, travelling from guru to guru the length of the land, until eventually he found what he sought. His comments fascinate: 'I prefer Christ's wisdom to his commentator's ignorance.' 'I contain within myself the two elements of scientific scepticism and spiritual sensitivity.' He accepted the reality of the Divine: '... not by argument but by the witness of an overwhelming experience'. He learnt of the telepathic power of the mind accepting that 'there is a spiritual evolution running parallel with the physical one'.

Brunton met holy men who claimed to communicate mind to mind, a form of telepathy certainly accepted by Oliver Lodge. One guru stated: 'The time is soon coming to give mankind a universal spiritual belief which shall serve all races of people and all countries.' But Paul finds, too, self-important and unreliable teachers. Recognising them as such, he passes on elsewhere but learns meanwhile about breathing, postures, exercises, all the bodily practices of value.

I would love to expand on the eloquent and absorbing words of this man, but others deserve mention too. Do read, though, of his spirited voyage through India. I see I have written in my copy: 'It is a moving and uplifting story that he tells, an inspiring journey of both body and soul.'

## Four Legs, Two Legs

Now I will tell you a tale of two women. Women seem to possess an intuitive quality that lends itself to healing: when men heal, it is the feminine element in their natures that comes to the fore.

In October 2006 my dear wife and I celebrated fifty-two years of an idyllic marriage. At about that time she suffered a fall when we were guests of the Hare Krishna Centre in Letchmore Heath. That fall triggered off more hip problems. She had had replacements and a number of dislocations, requiring each time an emergency rush to the local hospital. The experts agreed that she should have an operation that hopefully would secure the offending joint.

What had to be done was done and I anticipated bringing her home on 20th December. On that day the whole of her digestive system rebelled, a perforation followed, and no further operation could be undertaken with any chance of success. And so my poor wife deteriorated in the fortnight that followed. I cherished her greatly; she was a person full of love, truth and a sweetness of nature. What could I do to save her? There seemed to be no hope in the medical world. It is possible the anaesthetic and hip surgery were too much of a shock to an already weakened system. I thought of healing, though without too much hope.

My enquiries brought me to one Irene Sowter, someone previously unknown to me. She had the same down-to-earth qualities as Leslie Flint. She gave me her book *Tails to Tell*, and I realised that her healing gifts were clearly evident, especially with animals that were smitten: hence the four legs of this section's title. She and her husband were actually helped by a former vet, who had since passed on.

There is a great love of animals in Britain. We had always kept dogs and cats as pets and our daughter had rabbits too. Once she even brought home an injured goose, but I would not recommend that creature in home or garden. Horses too, were, and are, a part of the family scene.

I had had experience of a veterinary surgeon, a man who became a good friend. Just as Alfred Russel Wallace is little known publicly as a propounder of the theory of evolution, so John Carter is little known for his wonderful efforts for cancer patients, beginning with those who had four legs. He had lost a pet through cancer and decided to study the causes and treatment of this disease. His methods proved successful and soon all the vets in the district were sending their cancer-ridden animals to him. He achieved almost miraculous results in twenty-six recorded cases.

The four legs then became two legs. His achievements had become more widely known, and soon he was inundated with ill people. They came from far and wide. He helped many, prolonged the lives of many, using a special mixture (C247) composed of minerals and vitamins alongside a specific organic diet. He reminded me of the achievements of Dr Max Gerson in the USA.

Carter's treatment was investigated by experts with positive results. A company promoted the treatments, but sadly John became ill himself and passed away. His non-invasive cancer treatments are still being used in the UK and parts of Europe. Whenever a cancer charity sought a donation from me I agreed to make a payment after they had investigated John Carter's claims and achievements. I never heard a word from them after that.

Thus John Carter, a gifted unknown, was a notable help to both humans and animals. I wondered whether Irene Sowter could do the same for my wife. I spoke to her. I read her book. What did she say? 'Healing energy comes from the Godhead.' She recounts all manner of help to animals from spiritual beings, and describes the wonderful colours used in the healing process. She was delighted when the Royal College of Veterinary Surgeons had no objection to animal healing. Her guide, Charlie Kemp, stated: 'Animals are psychic and very aware indeed of negative or positive thoughts.'

Irene Sowter's book gave case history after case history. She achieved so much for the animal kingdom. She believed in a balance of mind, body and spirit in harmony. Again we have a healer stating that 'there is no such thing as death'. However she could not help my dear wife, much as she wished. Sheila passed to the next phase of life on 5th January 2007, uttering the words: 'I am so lucky. I have been so lucky…', words which reduced me to tears. It was not too long afterwards that Irene Sowter joined her.

Another person who believed in living a balanced life was Elizabeth Farrell. In her book *The Unfolding Journey* she refers time and again to the need for balance. She had a guide, Nemerah, who 'advocates balance in all things', insists on 'balance when he teaches about love'. Elizabeth Farrell, medium and healer, states clearly 'balance in all things'. She looks forward with great hope to man's increased power to heal, from skin grafts to Alzheimer's. She refers to a dream, a vision, and reality, adding: 'I must retain a balance with everyday living.' This reminds me of Rabbi Nachman's statement that life was a narrow bridge, and the important thing was not to lose one's balance.

Elizabeth's story is similar to those of all these empowered beings – one of overcoming difficult circumstances, above all overcoming oneself, whilst always keeping one's feet on the ground. It must have been in the early 1980s that I met this fair-haired, smiling soul in the College of Psychic Studies. I had been so enthused by my healing experiences with the Knightsbridge hairdresser, with my healing sessions in Essex, with help to others, that I went, on advice, to the College to enrol on one of their training courses for healers.

The receptionist took my details and sent me along to the room where the courses were held. Elizabeth Farrell was the teacher. She had an easy, relaxed manner. We spoke. I explained why I was there. After some time talking, two unusual things occurred. First, Elizabeth had a kind of trance or at least some contact with the world ahead and confirmed that my mother was there with us. It was wonderful to be in touch with this most splendid of mothers. She had been born in Poland and had stayed with her grandmother when all the family had left for England. Her grandmother, whom she adored, had passed on in her late nineties, and Esther, my mother, then came to England in 1902, alone, aged sixteen. Her grandmother had been the town healer.

Then, to my surprise, Elizabeth turned to me and said: 'You are a natural healer. You need no course, no tuition.' We spoke further, then I left the College, encouraged by her words. But I wanted to learn more about her, so read her book. She had led a conventional middle-class life until her forties, as a daughter, wife, mother, later grandmother, a great support to her businessman husband.

But mediumship beckoned her. She learned the skill over the years but in the process had to overcome difficult problems within herself. In an early chapter she wrote: 'I awoke one morning to find myself standing by my bedside looking down at myself and my husband asleep.' She realised that some part of oneself, etheric, astral, leaves the body during the sleep state and functions in a different dimension. Thereafter others came into her world, mediums such as Ursula Roberts and Ivy Northage, also Brenda Marshall, later President of the College. I had the pleasure of a long contact with Mrs Marshall, an especially kind, helpful, and most practical lady. Elizabeth mentioned too Gordon Turner, who healed those with both two and four legs.

But all was not plain sailing. There were depressive and obsessive periods, there were unhelpful spirits about, there was fear, there was herself to overcome. But she had the qualities needed. She referred to her wartime career as a radio operator in the Royal Air Force. She met Harry Edwards and saw a golden light about him. She heard words that came from a colleague trance medium to the effect that 'the existence of the spirit world will be proved, not by the Spiritualists, but by the scientists'. This remains the hope of many, but so far scientists have made no move to investigate the evidence that exists. Through Elizabeth came contact with Joyce Grenfell and Aldous Huxley from the next world. She also became fascinated with Carl Jung's views about the collective unconscious.

Having regarded herself as a Humanist in early days, her experiences confirmed her guide's view that 'at no time can we be separated from the God consciousness for we are part of it', as well as the fact that 'life here has meaning, and death [is] but a doorway to further experience'.

She looked back on her life and concluded that 'the most salutary lesson I have had to learn is to accept how very little I really know'. That may be, Elizabeth, but with your humility, you have been a great help to many and a source of light and understanding in your chosen field.

## Faith and Hope Eternal

With the word 'balance' still echoing in my mind I thought it time to mention some practical affairs. These are described more fully in previous books, particularly *The Rainbow Never Ends*, but I want in this and the following chapter to extend this narrative to matters which have the ring of eternity. First, though, let me make mention of my own background.

I was raised in London's East End by immigrant Jewish parents in an intensely Jewish way. Conditions were not good. A bath meant a mile walk to the public baths. Our terraced house, with cellar kitchen, contained my father's tailoring workshop. Came the war, a year or two were spent out of the capital followed by a return to north-west London, to the bombs, the air-raid shelters, and the constant peril. We survived. Next for me came two years in the Army, from which I emerged unharmed and thence wandered about Europe before qualifying as a solicitor in 1951.

At the age of twenty-five I hadn't the faintest inkling of mediumship, of healing, of the spiritualist world bubbling around. Soon after, in 1952, I opened my own legal practice in Fleet Street. It blossomed and later this led to amalgamation into a larger unit, with me as the senior partner (because I was the oldest not the brightest). Meanwhile I had the good fortune to marry a wonderful wife. We had three children, moved first to Highgate, then to a delightful Georgian house on the heights of Monken Hadley, at the northern tip of London. This house, incidentally, was the one in which Dame Cicely Saunders, founder of the Hospice Movement, had been raised.

During this active period I was involved in the many practical affairs of my clients, in communal and national and international organisations, in travel: my life was full to the brim. We sadly lost family members at various points – uncles, aunts, parents – but, saddest of all, we lost David, our twenty-one-year-old son.

In due course, I became less involved in the matters mentioned above. Son Jonathan and daughter Esther married. We moved to a smaller house. Then in January 2007 my dear wife passed on. She had all the qualities I lacked, especially patience and a natural gift with technology and machines. I tried to do justice to her memory in an earlier book, *Letters to my Wife*.

So that is me. I have been lucky, not only in my practical daily life, but in being given the chance to learn of the wider world of the spirit. Now that you know all about me, I turn in the following chapters to the story of two people – Sir Arthur Conan Doyle and Jesus of Nazareth. As far as Jesus is concerned the story is strange indeed, almost unbelievable. As to the first-named, my interest in him was aroused by what was said at one of the sittings with Leslie Flint.

## Sir Arthur Conan Doyle

Of course, the creator of Sherlock Holmes was a world-famous figure, but I decided to find out all I could about him, as well as read his adventure stories. Like John Podmore, he was a big man in every way, but also a doctor, sportsman and playwright, a bold figure of courage and enterprise who gave himself fully, without stint, to many humane causes. He was born in 1859 in Edinburgh and died in 1930. His seventy-one years saw him produce forty full-length books, including histories of the 1899-1901 South African War and World War I, as well as innumerable short stories.

Conan Doyle was proficient as a boxer, played cricket for the MCC, was a billiards expert, and even introduced skiing to Switzerland. That was life on one level, but the agonies of the 1914-18 war made him look further. 'I suddenly seemed to see that this subject with which I had so long dallied was not merely the study of a force outside the rules of science but that it was really something tremendous, a breaking down of the walls between two worlds, a direct undeniable message from beyond, a call of hope and guidance for the human race at the time of its deepest afflictions.'

Thus began his crusade, his mission, to spread the truths of individual survival and communication, touring the world, speaking in city after city, until the body could take no more. Biographies of him were written, one ending with the words: 'Let no man write his epitaph. He is not dead.' And indeed he was not dead. I read and read about this man until there came into my hands a most inspiring book called *The Return of Arthur Conan Doyle*. Here I studied his detailed messages, his faith, and his hope for the future. But, *mirabile dictu*, there was also a photograph of him as he materialised. I had had personal experience of this phenomenon.

When I was helping Gladys Hayter in her Ilford healing clinic she spoke to me about psychic photography, a subject unknown to me. Gladys showed me photographs of beings who were around us but whom we could not see. It was mind-boggling. Just as a certain force or power enabled Coral Polge to paint a portrait, so Gladys, or in Conan Doyle's case, Mrs Caird, had the power to photograph a person who appeared from beyond our material bounds. I have read and re-read the messages from Conan Doyle. There are so many I would wish to record here: I mention but a few.

'So long as man remains enmeshed in intellectual pride he can never find truth.' Like so many other messages he emphasised the actual power of thought, as well as the need for balance. A medium had to be 'well-balanced, sane, sound and true'. He understood how remote his ideas were from those of most people who were working hard to earn a living and trying to cope with day-to-day problems. 'Men's minds have to be prepared gradually for new ideas.' As a former doctor, he also states that 'until medicine deigns to study the laws governing man's spiritual being it will continue to be confronted and baffled by obscure diseases…'.

He refers to Jesus as 'The Master', but also speaks highly of Buddha. I wonder whether he felt drawn to them because they were never involved in the taking of human life, unlike Moses and Mohammed. He speaks, too, of a race of men who will 'evolve considerably in advance of the humanity of today', adding that 'a soul may deride, deny, or reject God but it can never escape from him'. This sentiment is in line with the teachings of many others.

Looking at my comments in the margins of the book (not quite so easy to do with current electronic versions), I see that I have trawled through and added to my comments and admiration for Conan Doyle on page after page, from 1980 to 2008 – twenty-eight years of study. His words can be read and read, again and again. They continue to provide hope and inspiration, and will be referred to later in more detail.

## Jesus

Sometime in 2010 I received a phone call from Florida. The man had the same initials as me – AR. His name, Alan Ross. He asked me for my comments on a massive book he had sent to me, *The New Testament of Spiritualism*, containing over 500 pages. But what else it contained would infuriate sceptics and secularists.

A certain Methodist lawyer in Washington DC, one James E. Padgett, received message after message from 1914 onwards which he wrote down, an example of automatic writing. What would have confirmed the sceptics even more in their disbelief were the nature of the messages and the names, famous names from across the centuries, across the continents, of the senders. These were listed under the following headings: Family, Friends, Strangers, Soldiers, Heads of State, Religious Reformers, Philosophers, Ancient Spirits, Old Testament, New Testament, and finally Jesus, including a new prayer composed by him.

I quote from Alan Ross's Preface:

'*The New Testament of Spiritualism* is a revealment from the spirit world of a unique and extraordinary nature. This is because, instead of the material originating from the usual one or two communicators, it is from a great array of spirits who lived throughout history. Many of the spirits are famous and will be known, others are not. For many of the spirits English was not their native language, it had to be learned in order for the medium to understand their thoughts. *The New Testament of Spiritualism* is a book that contains revolutionary concepts that, to my knowledge, are not found elsewhere. Therefore, I ask when reading to keep an open mind to things you have read before.'

It is all very well for Alan Ross to ask readers to keep an open mind. More likely there will be open mouths at the 257 separate messages, including 31 from Jesus which would disturb orthodox Christians, since long-held dogmas are stated to be incorrect. In referring to the Biblical account of creation, Jesus states: 'There never was a time or period when there was void in the universe or when there was chaos. God never created anything out of nothing.' There are no miracles, only 'the result of the ordinary workings of God's law'. There are also no devils and no Satan, but 'my truths are plain and my teachings can be understood by the simple'.

Not only are there the words of Jesus but also messages from the writers of the Gospels and from Old Testament prophets. Whether genuine or not, the words contained in this volume are remarkable. So I ask myself, why should Padgett and later on Daniel Samuels, both highly educated people of standing, concoct this massive collection of words, and why should Alan Ross do so much to publish them? There was no real financial incentive, no attempt to assert personal importance, no ambition beyond that of passing on words they felt to be of significance.

Having read through his weighty volume, I then received from Florida another book, in draft, entitled *Spiritualism and Beyond*. Alan Ross asked for my comments, which I sent him. I also spoke to him again. He seemed a very sensible, level-headed person, with a limited interest in material things, and quite sincere. This second book represents a collection of lectures he had given over the years. Its sections are headed: History, Mystery, In The Beginning, The Human Soul, The Spirit World, God and Divine Love, UFO and Akashic Records, and Reincarnation.

Many of the ideas expressed would commend themselves to Conan Doyle and most of the people I have highlighted. Again, the word 'love' appears again and again. The book is very much a description of Alan Ross's personal experiences and search. But he had not finished with me as far as books were concerned: next I received a published book called *The Genuine Jesus: A Channelled Autobiography*. It was fascinating. Imagine that: an autobiography of Jesus!

In the preface, Alan Ross refers to the book as unique, containing the material that came via Padgett and Samuels over a period of years. 'All the material', he states, 'originated from Jesus. There are two hundred Bible references, and in the book there are concepts abut Jesus's life and teachings, that, to my knowledge, are not to be found elsewhere.' There is even a description of Jesus's appearance. In his orderly fashion Alan Ross divides the contents into sections as follows: Birth and Youth, The Ministry, The Last Week, The Reappearance, The Second Coming, and The Teachings.

Again, regular church worshippers and priests would be taken aback by the adverse reflections on some of their cherished dogmas and rituals. There was no virgin birth. Jesus did not die for the sins of the world or of others. Jesus, his parents, brothers and sisters lived in Egypt for some years. He never, aged twelve, expounded the law in Jerusalem. He never travelled to India, Greece or elsewhere. Baptism is man's creation and means little. He did not fast for forty days and nights and he was never tempted as there is no devil or Satan. He refers to 'distorted writings' in John's Gospel. He describes the nature of the Pharisees and Sadducees and is more sympathetic to the former than the latter. Above all, God is not the god of one nation or race.

By this time, the dedicated Christian would be wiping the sweat from his or her brow and might well throw the book down as containing a farrago of nonsense. I wonder what the Humanist would do. Jesus continues: 'In the Gospels, there are a number of blessings that are never used at all.' Tom Paine would agree. Interestingly, Jesus confirms what Harry Edwards taught about the nature of spiritual healing. Of course I am reflecting denials here. There are also positive comments on the meaning of his words and blessings, but: 'I am not a part of the Godhead. I am a man as other men are men.' This reflects on the Trinity idea. But Jesus clearly was not like other men.

There is something arresting and wonderful in Jesus's faith in God, in his own passion, in his actual teachings, in his emphasis on love, 'love one another as I have loved you'. The Eucharist of blood and wine, flesh and bread, does not come out well in Jesus's words. He referred to the idea as being of Greek origin. His comments on Judas and his brother James are also interesting and unusual.

I could go on and on, and meanwhile the blood pressure of orthodox Christians would be rising and rising. Ross refers to translations and reproductions added to and eliminated from the original writings, until the Bible became filled with false doctrines and teachings. But then, atheists and agnostics might say that of all religious books. Reading this volume would, however, be a challenge, to atheists who deny the existence of God, to agnostics who are uncertain about various concepts, and to the orthodox in all religions. Jesus, if his words here are correct, continues to be a challenge to the world.

## Sacks and Dawkins

I would like to end this part of the book with something more up-to-date, more twenty-first century. So far I have either described personal experiences with largely unknown individuals or figures of universal fame. What better way to redress the balance than with a note about a couple of highly respected individuals, well-known figures, especially in Britain, who represent opposite sides of the endless debate about God, belief, science and religion.

In the long run their names are unlikely to be compared to some of the personalities already mentioned but in themselves they seem to me to typify and summarise the high intellectual level of the debate setting out their honest opinions, publicly expressed, with notable eloquence. So here goes.

Sacks and Dawkins. Sounds like a double act or a firm of lawyers, doesn't it, but these names actually belong to two of the outstanding brains of this generation, both of whom are locked in a fierce debate as to the existence of God.

They deserve a fuller appellation. 'Sacks' is Lord Jonathan Sacks, a former Professor of Philosophy, a member of the House of Lords, and, for many years, Chief Rabbi of the Jewish Communities of the Commonwealth, a person admired and respected by members of all faiths and none. And then we have 'Dawkins', Professor Richard Dawkins, of Oxford University, a Fellow of the Royal Society and Royal Society of Literature, a man garlanded with prestigious honours and awards. (I hope they don't mind if I adopt the habit of legal terminology and describe them by their surnames alone from here onwards: no disrespect is intended.)

Both men are deeply learned, Sacks in philosophy, Dawkins in science. Both are public figures, heard and seen regularly in and on the media. Both are prolific writers. For example, *The God Delusion* by Dawkins amounts to 420-odd pages, whilst Sacks's *The Great Partnership* struggles to a mere 300 pages. However Sacks has one up on Dawkins. The books the latter recommends us to read number 168, whereas Sacks longs us to make the acquaintance of no less than 288 books. Publishers must be delighted.

Needless to say, Dawkins denies the existence of God, whereas Sacks believes in the reality of God. Both writers exhibit sincerity of belief, enormous erudition, alongside eloquent facility of expression and deep human perception, though Dawkins occasionally bares his teeth and bites.

These two gentlemen have set out their reasons, their conclusions, in clear terms, though Sacks is given to a love of generalisations and assumptions that demand more evidence, at least to me. Dawkins is also a generaliser, very definite in views, almost a militant atheist.

Dawkins acknowledges that his views may deny the bereaved the comfort afforded by religion, but such comfort is founded 'on the neurologically highly implausible premise that we survive the death of our brains'. Indeed, 'to be an atheist is a realistic aspiration, and a brave and splendid one'. He spends the rest of the book justifying that belief.

Of course, to be an atheist, one makes an absolute statement, a truth for all time: surely a dangerous proposition where new discoveries tumble over one another, from Newton to Einstein, Planck to Crick and Watson, big bangs to black holes, Darwin and Wallace. Dawkins merely mentions Wallace's name twice and says absolutely nothing at all about him, even though he was a botanist, a scientist of great standing, whose theory of evolution by natural selection was presented to the Linnaean Society in 1858, jointly with Charles Darwin.

Interestingly, both men call to their aid the words of Einstein, but Sacks, steeped as he is in philosophy, quotes philosophers galore, from the ancient Greeks to Nietzsche and beyond. Reading these two books is a university education in itself. I am a little concerned about Sacks's love of philosophy. A great Jewish teacher, Rabbi Nachman, warned against involvement in that subject. Sacks loves aphorisms: 'Science is about explanation. Religion is about meaning.' What I like about Sacks though is that he never condemns anyone for their doubts or their atheism. He shows understanding of the problems of modern man and appreciates the great value of religion in creating identity, a sense of security, a feeling of family cohesion and unity, creativity in all forms of art, and above all, an explanation of how man got here and the way he should live.

Religion, he feels, gives a sanction, a backing, for morality, for good behaviour, for the good life. Dawkins, however, indicates that belief in God, in religion, is not necessary for man to be good. He points out the terrible inhumanity of the Crusades, the Thirty Years' War, the Inquisition, and more recent monstrosities committed in the name of religion. Sacks's list of secular, non-religious horrors include Nazi Germany, the Holocaust, the millions who perished in Communist Soviet Union and China, indeed the tens of millions.

Dawkins notes that, unlike the India-based religions, the Abrahamic faiths, particularly Christianity and Islam, were spread by the sword. For some reason the English radical, Tom Paine, a great figure in the American War of Independence, is referred to by both experts. Dawkins calls him a deist. Sacks, surprisingly in view of *The Age of Reason*, describes Paine as an atheist.

As might be expected, Sacks quotes at length from Biblical, rabbinical and Jewish sources, and gives the impression of learning combined with tolerance. I didn't write any comments in his book as I read, which I usually do, since I had borrowed it, but at the end of *The God Delusion* I wrote as follows: 'Dawkins is an honest, learned, lively man. He perceives deeply. Perhaps he doesn't quite see the powerful social group pressure of religions, the performances they put on. He does recognise the power of early indoctrination and habit. He has a mixture of arrogance and humility, but is not afraid to say what he thinks. He cannot conceive of a separate spiritual world and hence says nothing about it. He would regard it as a comforting illusion. He, being so honest, deserves to consider the reality of that world, about which I write in this book. He may still dismiss it, probably will, but should at least look at the evidence.'

And that, dear reader, is how, in one way, the book you are reading came about; in fact, it is the reason for this chapter being included. Neither of these learned authorities really defined God. Sacks refers to attributes of God, but largely assumes that God exists, as a matter of both faith and reason. Dawkins has little time for the reasons. Sacks sees God as the *sine qua non* of existence. I quote him: 'Without belief in a transcendent God, the God of freedom who acts because he chooses, it is ultimately impossible to sustain the idea that we are free, that we have choice, that we are made by our decisions, that we are morally responsible agents. Science leaves no space for human freedom.' I wish Sacks had quoted the words of ancient Rabbi, Akavya ben Mehalalel: 'Know where you have come from, where you are going to, and before whom you will have to give an account of your life.' Which thought brings me to the real point of this chapter.

After reading all 720 pages of accumulated wisdom, I am amazed that neither author, courageous though they both are, has even ventured into the wonderful evidence of the reality of the world of the spirit that has emerged in the last 150 years. I am not talking about whether there is or is not a God. That debate is endless, stirs the blood, raises the temperature, often sparks wars, sets faith against faith, faith against non-faith, whilst each side luxuriates in its own self-esteem and self-belief. No: I am talking about the reality of the world of the spirit, whose existence I'm sure Dawkins would deny as an illusion, whilst Sacks would say that it is not a matter for investigation. Yet, since 1850, there has been a wealth of revelation, indeed of hard evidence, that is vital to the future of mankind: for despite all the influence of religions and secular creeds, man descends ever deeper into a moral and material morass.

How on earth can two brilliant men ignore the mass of evidence that man survives death, that there is communication between the world of the spirit and our material world – apart from the sheer wonder of spiritual healing? Significantly, the evidence for the reality of the spiritual world has been accepted by leading scientists, such as Sir Oliver Lodge, Sir William Crookes, and even Alfred Russel Wallace of evolution fame.

I have waded through the indexes of both books. I note a bleak reference to Wallace by Dawkins, but no word by either writer about Lodge or Crookes, or the greatest healer since Jesus, Harry Edwards, or the gifted direct voice medium Leslie Flint. How can you talk about God and make no reference to the lives of these individuals? They are but a few names among hundreds, too.

I would advise Dawkins to study the thousands of tapes of conversations between the two worlds. I would love him and Sacks to investigate the seeming miracles of healing performed in public by Harry Edwards over decades. The evidence is powerful, and I state this as a lawyer, but the conclusions would undoubtedly disturb the settled world view expressed by both men.

As I have stated elsewhere, I have merely, in this book, touched the surface of the subject. A study of the evidence may lead to a conclusion that there is a force, a presence, a being, a source, to whom the word 'God' can be applied. However, it may be that, as both Einstein and Darwin implied, the nature of God as the home and origin of eternity is not something we, at our present stage of development, can possibly comprehend.

One is tempted to quote Hamlet's words to Horatio: 'There are more things in heaven and earth…' – Dawkins and Sacks, brilliant though you both are – '… than are dreamt of in your philosophy'.

# PART III

## Introduction

Those of you who have managed to read Part II may wonder why I include Part III. Some may now be convinced of the reality of spirit survival and communication whilst others, particularly those of a scientific turn of mind, may retain their scepticism and doubt. That is perfectly healthy. These additional items however, may be of help. All I write is subjective. I used to joke with people saying their views were subjective whilst mine were objective, but really what emanates from a person can rarely be purely objective. Even an elevated High Court judge brings his own experiences, possibly prejudices, to his eventual decision, whether he is aware of it or not.

So, you now have a third part of the book to face. Indeed, I hope it will be no problem, and the reading of it goes swimmingly.

A gifted friend once referred me to the theory of parallel universes, observing that my life consisted of such a phenomenon, and I suppose she was right. (Incidentally, there are many more 'she's' in my life than 'he's'.) If you have read *The Rainbow Never Ends* you will know of my daily involvement with an array of practical affairs and active public organisations; yet alongside these, I maintained my constant interest in the parallel universe of the world of the spirit. I hope you don't mind, therefore, if I bring to your attention some writings of mine, and of others, which may be a kind of supplement, possibly support, to what has already been described. A short introduction to each may be helpful by way of explanation.

Aubrey Rose

# The Creative Spirit – Whence Does It Come?
## Talk to College of Psychic Studies
(31st March 1987)

*I have previously referred to this lecture of mine, but I include it as a continuing tribute to our son David, since much of the talk revolves around his remarkable poems, lyrics and thoughts.*

Tonight is also a privilege, for me. I have never before spoken to an organisation whose objective is to perceive the links between two realms, whose studies bestride the worlds of the body, the intellect, and the spirit. I have read your programmes, with wonderful speakers on profound subjects, dealing with the dimensions of space, time and eternity, and levels of perception and development.

I am honoured, therefore, to have been asked to present one of these programmes, and am so pleased that my wife has agreed to participate. The subject I have chosen is the source of creativity, illustrating it particularly with the works of our son, David, in his twenty-one years with us. Since he died in 1978 I have been in continual dialogue with him. Before that date, I knew not a thing about communication, messages, healing, not a word. His passing opened a door into a new world, and I reflect my gratitude to him tonight.

Many gifted people have helped me in this journey of discovery: Leslie Flint, our good and close friend, Nan McKenzie, that rare angel of healing, Albert Best, your own outstanding Elizabeth Farrell, and many others.

In 1984 there took place an exhibition of David's paintings and writings in aid of Cancer Relief at the Arts Centre in Barnet. We also organised three meetings in conjunction with the leading scientists from the Imperial Cancer Research Fund. The second was a talk by Dame Cicely Saunders, who incidentally was brought up in the house in which we now live, on The Hospice Movement, and the third was a panel of prominent writers and artists on the subject we are discussing tonight. They considered the source of their creativity, described how they worked, got ideas, translated them into books, paintings, sculptures, but came to no conclusion.

And it is a subject many of us have pondered. In the spring programme of the College, tonight is the concluding date. Interestingly, the opening date on 20th January was a lecture by Ivy Northage entitled 'Are our gifts pre-ordained?' Whence comes the spark of creation? In the beginning God created, and everything we create is in the image of this original creation.

If you ask the question as to the origin of the creative urge, as I did, of a distinguished medical scientist, you will receive the response as I did, that it is all a question of genetic material. In his view this was the basis of Shakespeare's thirty-seven or more plays, some of surpassing beauty and perception, or of the memorable sounds of Mozart and Beethoven. The musical tradition was evident in the generations of the Bach family. And if you ask 'From where did Rembrandt derive the urge to reflect the depths of a soul in the gaze of eyes, the expression of hands?', you will receive the same reply, 'it is all in the genes'. And similarly, with the origin of the ideas of Euclid, Pythagoras, the scientific perception of Copernicus, Newton, Einstein, the medical discoveries of Lister, Jenner, Pasteur, Fleming, Salk.

From a strictly scientific, materialistic, point of view, all these were the results of heredity, a happy combination of DNA and genetic material, expressing itself in a suitable environment, the loftiest peaks among the surrounding heights, reflecting in themselves, the evolutionary spirit of their age.

If you then seek other explanations, you may find, as with Gurdjieff, that by self-development that same genetic material could acquire psychic qualities, so that the finer the matter, the greater the intelligence, akin to the teachings of inner development in Hinduism and Buddhism.

And so I continued to ask questions.

From where came the thoughts of philosophers – Socrates, Confucius, Spinoza, the analysis of Freud, the experimental reflections of Jung? How did Charles Dickens and Leo Tolstoy conjure up a world of make-believe that seems more alive than our tangible reality? Whence derived that passion for human freedom, given immortal expression in the words of Jefferson, Tom Paine, Lincoln? Above all, whence came the inspiration of those great religious teachers, Isaiah, the Psalmist, Buddha, Jesus, St Francis, the creators of new values and messengers of the spirit?

Some say there is an existing store of universal energy, which can be tapped by people of a particular sensitivity and receptivity. This was apparently the view of Albert Einstein. He is reported to have said that Beethoven created and fashioned his works but that Mozart's music was so pure that it seemed to have been ever-present in the universe, only waiting to be discovered by the master.

And while mentioning Einstein, the bearer of possibly the profoundest revelation in the last century, it is worth noting his words, 'He who finds a thought that lets us penetrate even a little deeper into the eternal mystery of nature has been granted a great grace'. And Einstein, like other great creative people, was helpless in the grip of an inexorable compulsion. The creative gift just had to find expression, an outlet, just as Rembrandt had to paint, and Michelangelo had to create his masterpieces in marble.

So I turned to the many religious and spiritual traditions. Coming as I do from the Jewish tradition, in my studies I thought I would look into that tradition for my answers, and I stumbled on an eighteenth century rabbi, Rabbi Nachman of Bratslav. He died aged thirty-eight in 1810, one of the Chassidim, or pious ones, part of an amazing movement in religious history. Yet outside his own little world, and in his day, few had heard of him. There are many such unrecognised geniuses of the spirit in all religious traditions.

I was excited by my discovery of this Rabbi. He said much that would fit in with the teachings from the world of the spirit, teachings so often studied in this College. I quote a few of his sayings:

*The only time a person can think clearly is when he is dead.*

*Man is a miniature world. His essence contains the world and everything in it.*

*Guard your thoughts carefully for thought can literally create a living thing.*

*In the transcendental worlds, the lowest of an upper world is higher than the highest level of a lower one, there are levels above levels, high above high, without limit or bound.*

*There is a light that shines in a thousand worlds. This light is so intense that the average person cannot accept it.*

*Before a tzaddik, a righteous holy leader, can rise from one level to the next, he is first tested.*

*All of your future life is determined by what you find during the time of exploration.*

*The main thing is not study, but deeds.*

*The true goal of knowledge is the realisation of one's ignorance.*

The Rabbi once told someone, *I will tell you a secret. Great atheism is coming to the world, as a test from on high.*

From these few quotations you can see that we are dealing with no ordinary person. He had views on the origins of creativity. I quote from a biographer:

'"In the beginning God created heaven and earth". Nachman thanked God for such a simple statement. To the Rabbi, philosophy was not highly regarded. Simplicity, however, was the highest possible thing. On creativity he commented: "The thoughts in one's mind are truly among God's wonders. An original idea is a revelation of God, bringing something from nothingness to existence".

'I conclude my quotation from Rabbi Nachman as follows: "All scientific discoveries and inventions come from on high. Without such inspiration, they could never be discovered. But when the time comes for an idea to be revealed to the world, the necessary inspiration is granted to a researcher, from on high. A thought enters his mind, and it is thus revealed. Many people may have previously sought this idea, but it still eluded them. Only when the time comes for it to be revealed can the inspiration be found".

'That is the view of Nachman as to the source of creativity. Incidentally, before he passed away Nachman said: "I have already reached such a level that I can no longer advance while still clothed in this earthly body. I yearn to put this body aside, for I cannot remain on one level".'

He was remarkable, but I am sure had I the time to search, I would find Nachmans in the other great religious and spiritual traditions.

Each of us, like this Rabbi, may have our own idea of the source of creative action. We all create something, a family, prosaic things, a meal, a garment, wealth, happiness, confusion, so from where does the original artist derive his or her inspiration to create music, sculpture, poetry, painting?

From genetic material, from sublimation of sexual energy, from the life force, from self-development or as Sir Arthur Conan Doyle related: 'From spheres beyond the dull earth environment, from heights outside the compass of human mentality'.

As an illustration, let us take a look at one young man, at some of his words and paintings. He did not live longer than the age of twenty-one, but he began to show early signs of an unusual spark of creativity, that gift that seems instinctive, that compulsion to create.

Very often we find a young person has a gift for something and we don't know where it comes from. David Rose had a poetic instinct, a love of stringing words together to create impressions, to convey feelings. You have probably never heard of him or read what he has written. He died too young.

But some well-known people have been impressed not only by his creativity, but by his manner of facing adversity.

A prominent writer and broadcaster, director of The Man Booker Prize, and administrator of the National Book League, Martyn Goff [who has since passed, on 25th March 2015 ] said of him: 'David Rose, an extraordinary person who deserves to be very widely known. His story, while inevitably sad, is also life-enhancing. If this is the quality of which human beings may be made, then humanity is indeed worth saving.'

The celebrated novelist, lecturer and Doctor of Literature, George Lamming, wrote about one of David's poems 'Drought' as follows:

'Poetry is a way of ordering feeling and making it known through language that is memorable. Such is the case with his poem "Drought". There is more to the title than a literal failure of rain.

'It is a stark image of slow dying, of crucifixion by nature. The occasional infelicities of the verse are negligible beside this gift of the feeling eye and the inner ear. And it seems to be quite remarkable in one so young.

'It is impossible to say where this way with words would have taken him. His courage in death had made his family all the more aware of the fact that he had brought to their ordinary affections a quality that is rare.

'He was specially blessed with the gift of moral feeling.'

Perhaps in the light of this comment it would be interesting to hear this short little poem. David had never seen drought, and the famine it brought, as vividly as we have on our television screens, but he felt deeply, and, with the artist's gift, re-created through a handful of words, the horrors of famine. This is one of the creative gifts, to communicate feelings of others, whether of suffering or of joy, which you may never have experienced yourself, a process of projection.

Think of this as the poem 'Drought', written at the age of thirteen, is recited. It refers to India. It could have referred to Africa.

### Drought

> The people ask for rain
> The children pray for rain
> Old women cry for rain
> And yet it does not come.

The heat is getting worse
The maddening heat and dirt
And yet it does not come.

The crops they brown and die
Cow's bones show through their thigh
Men in hell's dirt do lie
And yet it does not come.

The villages are in dust
A death had come that must
Make great India bust
And yet it does not come.

This love of using words emerged at the age of seven. He wrote some sweet childish poems, little images, with rhymes sometimes forced, but still, simple lines that cast their shadow ahead.

### The Blackbird

A blackbird sitting in a tree
Sings his song of melody
He sings his song so loud and clear
So all the people round can hear.

But the people hurrying by
Do not hear the bird on high
They are too busy with other things
To hear the song the blackbird sings.

But the blackbird does not care
About the people hurrying there
He sings his song himself to please
Sitting there amongst the trees.

Note the repetition of the same words at the beginning and the end of this little poem. A blackbird sitting at the beginning, and at the end – He sings his song … Sitting there …

The repetition of the words is like an echo. You will notice it in other poems. It comes instinctively, but it is also a form of artistry.

Then there is the sensation of 'Twilight', dusk, a time of the going down of the sun, when vague impressions form to which you rarely give expression.

This eight-year-old, in simple language, conjures up this haunting time of the day:

### Twilight

Now the sun is going down
All about old London Town
The sky above is very red
And little children go to bed.

Half in shadow and half in dark
Are the people in the park
The weird insects are the trees
Waving their leaves in the breeze.

The cars rumble in the street
We hear the pitter-patter of people's feet
As they quickly hurry home
No longer will the streets they roam.

As it grows a little darker
Each light shines like a yellow sparkler
The sky is now a bluey-grey
As the light fades away.

The sky starts off as red, then there is half-shadow, half-dark, then the sky is blue-grey, and finally the light fades away. Recall George Lamming's words, 'Poetry is a way of ordering feeling', giving order to impressions, and this little poem is an example.

The eight-year-old grew into a twelve-year-old, with the same interests of any normal youngster: sports, travel, music, study. He went to the City of London School and had the advantage of imaginative teachers.

From within him there burgeoned a love of natural things. Instinctively the budding poet felt man was trespassing on the rights of nature, assaulting the trees and the grass, with our smoky factories and looming buildings. And he wrote a poem of some intensity when just thirteen. Listen again to the dramatic effect of repetition:

### Humans v Nature

All is quiet, all is still
The trees have leaves
The grass and hill
Do not make a noisy sound
Until the day men came around.

Black smoke so early in the day
That all the day is turned away
With day and night and day and night and –
Nature must go by the way.

Black pillars for those beauteous trees
Man gives nature this grave sight
Of death, destruction and of blight
And death and death and death and death
Of nature, goodness, and of ... MAN.

When man is under graves of earth
The country will be quiet and still
The trees have leaves
The grass and hill
Do not make a noisy sound
When men are underneath the ground.

The title denotes a contest, humans versus nature, man destroys: the word death appears four times. All is quiet and still until man, acquisitive, destructive man, bursts onto the scene. When man is gone the early Eden will return and again 'The country will be quiet and still'.

This is a protest poem, as are the next two poems, both also written at the age of thirteen.

Not only did man attack nature, he also attacked himself. He created weapons of destruction, he trained people to kill and destroy. The prophet

Micah, 2,500 years ago, looked forward to the day when 'Swords would be turned into ploughshares and man would learn war no more'. Just look around today, and survey the horrors of war and constant conflict,

    David had an option at school of joining the Cadet Force and training as a soldier-cadet, or decorating old people's homes. He did the latter. That had purpose. It was useful, constructive. But he watched the Cadet Force drill, and reflected on what he saw in a pointed poem, written with the rhythm of a parade or a march, called 'Tin Soldiers'. Notice the repetition and the rhythm designed to suit the subject:

### Tin Soldiers

Little tin soldiers
Standing in a row
Left right, left right
Up and down they go.
Sergeant giving orders
Booming with a will
Fourteen-year-old soldier boys
Learning how to kill.

Violence breeds more violence
Monday afternoons
Regimented soldier boys
Learning war too soon.
Wearing pretty uniforms
Duty to the flag
Belt and buckles shining
Don't let your spirits sag.

Standing there like robots
You must not think at all
Thought is a grievous crime
Just hear the sergeant's call
Good for moral fibre?
Is it really so
When you're taught not to think
How can your minds grow?

# BEYOND THE RAINBOW

> Parading there so smartly
> Standing there so still
> Fourteen-year-old soldier boys
> Learning how to kill.

But of course soldiers need weapons, guns. The tin soldiers need … toys. The result is destruction.

   The next poem is passionate. The repetition, the echo, is still there, there is also a sudden sense of drama in the middle of the poem which transforms the mood. It is interesting to see how the poet changes key suddenly, like a composer, and of course David also composed and performed his own music, and thereby rivets our attention :

### The Toy

> When I was just a little boy
> A sweet five years of age
> My mother gave me a gun, a toy
> Of plastic; it made a clicking sound
> At which you ought to … all fall down
> But always to get up again.
> It never let you drown
> In anguish, sweat and dirt
> And blood … and what's the word?
> For it couldn't kill
> A man, a child or boy
> For though it looked so real
> It yet was but a toy.
>
> When I was eighteen years of age
> As innocent as a child
> My people gave me a toy
> And warned me it was wild.
> But I did not understand
> What it could do to boy and man
> It made a funny clicking sound …
> They did not rise up from the ground.
> For the ketchup was too red

> The mess of gut and blood and dead
> Dead! That's it, the word is dead.
> The bloody frozen muck of flesh
> Lying there so quiet and – dead.
> I was crying as I saw
> I'll hear that clicking sound no more
> For men must learn to get no joy
> From playing with this deadly toy.

Contrasting moods and words emerge: sweet, innocent, a toy of plastic, a clicking sound, even 'all fall down' – like the refrain in Ring a Ring o' Roses – all very childish, innocent, harmless. Then, suddenly, the fierce impact of a dreadful reality. 'They did not rise up from the ground ...'. And he concludes 'I'll hear that clicking sound no more'. The sound began as innocent, but it became deadly. And the conclusion, for a thirteen-year-old, is perceptive. He realises that people do get joy from using a gun, a sense of power. Consider what a gun did in Norway in 2011, and in the USA in 2012, when innocent young people were murdered by disturbed individuals.

On a world scale today, the gun – the toy – is now the atomic weapon, the mass destruction instrument. They are still toys, only more deadly. Their nature is the same.

And at the same age, David worried about famine and in the poem 'Drought', which you heard, he recreated an intensity of suffering, of hunger, that he personally never knew.

David carried on studying, playing, enjoying life, wandered through his O- and A-levels, began at university. An illness hit him just before his twentieth birthday, unfortunately not one the doctors could cure. The young philosopher in him commented that 'it was just bad luck'.

He had played the guitar from an early age and now he formed his own group, and despite his affliction, began composing songs, words and music. In three months he composed fifteen songs, which his group performed to audiences: another form of creativity. Words for songs often mean little. They are subsidiary to the rhythm and melody of the music.

Incidentally, the world-famous guitarist, teacher and composer, Bert Weedon, said this about David's music:

*The music that he created represents so clearly the drive, energy, and frustrations of his generation. Through it we hear many things – the reaction of a sensitive, thinking young man to the world about him.*

*His rhythms, aggressive and strident, are the sounds that so many young people find express their own feelings, and then the music changes to long passages of solo guitar-playing that show a great depth of emotion and passion – the music of a young man pouring out his heart into florid musical phrases.*

*I am amazed at his dexterity as a performer. His flights of melodic invention are so adventurous and promising. I only wish I had known him – he had so much to say.*

One lyric shows David's concern at the misuse of power, by politicians or bureaucrats. (Remember, this is not a poem, the words are linked to the music.) He called it 'Man From The Ministry'.

### Man From The Ministry

See the man, with the gun in his hand
Tired, yet alert all the while
See the hate and the humour there
See the cold burning smile.

He lived for himself and the wet drips of death
He lived for excitement and thrills
He lived to see fear in the eyes of men
Whom he never 'really' wanted to kill.

He was born in a bad part of Hampstead
Where he grew up to be a great power
He lived his whole life in business and strife
And killed with his pen every hour.

In the morning he shines of cold lightning
His car it burns down the road
But what he can do, to me or to you
Depends on the power that you hold.

He wrote another song called 'The City', in which he contrasted the pleasure and noise of the city, with its loneliness: 'It's so cold in the heart of the city'. Of course, the songs included love lyrics, touching and alive. For one he created a new word, 'Silvren'. It fitted his lyrics and melody. The whole song is but a few lines, yet the development, the form, is interesting – sunshine, stardust, moonlight.

### Silvren Lady

Sunshine, in her eyes
Flickering gently, flickering bright

Stardust, in her smile
Spreading sweet magic all the while.

Moonlight, floating in gold
A single strand of her hair, it glows.

She's a Lady, silvren you see
Burnished amber, she'll set you free.

Silvren lady, silvren child
Come to me gently, come to me wild.

Perhaps the next lyric shows him as a quiet observer, one who knew his time was running out. He called the song 'Drifting'.

### Drifting

When the river flows past my door
The crowds all call on me for more
I don't follow the road or the sky
I see the fires burning in their eye.

*Chorus*
I don't need to follow
I just sit right down
Tomorrow when it comes will be tomorrow
I'll still be around.

Green meadows roll on by
Gently till the time it comes to die
I wake each day, still to see the sun
Lazily I watch the passing fun.
A drifter to you I may seem
A child lost in a dream
But I rarely need to cry
Don't see such sadness in my eye.

Some of the songs had powerful rhythms, and the lyrics reflected the forcefulness of the music. The words often seem strange and mystical. Here is one called 'The Pattener'.

### The Pattener

The seven isles knew his fame
Kings and princes to him came
None of them were quite the same
They didn't understand his game
They never learnt his name.

Power over words he had
Power over deeds of man
Kept the circle in his hand
Saw to it that stillness ruled the land
Life he formed out of a grain of sand.

Secretly he passed his years
Living with no need of fear
Secure in power was he here
Until the thought of his death did appear
Crisp upon the glass were his tears.

Death it came, it called his name
The Pattener he had to change
For all in all he was the same
As all the cowering peasants that he spurned
Yet here was something that he had not learned.

There is a similar mystical allegorical poem called 'Chess', its rhythm strongly linked to the beat of the music.

### Chess

The black magician, sits playing boisterous games
Juggling with the feelings of the ladies that he tames
Smoothing curving pathways through their gently tear-stained dreams
Strumming on their beings, composing one-note themes.

The red Queen , she lays tin soldiers on her board
Standing them in ranks, stacking them in drawers
Leaves them dead and dripping, drying in the sun
Laughs at the crippled images as she grabs another one.

Pawns spinning, turning circles
Caught in a spiralling net
Endings never lead to dawn
Beginnings to sunset.

Magician and the red Queen, sit in the lighted hall
Moving knights and bishops adroitly round the floor
Who in turn string their puppets, gaily painted dancers
Who sing and ask their questions, but never find the answers.

The blue King in his castle lets all his mirrors spin
He daubs them with a paintbrush as the images begin
He controls the red and silver, he knows the secret way
But now he finds he cannot stop his blue from turning grey.

Perhaps this is something akin to us as humans playing out our lives, asking questions with no answers. Perhaps he saw us human beings as :
> Pawns spinning, turning circles
> Caught in a spiralling net
> Endings never lead to dawn
> Beginnings to sunset.

And interestingly, Nachman described the world as 'A rotating wheel where everything goes in circles'.

The lyrics were as strange as some of David's paintings. In the last six months of his life, when music became impossible to play or create, he drew hundreds of coloured drawings, which have been turned into tapestries and reproduced on pottery. Perhaps there is an affinity between the strange words and drawings. Perhaps there is a feel for religious truth.

The problems of religion prompted him to write an article on the subject just after his barmitzvah at the age of thirteen. It is in the form of an imaginary discussion between two youngsters. Again it raises many questions, with no answers.

## WHY RELIGION?

'But I tell you it is hypocritical to say we need religion as God cannot exist,' said Michael. Richard and Michael were having a heated discussion of whether religion is necessary today. They are both Jews, but Michael is an agnostic, leaning toward atheism, and nearly does not believe in God.

'Why?' retorted Richard. 'Think of the human body. What are we made out of, carbon, hydrogen, these elements do not laugh, live, think, but we do, why?'

'Yes, but ...'

'And also how come that in so many religions there is oneness. Is this a coincidence?'

'Where is God?' says Michael. 'We have been to the moon, we cannot see him, our electrotelescopes cannot sense him. And what about the creation, what a fairy story! And also how could God exist in time, when time moves so fast?'

'When you have quite finished', said Richard, 'I will answer those points. First science, space and time. God cannot be within time and space. He must be in another dimension outside. God is nowhere and nothing as we know it. He is outside the imagination of a tiny brain like that of the human, in a fifth dimension which has not time or material, just a lot of nothing which has everything. Next your point about creation, you must remember that the people who wrote the Bible lived before the time of scientific instruments and did not know all the facts, so how were they to know how the earth was created? They got it in the right order anyway, so I think they did very well.'

Michael was rather taken aback with these arguments. He thought he had played an ace, but it was a deuce. Then his brain started to work again.

'Religion has been a great help to man, I must say. Look at Northern Ireland, the pogroms, the reign of Mary Tudor – just a few examples, where religion has brought mass murder!'

'Yes, but this was not religion', said Richard. 'It might be in the name of religion, but it was not religion. And what would ethical standards be without religion?'

'Just as high,' said Michael. 'Look at humanism!' Michael clutches at a new idea. 'Anyway religion blocks the facts of life, and produces an illusion of safety. It suggests that if you are good, you will go up to heaven.'

'Does it hurt people not to feel scared all the time?'

'But you must admit prayer is a waste of time. If by any chance God did exist, what is the good of, as you call him, puny little man, blessing God?'

'But man needs prayer and worship, it helps with life, gives him a safe feeling and satisfies his need for prayer, which even you have.'

'And the money spent on priests and places of worship, this could be given to charities and used in much better causes. For instance, in the Middle Ages when people lived in immense poverty, and priests adorned themselves and their churches with gold.'

Silence. This was a new line which Richard had not come across before.

'But to supply comfort to people is worth its weight in gold, and Michelangelo's paintings give immense pleasure to many people. And in times of great stress even atheists turn to God and find comfort there.'

The bell went and the argument ended.

The unanswerable question was left unanswered.

This search for truth is probably hinted at in David's poems and lyrics. The last thing I quote is the most unusual of all, written in a Biblical style, again with graphic use of words, and again his search for truth and reality. Shortly after his death on 5th July 1978, a scrap of paper was discovered with the following strange words scrawled across them:

'And lo! Man created politics and religions and social values, and traditions; many great and awesome Gods he created him. And seeing his work prospered he created many lesser Gods and these he named "isms".

And, over all his work, man created one all-powerful omnipresent Lord, Dogma, Lord of all. And he ruled and shone in his colours of Black and White. And man saw that all was Good, for he felt safe and all was simple.

Yet verily, a being came out of the shadow, and placed before man – grey. And he came with his disciples, reason, understanding and logic.

But man saw that it made him unsafe, and made him think and so was Evil, and man cast out grey into a void so that few could reach him.

So the Gods ruled and man was content. And lo, there was great destruction, but man named why he destroyed, and it was justified. And man named his causes and the destruction was righteous. And man saw that any that opposed him were evil, and so destruction was Holy.

And man saw that all was still not perfect, so he saw that to be truly safe he must create great organisations into which he can flee. And these he named with many names. And into them he breathed all his powers and these organisations grew, swallowing man, and man was dark and safe, and so he saw that it was good. And soon man saw that if he snuffed out man altogether then he would be safe, and he did, and it was good.'

There you have the thoughts of a young man, who believed words could mean things, reflect things, that words had a power and a life of their own.

Since his death he has described his passing at his young age as if it was in some way ordained, for some purpose. He has described his colourful drawings as having been inspired from the other side. He added that the balance of shapes and colours had special significance of which he was not aware when drawing them. And amidst all this, he has retained, indeed enlarged, the sense of humour and fun he had whilst physically with us.

You have listened patiently to a long tale, from Rabbi Nachman to David's poetry. I hope what I have said may have thrown a little light on the source of creativity, the material emanations and symbols of the world of the spirit, that constantly amaze and delight yet puzzle us.

Certainly David's short life transformed my own perception of reality. This has happened in other cases where a gifted youngster dies early, leaving behind timeless echoes.

Certainly, in David's case, the creative spirit was beginning to bud, and perhaps, in the world he now inhabits, continues to blossom and bear fruit.

If ever we needed a new burst of moral creativity it is now, to combat the seeds of destructiveness daily sown around us. George Lamming said that David 'was blessed with a special gift of moral feeling'. We need in some way to develop this moral feeling as the main feature of our creative efforts, calling for help from the source of all things, so that our human species, like Nachman, can rise to a new level of existence where creation, not destruction, is the constant theme.

AUBREY ROSE

## CANCER – A THEORY

Paper presented to Imperial Cancer Research Fund London
(13th February 1979)

*I had many fruitful meetings with medical experts on the subject of cancer, particularly the epidemiologists. Obviously my interest arose mainly from my son's illness. I had noticed in my daily work the onset of cancer in women who had been involved in stressful marriages and divorces. Hence mental and emotional contributory causes seemed to me relevant in some types of cancer, apart from any genetic aspect.*

*This copy of my article below bears my comment as follows:*

*'This was a further paper sent to encourage wider research by the national cancer research bodies. It bore fruit.' This article was considered by the scientists in the main cancer research body in the UK.*

In trying to break the code that will lead to an understanding of the true origin of cancer, scientists and research institutions are now prepared to look at ideas they would not formerly have countenanced. This arises from a number of factors. First there is now evidence of sufficient volume, depth, and precision, to link in pre-disposed or suitable subjects, cancer of certain organs with the external stimuli and chemical penetration from outside the body. This is particularly evident to research experts in the proximate link of lung cancer to sustained smoking of cigarettes, the development of skin cancer from repeated exposure to external rays from the sun or from other sources, and the effects on different organs of specific substances such as asbestos.

These findings do not follow the lines of thought that might have logically been derived from nineteenth century medical science, namely the importance of bacteria and the virus in disease and illness. I do not know of any present-day research that links cancer to any bacterial origin, although there appear to be divided views as to the importance of continued research into the viral foundation of cancers.

A further reason for looking more closely at new ideas is the increasing evidence, from many sources, of the general effect of external and internal environment on the body and its many parts and systems. Externally, many studies have revealed the growing impact on disease and illness of the daily influences to which we are subject, particularly in industrialised countries. One study reveals the increased lead content in the air from motor vehicle exhausts and its harmful effect on the brains of young people and children. Another report shows the adverse effect on the unborn child when the pregnant mother consumes alcohol, smokes cigarettes, or takes prohibited drugs. Doctors have also seen how tuberculosis, so prevalent here earlier this century, has been affected by a change in housing, sanitation, and dietary factors, as well as new drugs. Thus it is right that medical science and research should continue to seek the external stimuli that lead on to cancers. Another reason for throwing wider the net of enquiry is the absence of any real breakthrough despite the expenditure of enormous funds, especially in the United States, and the efforts of a large number of research workers. That such funds, and such work, should continue is absolutely necessary, even though progress has been slow, and hopes are repeatedly frustrated, and this continuation is important despite the views of some people that the key to the problem will suddenly present itself to some individual, sitting quietly, and musing on a strange association of seemingly disparate facts or results which startlingly lead on to a new vision.

Examples of these revelations to individuals abound, and the names of Archimedes, Newton, Pasteur, Fleming, Einstein, are mentioned. But as every scientist knows, these individuals are the peaks of solidly and slowly built foundations, of generations of patient research, of the ratifying process of inclusion and exclusion of theories and facts by innumerable experimenters and theorists, of the general evolution and widening span of scientific knowledge.

When we talk of environmental factors, we mean in effect all physical factors that are external in origin to the human being. These include traffic and transport, housing and place of work, the condition of the atmosphere, whether it is clean or polluted, the presence of parks, gardens, trees and flowers, the pressure and level of noise from natural phenomena as well as from man-made apparatus, the strength and movement of artificial lighting, the density of population surrounding us, and the combination of all these factors in the daily pattern and habits of the human organism.

But there is also an internal physical environment. The factors that bombard or soothe us externally also, in their own manner, have their counterparts internally. My limited medical knowledge restricts and inhibits a more detailed explanation, but some points are clear on the basis of published and accepted knowledge as well as of common sense. Thus the internal environment is as prone to influence and change as the external. A heavy meal affects the digestive organs, excess of alcohol affects balance, decision, control as well as the liver, smoking affects the chest and lungs, drugs affect the appearance, the eyes and movement.

Similarly any imbalance or stoppage or malfunction in the internal environment are changed by a similar process of imbibing or taking into the organism by mouth or injection or inhalation a large variety of medicaments or substances to relieve pain, assist diabetes, disperse stones, thin the bloodstream, assist the waste-expelling organs, aid breathing, create a glandular balance, destroy bacteria, combat viruses, reinforce the defence mechanism, and rescue defective organs be they the ear, the heart, the hip or the kidneys.

Gradually in this century, more and more attention has been given by doctors and experts to the most potent and regular of the items affecting our internal environment, namely what we eat and drink. The earlier general view was based on the old music-hall song affirming that 'A little of what you fancy does you good'. Many people remembered the phrase 'what you fancy' and forgot the words 'a little'. Some groups like vegetarians or vegans have made the nature of food and drink into an article of daily faith, separating themselves noticeably from the vast majority of the population around them in practice and often in sympathy. Complaints about new forms of mass production of food called 'factory farming' in the case of poultry, pigs and cows, and concerning the pollution of the earth and growing things by chemical stimulation, made little impact until recent years, due largely to the fact that the new processes gave many people a sufficiency of food they had never had before, as well as meeting the insatiable demands of an escalating population.

But the advances having been made, some dietitians and researchers have had time to pause and consider the effect of the new revolution in food production, preparation, and consumption. Within the last two years official government publications in the USA and the UK have indicated misgivings as to the pattern of diet in their countries. These reports have recommended an adjustment of the proportions of fats, proteins and carbohydrates consumed, advocated increased use of fresh, uncooked foods, especially fruit and vegetables, but above all have taken a definite step in linking the nature and pattern of food and drink consumed with health and illness.

This may sound an elementary advance or a statement of the obvious, a fact clear to every general medical practitioner. It is not, however, a fact that is as widely accepted as is often thought. I would like to know how far the link between food and drink with health, illness and behaviour, has influenced those who design diets for institutions like schools, hospitals, prisons, etcetera, and even more important, has influenced those who actually prepare the meals. How far are social disturbances, riots, strikes, and unrest based on the stimulus or deficiencies of defective diets?

When various old religions proscribed certain foods they linked these prohibitions to questions of moral behaviour and sin. Although such linkage may seem ridiculous nonsense to our century, it may be that the ancients had certain insights we have neither understood nor investigated objectively.

It is therefore encouraging to see that official cancer research bodies are including in their programmes consideration of the link between what we consume and the incidence of cancer. I hope that this area of research is extended, and the research experts carefully consider the many books, investigations and treatments by doctors and others, who see a link between food and cancer as definite and clear as that between cigarette-smoking and cancer. The accumulated claims made by such people deserve study, probing and detailed questioning. The limited progress made in existing avenues has encouraged research bodies to widen their approach, for the simple sake of finding a solution, and not merely to meet external criticism. Those experts I have met working in official cancer research bodies have all been people of the utmost integrity and concern, and do not deserve the sniping to which they are so often subject.

It is imperative that lines of research continue not merely as to the effect of the external environment on cancer in the human being, but also as to the effect of the internal physical environment, including the relationship between diet and the origin, growth and treatment of the disease.

But I have wondered whether there is not another element or dimension in the origin of the malfunction of cells. If we could project our own mental processes with all our modern computer aids and equipment, into the heart of one cell and monitor its progress from normality to disarray, and the influences that are there in combat, we might obtain a clearer picture from the inside of the process, rather than as external observers. We can only therefore speculate from outside observation, using our scientific know-how to witness and test, as fully as we can, what is happening.

In order to understand this procedure, researchers frequently use rats, mice and other animals to assist in their experiments. The results may be useful in the strictly physical sense, although some scientists, apart from animal lovers, have their doubts even as to this. Occasionally some human volunteers, especially those in prison or dying in hospitals, allow themselves to be used for experiments. I wonder whether any conclusive facts can emerge from experiments either on animals, or even on people in extreme conditions of health, that throw light on how a seemingly normal and unaffected person suddenly appears to be smitten by cancer.

And I have also wondered how, despite the theories of vegetarians, there are some people who have lived to a ripe old age, in good health, on a diet that contains all the ingredients that would appear to make for illness and early death. Winston Churchill and George Bernard Shaw both died in their nineties, yet their diets were as different and as contrary as any that could be imagined. One consumed meat and alcohol (and smoked) with relish, the other was a strict vegetarian and shunned strong drink. It might be objected that these were exceptional individuals, but we come across these 'exceptions' sufficiently to know that while food and drink (and smoking) are of vital importance, there must be other forces at work in the prolongation, the durability, and the quality of life.

I do not think those other forces revolve around the discovery of some mysterious substance so far undiscovered in the cellular composition. I know research continues to consider this possibility, and rightly so, because all possible avenues should be explored if resources permit, and a dogmatic approach is the most censorious in this field of research, but I have almost an instinctive feeling that this line of activity will not bear fruit. Against this is the dramatic results of research into matter and composition of the cell. When ancient Greeks referred to molecules or atoms, they could not have foreseen the world of protons, neutrons and electrons, let alone the wonders of DNA and the raw materials of living cells. Perhaps continued cancer research may provide a parallel advance although the task is uphill indeed.

There is now in medical science a growing view of treating 'the whole person', of relating a particular organic problem to the general background and life-style of the individual, and to see whether the illness has but a single, simple cause, or is the result of a combination of factors. Thus when a person lightly says 'you are what you eat' the more profound doctor would recognise the element of truth in that statement, but would relate it to the wider external and internal environment of the patient.

There is, in my view, a perspective wider still that may be relevant in the origin of illness, including cancer. It is I believe, correct that where a virus strikes it is usually linked to a particular organ, the lungs, the nose, the throat, etcetera, but cancer or the explosive malfunction of cells, akin perhaps to our population explosion, is no respecter of organs. It may strike at any part or parts of the body, at tissue, bone, cartilage, brain, or the blood. It may grow slowly or speedily, depending on the part affected, or it may, in a few cases, unaccountably decline, or even disappear.

Just, therefore, as the medical healer may try to cure 'the whole person' so cancer may attack the whole person. This, of course, is the theory of many of the unconventional therapists of the last hundred years who say that cancer is the ultimate manifestation or symptom of a long-standing toxic build-up in the blood stream, flowing from dietary, environmental and mental abuse of the body, evidencing in previous lesser symptoms, but finally emerging in the most susceptible and least resistant part or area of the human organism.

But our advance in knowledge has also taught new lessons as to the extraordinary communications system that inhabits us. Many systems are operating simultaneously in the universe that is one human body, the heart pumping the blood around, the digestive and evacuative process, the respiratory movement, the glandular control system, the undulations of sexual impulse, and also the amazing nervous system that transmits pain and pleasure and all sensation.

I have recently seen and discussed the problems of young people who have been affected or damaged by certain vaccines given to them in the first years of their lives. One tall and fast growing twelve-year-old, a lovely youngster, had his nervous system so affected that he could not co-ordinate his hands, his urinary functions, his eyes, or restrain the fits that overtook him at intervals. In these sad cases, the control mechanism is malfunctioning, and a mild sort of anarchy has taken over. There is no set rhythm to movement, no settled pattern of behaviour, as much the mark of civilised society as of civilised man, because the message cannot pass in its wholeness from the seat of the central system along the nervous media to the ultimate organ or limb.

It is not always the control mechanism that is to blame, but sometimes the nerves themselves may be blocked or ill or affected. In the East, systems such as acupuncture were brilliantly devised to do a job of repair by releasing the accumulated tensions and physical blockages in the system, and by relating the course of the nerves themselves and their crucial 'junction points' to illness and distress in particular organs, often far removed within the body from the cause and origin of the malady.

I have more and more in my own mind tried to relate the problems of the origin of cancer to the behaviour of the nervous system. It is possible that research has already been done on a possible link, I do not know, but many things seemingly unrelated make sense once the assumption is granted.

The latest research on cell composition has been emphasising its electrical basis and the passage and movement of chemicals or impulses from within the cell to its outer environment. There is a control source in the human entity, at the core of the nervous system, that relates not merely to legs and arms, but also to non-mobile organs, and to the smallest parts of our being, including cells. Just as specific areas of our brain are now accepted as controlling or relating to movement, to vision, to hearing, even to aggression, is it not possible that there are other parts of the control mechanism, possibly as yet undefined or undiscovered, that are in charge of the movement, change, proliferation and functioning of cells in different areas of the body? And if the nervous impulses and messages are affected, might that not lead to a state of cellular disorientation or disintegration, a kind of 'physical schizophrenia' within particular cells? And those cells would be in that part of the body, including the blood, that are normally most effectively controlled by the specific area of the control mechanism that has itself become so disturbed. It is as if the transmitter has been damaged and is therefore sending out disturbed or disturbing signals, or possibly has ceased to signal at all.

This might explain the possible rise of cancer anywhere in the body. It would be a reflection, a system if you like, of the collapse or malfunction at the control headquarters. The analogy is buttressed by the artificial attempt in cancer treatment to encourage the growth of the defence mechanism in the shape of the white corpuscles, or to attack the wayward cells by the direct assault of radiotherapy or the internal attack of chemotherapy and the new toxic drugs.

The view put forward might also explain some of the problems of the present therapies. Why is the removal or destruction of an affected organ or area so often only of temporary value, with the renewal of the attack elsewhere or in an associated area? It may be that the diseased element in the control system, having been denied the completion of its wrong message in one spot reacts on other messages and systems, which were otherwise behaving correctly and normally. If there is any substance in this theory, it would be the basis of the internal cause of cancer, the counterpart of the external causes previously mentioned.

The problem always with any theory about cancer, as with religion, is whether one can accept the premise. In the latter case, if you grant me a premise, I can erect a religion. The same with medical research, the essence of which is not only what questions you have asked, but also what assumptions you have not questioned.

If, therefore, there is any substance in this premise, the next vital question is not merely to ascertain the specific physical part of the brain responsible for the malfunction, but to consider what are the influences that lead to such a condition.

On the purely physical side, research might be useful into whether there are categories of people who seem to be less affected by cancer, all other circumstances being equal. I am told that mental patients, particularly schizophrenics, suffer less from cancer than the average population. Is there any substance in this claim? Would research here be fruitful? The same applies to the prison population, especially those guilty of violence. Similarly, is there any distinction between peoples who inhabit different parts of the world? I am told again that Eskimos in their traditional environment do not often suffer from cancer, nor do the Hunzas. Is there any statistical basis for this? All these are, or have been, subjects for research.

What then are the influences that may give rise to a diseased control condition that in turn will appear in a cancerous form? It may be that the dietary and environmentalist therapists have a good point, but not necessarily the one they are ostensibly aiming at. The right food and environment may be very relevant to the condition of the nervous system, but in all the cases I have read about, in the useful treatment proposed by the naturopaths, the Nature Cure adherents, the Gerson Therapy advocates, there has been an exercise of will and determination by the patient that has been remarkable, with a complete change of mental, if not spiritual, condition and approach. Although the therapists mention this in their books and reports, they attribute success to the change of diet and regime.

This may be true to a limited extent, but the adherence to a most difficult diet and regime may itself be only a symptom of a change in the central nervous mechanism, a change that colours and floods extensively the body and its processes.

When I read that Mormons and Seventh-day Adventists are less prone to cancer than the population among which they live, does this mean, assuming the accuracy of the statement, that it is the difference in their diet that is the effective cause, or is the diet not a symptom, an effect, of a different state of mental and spiritual wholeness? These are very deep waters, and we may not know the end of the thing thereby begun, but it is surely a path to examine much more closely than has been done previously by bodies devoted to research into cancer and other afflictions.

I was struck by a sentence in a letter I received from a distinguished medical scientist. The letter deals mainly with the problems of suggesting new avenues, the limitation of our present forms of cancer treatment, and the writer then states:

'It is quite possible that prayer and the development of a strong faith of some sort might influence the development of at least some tumours. Probably the extreme difficulty of carrying out statistically acceptable surveys discourages work on this possibly important subject.'

This sentence prompts a consideration of the efforts to cure drug addiction and alcoholism. Both may have physical causes and pre-disposition. Indeed alcoholism is often referred to as a specific disease with a chemical base, yet the various 'anonymous' organisations founded their frequently successful approach first on a sustained group therapy, but more deeply on making an addict understand the spiritual springs on which true life rests, and the supreme importance of adopting the right values in life, including self-discipline to avoid self-destruction (a destruction every bit as real as in cancer), concern and action for the benefit of others to overcome the dense fog of materialism and selfishness that blinds so many people in all countries. And, thank God, they have their successes.

In the same way, cancer research bodies in different parts of the world are taking a cautious look into this seemingly intangible aspect of cancer prevention and treatment. Adapting the old Roman ideal of 'a healthy mind in a healthy body', they may well seek to discover whether, on many occasions, a healthy mind creates a healthy body.

These doctors and researchers are, I am sure, as intrigued and as thrilled as I am when they see famous spiritual healers deal successfully with physical problems that seem intractable to conventional medicine and often incurable in normal medical terms.

In these cases, and they include cancer, it seems to me vital that research is undertaken as to what is actually happening between healer and subject, within healer and subject. Can the process be compared, in prosaic terms, to the recharging of an almost extinct battery, is there an injection of what Shaw called 'the life force' from one to another, does the spiritual link possess an electrical or other property, and from what source does the healer receive such a power to heal?

It is possible to answer these questions in conventional religious terms, but again, I do not think that is scientifically satisfactory. Something wonderful, curative, real, takes place, but what precisely is happening are questions for cancer researchers and not for cancer researchers only.

In conclusion, we are all of us, laymen, experts, scientists, patients and doctors, seeking together some further insight into the cause and prevention, cure and treatment of cancer in its manifold forms and expressions. Having had personal experience within my own family, like so many other families these days, of the problem of cancer, I have tried to find some clue, some common starting point, that might lead along a useful avenue of research. My reading of many books, and discussions with many experts, and the turning over of the problem in my mind, has led me to the theory that I have tried to describe. Research may already have discounted this theory, it may do so in time, but the expression of these views, brief and in the most general terms, may stimulate trained minds and open spirits to widen the scope of their research.

There is no mathematical equation that can encompass what I have tried to say. In linguistic terms the view I have here expressed can be summarised in the statement that cancer begins in the brain. The malfunctioning of the cells, wherever they are, is merely a reflection of a disturbance within the nervous controlling centre of the body. Any ultimate solution to the problem of cancer must address itself to the seat of the problem, and not merely to the symptoms.

# AUBREY ROSE

## THE HABIRUS OF OUTER SPACE
### Notes of a newly discovered inter-planetary Jewish community
(16th March 1994)

*Having been involved in Jewish communal affairs, I was fascinated by the different streams in Judaism as in all other religions, so I imagined a kind of fantasy, namely the discovery of a planet inhabited only by Jews. Of course the same speculation could apply to those of other faiths.*

I had been to a committee meeting. Most Anglo-Jewish autobiographies could begin with this sentence. Work, life, family, at times seem to be mere interruptions of one endless committee meeting. Among many blessings in our tradition, on bread, wine, first fruits, I notice one siddur (prayer book) contains a specific prayer for committee meetings.

The one I had been to had been hard going – long, tedious, argumentative. Every subject under the Jewish sun had been raised.

How were we to deal with threats to Shechita (ritual slaughter of animals). Were we for or against the *eruv*, the poles and wires, kerbs and streets, substituting for a walled city? How could the organisation be kept going when funds were in short supply? What should we do to members who did not pay their fees? Was there anything we could do about Rabbis who argued with each other, did not speak to each other, who fought with the lay leaders of their synagogues?

Other issues arose. What was our attitude to the Israeli-Arab peace process? How could we encourage Jewish education and Jewish continuity? And could we cope with an ageing community and demands on our welfare organisations?

There was barely a communal issue that was not raised. To cap it all, some members kept moving resolutions, raising points of order, referring to our over-long constitution. We Jews are great constitutionalists. Moses somehow, with outside aid, seemed to have kept it all within ten points. No one moved an amendment to that original charter. Aaron and the rest may have voted with their gold and valuables, but no one raised a point of order. Some who later did, Korach and crew, met a horrible end.

As I nodded and dozed through the steady drip of speeches, glancing occasionally at the hands of the clock moving on inexorably, it seemed to me that the meeting would never end. I yawned. The faces around the table changed and gradually merged into one huge face, lips opening and closing, but no words came. It was strange, bizarre, unreal. The face grew larger until it dominated the whole room. Suddenly it disappeared altogether and was replaced by a warm, friendly light, whilst a comforting voice echoed in my ear: 'Welcome, Shalom, peace unto you. May I welcome you as one of our Earth brothers to the planet Habiru.'

I should have been astonished. Strangely, I wasn't. I seemed to be at home. There was something familiar about the speaker. He resembled one of my committee colleagues, but there was no aggression about him, no sense of assertiveness. He was dressed in a kind of long, white toga. His face seemed youthful and free from strain. I was puzzled. How could I be transported to another planet, yet feel no sense of motion?

'Who are you?' I asked. 'Where am I?'

'It is a long story', my planetary friend responded. 'Do you really want to know?'

'Yes,' I insisted. I was not only puzzled, but vastly intrigued. Yet I felt a sense of happiness and tranquillity. His voice was soft and encouraging. I felt I could listen to him for ever.

'Well,' he replied, and launched into an explanation that left me open-mouthed with amazement. It sounded so convincing and, despite my incredulity, I felt instinctively that what I was being told was true.

'You and I are related,' he began. 'We were both hewn from the same rock, had the same ancestors, but at one catastrophic period in the history of planet Earth, we parted company and evolved differently. We, too, or our forebears, once lived on Earth, and we, you and I, or those that begat us and our fathers, were part of one single tribe.

'We were then known, especially to the ancient Egyptians, as Abiri or Abiru, the Habirus. We possessed a secret and a code that no one else walking the Earth shared with us. There were, of course, areas on your planet whose inhabitants had acquired other types of special wisdom, for example in China, Tibet, India, Egypt, but no one had received, or were as uniquely receptive, as we were.'

I listened, fascinated, but managed to blurt out a further question. 'What was that secret, that code? Tell me.'

My informant continued.

'Of course. All this is so new to you. And new ideas and new facts are such a challenge to entrenched dogmatic views. Your world, you know, is full of people with closed minds, some of them, I regret to say, are prominent religious and political leaders.'

I listened. I tried to think of anyone to whom he could be referring. Closed minds? Maybe I was one of those he meant. I thought I would draw him out a little.

'Well, who do you mean: can you be a little more specific?' I enquired.

'Do you know your history on Earth?' he replied. 'You know how the bringers of new ideas were always condemned. You had astronomers who said that your planet revolved around the sun. They were pilloried, ridiculed, condemned, forced to recant, men like Copernicus and Galileo.

'You had a scientist named Pasteur who found that many diseases were caused by bacteria. Doctors laughed at him, scorned him. Your politicians, Wilberforce, Lincoln and others, sought to abolish human slavery, but so-called religious people opposed them, saying that slavery was divinely ordained. What kind of God would make you in his own image and then condemn you to be a slave for ever? I could give you many examples of pioneers facing the scorn of those with closed minds.'

I nodded in agreement. There was no note of condemnation in his voice, just patient regret like a father gently chastening a child. I was intrigued at his use of the word Habiru, and his reference to our joint origin. How could such a thing be – he on his planet, me on mine? I asked for an explanation, which he readily gave. There was still something familiar about him. He seemed to spread a sense of peace. I could even call it love.

'Millennia ago,' he continued, 'there was a great cataclysmic upheaval on earth, an environmental disaster. Vast areas were flooded, which remained in folk-memory as the story of Noah and his Ark, not only in Hebrew folk-memory, but in general Earth folklore.

'It was about this time that the advanced civilisation of Atlantis sank beneath the water that covered much of the earth. One day your Earth colleagues will find evidence of this.

'We were a small people. We had wandered about the area you call the Middle East, acquiring the wisdom and knowledge of the mysteries of many nations. Eventually we settled in a land bordering the Great Sea, which you refer to as the Mediterranean. We really believed that it was the centre of the Earth. Before the Great Flood there had been many minor floods and earthquakes, so that most of us sought to live on higher ground, and a number settled around a fortified walled city, later called Jerusalem. It was there that you and I shared a common ancestor.

'It became clear, however, that that city and land, a good land, would be devastated by natural forces and human tribalism. So some of us travelled to other lands in search of safety and food. Others, more advanced, more adventurous, pioneers of both science and spirit, studying ancient wisdom, learned the secrets of the vibrational basis of all matter, and the means of transporting human beings, or even massive, normally immovable boulders, by vibrational sychronisation. We also studied the skies. We knew many things existed which we had not discovered and which yet remained to be discovered.'

I interjected. I was becoming increasingly puzzled by these strange references to vibrational movement, lifting of impossible weights, and especially discovering undiscovered things. I sought an explanation.

'I am fascinated, but find it difficult to follow. What do you mean by things that exist but are not discovered?'

'You can really provide the answer yourself,' he replied. 'Let me give you a few examples. Did not the blood circulate around the body for thousands and thousand of years, yet when did you learn about it? Just four hundred years ago. There has always been electricity, yet you only measured and harnessed it, understood it, some two hundred years ago.

'What you call matter is made up of molecules, electrons, atoms, all based on electrical impulses, facts you learned only in this century.

'I could go on', he added. 'Heredity, evolution, has been part of life for ever, yet you only became aware of them in the last century.'

'I know,' I replied, 'but what has this to do with planets?'

He paused for a while. He must have realised how strange I found our conversation, how difficult it was for me to take in all this information.

'When we realised,' he explained, 'that our future, and the future of our race was in danger, and more important, that our special secrets and codes might be lost to the human species, we began to search about in space for a world to which we could travel and live in peace.

'The special skills we had acquired showed us that in our particular universe there were many planets, some quite small, circling the sun, which could sustain human life, but which no conventional astronomer could perceive. We were even then far in advance of your own Earth knowledge today. Your scientists, you know, only discovered the planet Pluto as recently as 1930. They will discover further planets, with humans and other forms of life on them, some living at a higher level of behaviour and relationships than on present-day earth.

'We knew we had to act fast, that it was a race against time. By dint of intense study and prayer, an answer was given to us, an habitable planet was revealed, and, with the aid of our vibrational machinery, we transported ourselves, and many of our books of learning with us. We were able to overcome the force of gravity as well as extremes of heat and cold, and were overjoyed to find an atmosphere on our new home in which we could breathe and stand, in which plants grew, and food was available. It was so fortunate, like the heaven or Garden of Eden to which you often refer.

'Over the years we gradually adapted to our new environment. We even had a means of surveying what transpired on Earth since our departure, and this distressed us greatly. We retained a fond regard for the old hill-city, which had always had a special aura about it. At rare times we have been able to hint a message to you in that country and, in times of peril, we have been able to lend a modest hand when your survival was endangered, but of course our own hands were very much tied.'

I looked at my friend, who seemed so tranquil as he unfolded a story that stirred me, that raised a thousand questions in my brain.

'You mentioned secrets and codes. What did you mean?' I asked.

'We possessed,' he replied, 'the most advanced knowledge of the nature of reality. Whilst other peoples worshipped idols of stone or wood, rivers, trees or mountains, we knew that there was one single Eternal Spirit that pervaded all things, ourselves and yourselves included.

'We knew instinctively of this unseen, yet felt, being or spirit. We did not know what to call it, and used many names, Almighty, God, Eternal, The Holy One, even The Place. We felt that our acknowledgement of the Eternal Spirit gave us a special understanding and relationship. Perhaps our survival, and your survival, has something to do with that, but other people saw the relationship differently.'

Hearing this monotheistic view I felt I could now make common cause with him, but still queried his mention of codes and charters. He replied in a way I did not expect.

'The more we studied, (and we were great students and had endless curiosity), the more we realised that we were part of a great and wonderful experiment. We were being tested. We had evolved physically as far as we could. Now the challenge was to evolve spiritually. We had free will, but it was limited, which is why we could not help you or others on your planet as we would have wished. You have the same measure of that free will.

'We received teachings from great planetary teachers, moral teachings, that enabled us to evolve a world of love and peace. You received a reflection of those teachings through the heroes of your Hebrew history. You realise, I am sure, that Hebrew and Habiru are related words, just as you and I are related by the bonds of the past.'

I drew a deep breath. I could not easily or clearly take in all this new and extraordinary information. My mind was in turmoil. Teachings, reflections, Hebrew, Habiru, planets, vibrations, what was it all about? I must be dreaming, I thought, and pinched myself to prove it was all really happening.

I recalled that somewhere in the Talmud was the expression, 'as below, so above'. Was this what the Rabbis of old meant? I sought explanations. 'What teachings, what reflections?'

My friend showed no surprise. He had expected the question. He was prepared. He seemed to know in advance what I was going to ask.

'We did try to bring inspiration from above. It was not easy. Abraham bore witness to the single unseen God. Moses sought the people's freedom from physical and moral bounds and, through him, Ten Commandments were given that still seem, thousands of years on, beyond the capacity of the Earth people to practise.

'A series of prophets from Amos to Jesus taught about justice and compassion. Did you know that some of these advanced beings returned to their Habiru homeland here, from whence they had come? Enoch was suddenly taken, as was Elijah. Moses had no earthly grave.

'We, and they, had knowledge of universal laws. Those laws descend to other people through their own great teachers. Man had to evolve morals through his own efforts. Otherwise he would cease to be man, but as far as we could, or were permitted, we tried to give guidance.

'Of course, we had a special interest in our own people who had evolved from the Habirus, becoming Hebrews, Israelites, Jews, Sephardim, Ashkenazim. We watched, too, as the land around the old hill-city became Canaan, the Promised Land, Israel, Judah, Palestine, and Israel again.'

I wanted to interrupt here and learn more about the way of life of the Habiru, whether it was similar to our own. We had, after all, begun at the same point. Had we continued in the same way? I wondered.

My friend sensed my thoughts.

'No,' he replied. 'We have not evolved in the same way as you. You have sections of Jews different from other Jews because of their different history and environment. We have watched with interest how you developed, the many laws and practices you have established, and we have understood the reasons for this. You see, unlike us, you developed among other people and had by those laws and practices, to protect your identity in order to preserve the basic truths of the faith. Our development was different.'

'But surely,' I interposed, 'you must have the same laws, the same practices?'

'Why should we?' was the reply.

'Because we are all Jews,' I answered.

'Yes, but we came away from Earth at an early stage, and we are the sole inhabitants of our planet. There is no one else here.'

'I don't understand!' I exclaimed. 'Don't you practise Shechita?'

'We don't eat animals. They are also God's creatures.'

'How about the Sabbath?'

'We do observe the rule of the Seventh day and regard it as very special.'

'Good, I am glad to find out that we still have that in common. Do you carry anything on that day? Do you have an *eruv*?'

'The whole perimeter of the planet is our *eruv*', was the unexpected reply.

My Habiru friend tried to explain further.

'You see, we have our Hebrew traditions, just as you have yours. We study the Biblical stories, but we also have many, many stories and teachings that were never included in the Bible. And, of course, we departed from Earth long before you ever developed your Mishnah, your Talmud, your special Codes.'

This was a different kind of Jew, one I had not experienced before. I had always believed there was only one line of tradition from the Bible on through the Rabbis. 'Don't you have a Beth Din (Court of Law)? What do you do about debts and their release, Shemitah (not working the land), the seventh year change?'

'We long ago abolished money and all activities connected with its use. We have no need of money. Everything is organised for mutual benefit. One of our inspired messengers, whom you know as Isaiah, once spoke to you about this. You recall his words:

> *Ho, everyone that thirsteth, come ye for water*
> *And he that hath no money*
> *Come ye, buy and eat*
> *Yes, come, buy wine and milk*
> *Without money and without price.*

Little notice was taken of him.'

'Do you have synagogues?'

'Indeed we have places of prayer, just as you do. But we do not have the many different groupings you have. We all worship and pray, men and women, all equal, old and young. We have developed a pure form of Hebrew, from which your Biblical Hebrew derived.

'I have noticed that you on Earth have many forms of religion which you call Judaism, many labels, orthodox, reform, conservative, liberal, reconstructionalist, some working together, some ignoring or abusing the others. We find this very strange.

'None of these differences exist with us. We have a thousand different forms of prayer, to enrich each individual according to his or her stage of development.

'But we do watch with some amusement how several of your religious bodies, your Rabbis berate one another. Is this your form of Judaism?'

I was embarrassed and could find no words of reply, but was relieved, however, as he continued.

'I have noticed, also, with pleasure, much learning, much study, much writing and much lecturing among your people on Earth. Your whole society is filled with endless lectures and talks. You must love talking and listening. We here continue our joint tradition of study. But here we study more in silence. I am happy that this tradition of study remains alive in your world.'

He paused. He perceived the effect of his words on me. I had been digesting all he said with difficulty, words and ideas so different from all I know about our faith. Many questions and thoughts swirled around in my mind. I was almost at a loss for words. But he smiled so reassuringly that I hazarded a last remark.

'Are you awaiting the coming of the Messiah?' Indeed, I had been thinking of a group at home who put up posters and signs in public places, stating: 'We want Messiah now'. His reply was the last thing I was expecting.

'The Messiah has already been, not to you, but to us. He was one of the Messianic brotherhood, those who had advanced well beyond the level of planet Habiru, and who came to teach and guide us, and to approve and confirm what we had done in our world.

'Your world, your Earth-planet, is in no condition to receive anyone from the brotherhood. It has not evolved sufficiently. It is still full of murderous, impure hearts and minds. It could never recognise a Messianic visitor.'

I caught my breath at this response. I knew it would have deeply offended many of my colleagues on earth, those whose whole life and faith revolved around a Messianic coming. I felt I did not want to hear any more, could not cope with any more.

My head began to throb and pulsate. Slowly the pleasant face of my Habiru friend receded and faded away along with the soft white light into the far distance, and I could now hear however, the muted sound of familiar voices. My eyes were still closed, but I could make out a few sentences.

'Mr Chairman, I protest. Point of order. Closure. I insist on a vote. What about the resolution? I want my words minuted. I am bringing this discussion to a close. It is late. We will resume at our next meeting. Date of next meeting? Let us check our diaries ...'

Slowly my eyes opened. I recognised the strained faces I had seen earlier in the evening. One seemed strangely familiar, similar to the Habiru who had spoken so gently to me in my dream. Had it really been a dream? It had seemed so real, unlike anything I had ever dreamed before.

No one around the table took any notice of me. Clearly no one had the slightest inkling of my visit to the planet Habiru. None of them had changed at all, but I was no longer the same person I had been. Perhaps I had been privileged to peer into the past and the future and had seen what our planet and our Jewish people could become if we really tried, every one of us.

It had been a wonderful dream, and it changed my life for ever.

## JESUS THE JEW

### Westminster Cathedral Bulletin
(1994)

*My late friend, Israel Finestein QC, Judge and historian, and I sat with Cardinal Hume, leader of the Roman Catholics in Britain. Finestein and I were the elected leaders of the representative body of Jews in Britain. Such meetings of inter-faith character were frequent. I was fascinated by Cardinal Basil Hume. He had an aura of innocence and sincerity and faithfulness. We three sat and spoke together for what seemed like hours. Eventually we drifted into talk about health. The Catholic leader complained about a gout-like condition which affected walking. I had the temerity to advise him to eat a lot of celery and no rhubarb. He thanked me for my uninvited advice with some amusement. He was not only a fine religious leader but also a gentleman. He invited me to write something for the Cathedral magazine. Hence the following article, with the following brief introduction from the editor.*

Aubrey Rose OBE is a lawyer, practising in London, and active in the Jewish community as well as being a member of the Board of Deputies of British Jews. In the article below he gives us a glimpse of how a Jew of our own time looks at Jesus, and in so doing, allows us to consider afresh that mystery that we are all equal in the sight of God. In contributing this article to the Bulletin he would like it to be known that the views expressed are individual to him and not representative of the traditional Jewish attitude.

I am not a Catholic. I am a Jew, and therefore have a fellow feeling for Jesus. I am not an orthodox Jew but write, in response to your Editor, in terms you may find difficult to accept, as an individual who is proud of and close to our incredible Jewish heritage. For the Jewish story before Jesus, and particularly since Jesus, is remarkable, a world history, little known by many Jews, and almost totally unknown to non-Jews.

Your Bulletin describes the many fine things you do, the love and help, general and specialised, that come from you. To me this is more important than what you believe, although you would contend that without your faith, the acts might not follow.

One evening, recently, being in the neighbourhood, I decided to spend some time in the Cathedral. Outside it was dusk, and even darker inside. The great Cross made a clear statement. Candles flickered light and shadow over the grey walls. It was peaceful. A few people prayed. I glanced at the host of booklets. One was about Edith Stein. She had come from a strongly Jewish home. I thought of St Teresa of Avila and her Jewish background. In Paris today a Jewish Archbishop is enthroned, and I could not but ponder on the link between the two traditions.

I thought, too, of my daily work as a lawyer. So many connections with many Catholics, many Christians, including a Catholic school. I know how much we have in common and how much divides us. I appreciate therefore the vital significance of Jesus to true, not merely nominal, Christians.

But Jesus, seen from the Jewish standpoint, takes on a different image. My assumptions are not your assumptions. My experiences are not your experiences. My history is not your history. No Jew can regard anyone in human form as a God. Inspired? Yes. A messenger? Yes. Totally sinless? No. Hence there is not a figure in the Old Testament, from Abraham to Moses, David to Jonah, who is perfect. Some are quite reprehensible, most have an inevitable mixture of good and bad. It is what they strive to be that is important.

Here is a major difference. I see Jesus as a man, but of a spirituality, sensitivity, morality, perception, quite beyond the normal run of men and women. I could say the same of Buddha, whose story has much in common with that of Jesus. Neither of them, among religious founders, participated in violence leading to a person's death. They were both yea-sayers to life, cherished life.

Jesus, as a first-century Rabbi, spoke in parables, like his fellow Rabbis. Those parables Christians have erected into doctrines. Here we part company. Here we have our own separate interpretations. 'I and my Father are one' is no problem for me. We are all one with the Father, sharing the spark of the divine. Genesis states that man was made in God's image.

Jesus was resurrected. We are all resurrected. Life doesn't end with physical death. Jesus was crucified, a brutal Roman form of execution. Jews were crucified continually during his lifetime, and have been since, often at the hands of people describing themselves as Christians, but certainly not followers of the founder's teachings.

Jesus said he, or his way, was the only way. Other religious leaders have said the same. It was the way of moral teaching based on the Ten Commandments, vividly developed in the Sermon on the Mount, teachings clearly deriving from his Jewish inheritance, even to concern for enemies.

And, whether walking in Galilee, Judea, Samaria, or in Jerusalem, he maintained that same constant link with the world of the spirit so evident in the lives and utterances of the great Jewish prophets. I raise the question whether the human Jesus could have emerged from any but the Jewish tradition and how, depending on your answer, this should affect mutual regard between Jews and Christians.

The great problem in religion revolves around those who are so convinced that they have 'the truth' that any other claim to truth is discounted, reviled, or abused. It is through the fervency of such people that religious organisations have survived. It is through their intolerance and myopia that religious enmity, anti-Semitism included, has persisted.

I hope we are emerging from that long, painful period of religious childishness and adolescence into some kind of maturity. There is no guarantee that we are, but there are a few hopeful signs, not least from the perceptive, humane and understanding approach of Pope John XXIII and of your own Cardinal Hume.

I therefore see Jesus from a particular standpoint, as a Jew. Others see Jesus in their own image, as a revolutionary, or upholder of tradition, a white or black man, miracle-worker or healer, nationalist or universalist, as the fulfilment of prophecy or the creator of prophecy.

In my eyes, what Jesus had was a sense of identity, here and beyond this life, a sense of compassion and healing that shines through the Gospels, a sense of morality that derives completely from his Judaic inheritance, and a sense of Eternity that lifted him beyond our time-space dimension.

Jesus the Nazarene, Jesus the Jew, remains for me an heroic figure, part of my own inheritance as a man, the centre of your inheritance as the singular emanation of the divine.

## Articles from *Two Worlds*

*This journal was founded in 1887 by Emma Hardinge Britten. It is still going strong, mainly due to its editor, Tony Ortzen. It contains valuable articles but particularly details of the activities of the many Spiritualist churches around the country. The editor invited me to contribute an article occasionally, and three of them appear below. Incidentally, I was very pleased to have been invited to become a director of the owning company. Thus I am a director of two worlds, sorry, Two Worlds!*

### LEADING LAWYER BACKS CASE FOR AFTERLIFE

After thirty years of preparation, including, to a lesser extent, presentation, of evidence to courts of law, to tribunals of every kind, I am satisfied that the evidence for the existence of the world of the spirit and for the survival of the individual beyond death, and for communication between that world and our own, is overwhelming.

Death is a challenge to the living and to the dead. Those who survive face the problem of adjusting their deepest grief to the prosaic and urgent demands of daily routine.

For a period their very being moves between the ultimate and the trivial, each constantly recalling the other, intermingling the deepest loneliness, emptiness, and sadness, with the commonplace, the ordinary, and practical.

An ancient Rabbi once commented that his whole life had been nothing but a means of learning how to die. David (our son) had learned how to die. Had we learned how to cope with death?

Our life has very much the quality of an examination, a process of testing. Some are faced with unendurable questions, are searched too profoundly, whilst others seem not to suffer deeply in the process.

There is a mystery in this we cannot as yet unravel, a mystery that obsessed the Psalmist, and the great spiritual questioners of history. But to each of us at various stages come inevitable challenges to face, problems to confront, the crisis of birth, of growth, of retirement and of death.

We must fit ourselves so that we are prepared for them by taking thought, by the development of understanding and faith, by practical measures and training. Yet, however much preparation we undergo, the sudden reality of a personal loss strikes hard and wounds.

With problems of illness, money, homes, old age, there is always the hope of change, of improvement. With death the prospect of change is gone. We are overcome by its overwhelming finality.

I had not been a stranger to the problems of coping with death. My father had died in 1956.

I had watched him deteriorate from the same illness that had afflicted David, and the memory of his wasted form lying inert, lifeless, has never departed from me.

My mother died in 1967. I recall vividly the gentleness of her face and the softness of her dark eyes in her last weeks, as though she accepted and understood the approaching end.

In 1975, I had sat by the bedside of a 14-year-old son of close friends, held his hand and spoke with him, as he fought a brain tumour that took him away but a few days later.

In September 1977, the same wretched illness claimed the life of my wife's father. I sat by his bedside during the last days of his life, as he lay in a coma, making half-choking, incomprehensible sounds, as if to say something important, constantly reaching forward with his arms as though something prized lay just beyond his grasp.

But in most cases, those who had died, however much loved and cherished, were old, in their seventies or eighties, full of years, who had tasted the bitter-sweet mixture of life from decade to decade, and who had been given the opportunity to understand themselves and aim at achieving their potential.

Their bodies, too, had declined, conditioning and reconciling their minds and souls more easily to the onset of death.

But now, with this young man, so full of promise and of achievement, so wise in his youth, so steady in adversity, so serene in his last breath, the overwhelming tragedy of his being cut off from time and space, from family and friends, from creation and relationships, bore down and oppressed me, and shook every fibre of my being.

Tears and weeping, the great outpouring of inner grief, took hold of me, and it was many days before this well within subsided.

Where there is grief, there should be tears, although, in some, tears are no symbols of sadness, whilst grief, in others, may not always result in tears.

Where there are no tears, however, there may sometimes come further grief. A person should cry in times of sadness, and laugh and exult in times of joy.

The absence, or the prevention, of tears in the hour of distress could be a sign of danger. If you do not weep when stricken, you may not reap in joy. To everything indeed there is a season.

How does one cope with the death of a loved one? A perennial question, to which there is no standard answer.

Certainly give expression to your emotions of grief, certainly do such physical acts as to burial and mourning as seem natural and right to you.

If regular visiting of graves and placing of flowers give consolation, then it is right. If joining associations of those who have suffered a similar bereavement assists by the sharing of grief, then that is also right.

If the donation of funds or of personal services to charitable causes, such as cancer relief, is an outlet, and in a way, a kind of atonement, then that course is correct.

If ignoring formalities of any kind is what the survivors feel the deceased would have wished, that, too, is the right approach.

There is no standard way of coping with death. Whatever is right for the particular individual who strives is fully justified, provided it is honest and sincere. But the wisdom of the ages and the experience of centuries, confirmed by modern studies, point a few lessons. Grief should never be suppressed or bottled up; the stiff upper-lip is a vice, not a virtue.

A conspiracy of silence over the deceased is another form of suppressed emotion, and is harmful. Talk about the dead as naturally as you talk about the living, and keep their memories alive in your thoughts, in your prayers, and in your daily conversation.

If you need formal reminders of the anniversaries of their deaths, arrange for this to be given, even though it is sad if it is necessary.

Remember that death is as natural as birth, and is the inevitable consequence of living. There is not only a 'time to die' but also a way to die.

What we call fate may decree an early death or a late one, but it comes to us all, and is therefore part of the strand and fibre of life. Recognise, too, that even in our deepest grief, there is an element of selfishness.

The deceased may have, consciously or unconsciously, wished to die, but we, the survivors, have lost something by such death, the personal pleasure we have enjoyed in that person, a touch of egoistic sorrow, since in the death of one dearly loved as we loved David, we have lost a part of ourselves.

Recognise this and it may help to keep a balance. You will be told that time is a great healer, and it is. It may never heal completely, but it will help to create an equilibrium, and a sense of perspective.

Above all, your view of death depends ultimately on your view of life, whether you see purpose in human existence, whether you have faith in or understanding of our relationship with the Great Creator or Creative Force that surges through all things.

If your view is solely that of modern materialists, you will become a half-person who cannot acknowledge mystery in life and who rejects a fundamental area of human existence.

## SUICIDE BOMBERS AND THE BEYOND

Aubrey Rose has had a career as a lawyer, writer and in the field of human rights. His books include Journey into Immortality, an account of the life of his son David, in which he describes his experience of sittings with direct voice medium Leslie Flint. In this feature, Aubrey argues the case that terrorists will have to account for their actions once they enter the spirit realms.

*'I have set before you life and death, blessing and curse. Therefore choose life.'*
Deuteronomy

*'Store up for yourself treasures in heaven… If then the light within you is darkness, how great is that darkness.'* St Matthew

*'He who kills himself with anything, Allah will torment him with that in the fire of hell.'* Koran

*'Friendship is the only cure for hatred, the only guarantee of peace.'* Buddha

*'If we wish to create a lasting peace, we must begin with the children.'* Gandhi

Throughout the higher teachings of the faiths runs the theme of the supreme value – the gift of life. We are the blossoms on the tree of life. According to the Nazarene, we should try and live life more abundantly.

In spite of such teachings, the last century has witnessed endless crimes of the destruction of life.

The list is long, grievous and heartbreaking – the massacre of the Armenians, of Russian peasants, of the Chinese in the 1930s and 1960s, of millions in two World Wars, of Jews and others in the horror of the Holocaust, of whole peoples in Rwanda and Burundi, of millions in conflicts between Iran and Iraq, in Sudan and elsewhere.

How often is the flag of religion waved to justify and encourage such murderous acts?

The horrors committed in the name of religion century after century, in the Crusades, Holy Wars and genocide, church-inspired, are recounted not merely by historians, but also by those like Arthur Findlay in the Spiritualist movement.

The graphic words in the New Testament, 'in my Father's house are many mansions' and 'lay up for yourself treasures in Heaven' have special significance for those who cherish the inspired messages received from those many mansions over the last 150 years.

To anyone with knowledge of the laws of cause and effect, of reaping as you sow, in the relationship of our acts in this world to the consequences in the world ahead, the appearance of suicide bombers sends a chill of revulsion, indignation, almost of disbelief, down our spines.

We are often taught 'as you think, so you are' but this is a step removed from 'as you believe, so you are'.

That anyone can be so mentally indoctrinated, often those who are no more than children, to think, believe and act in such a horrific manner is the nearest thing to blasphemy against creation and the creator.

To destroy one's own life at the same time as that of others, in the belief that, in so doing, one inherits the blessings and joys of heaven is desperately sad and despicable, reminding one of the teaching to fear them that kill, not merely the body, but also the soul.

It is this same indoctrination and promise that drove Japanese pilots, to the glory of the Emperor, to crash into American warships. The same crazed motivation induced, more recently, Tamil Tigers to blow up parts of Colombo in Sri Lanka.

Now young Palestinian children are told they are heroes and heroines if they likewise destroy themselves and others in Israel, a country that has abolished the death penalty.

It is often asserted that education is the solution to this evil. It is not. Highly educated individuals assisted the Nazis. Those who crashed into the Twin Towers in New York on September 11th were not bereft of education. It is what is in the heart that matters, what is in the mind, the soul.

Crime in Britain, Europe and America has not declined as educational standards have improved. Education and knowledge are but tools for either good or bad ends.

The challenge to religious and moral leaders, and especially to those blessed with the insights of the messages so often set out in these pages, of knowledge of good and evil and of the two worlds, is how to warn suicide bombers and those who manipulate them that they are laying up for themselves great bitterness and grief in the world to come.

Who is there to explain and convince them that they will have to atone for their crimes and seek forgiveness from those whom they have deprived of life?

Is this a challenge that can be met in this present age when reality is so often smothered and perverted by self-interest and a perpetual electronic smokescreen of ephemeral words and images?

Those who carry out these unholy missions – and especially individuals who train and incite them – are committing a great blasphemy against humanity and the Divine Being, or Force, at the heart of all reality.

## IT COULD HAPPEN TO YOU

'I really have to get back to my office in London,' I said. 'There are people waiting to see me and I have to check what my staff are doing.'

'Well, if you so wish,' said the young woman, 'but while you're here, there are a few places that might interest you. It won't take long.'

I must say, I didn't quite know where I was. I recall getting on a train, as I had to travel some distance for my work. I was visiting a town I had not been in before. I must have fallen asleep and been woken up by the porter. Maybe this woman had been sent to meet me. I didn't quite understand what had happened.

'Oh, well,' I thought. 'It'll all make sense in a few minutes. I'll wake up properly and get on with my normal life, so why not look at what she wants to show me.'

I looked round. It seemed quite a pleasant place, well-lit, a bit quiet for a town, but maybe it was early in the day.

The young woman had taken hold of my hand as we walked along. This was unusual but somehow it seemed quite natural.

Normally, when a woman took hold of my hand it meant something. Normally, I would feel something, as I had a liking for women, but this holding of hands aroused nothing in me. I must say I was surprised.

She asked me if I liked music. I told her I did, and she took me into a large hall where a man was playing the piano. The tune was very peaceful but strange. I could have sworn each note seemed to trigger off a kind of colour that flew up from the keys. The woman explained. 'We have special kinds of instruments. You normally hear the music, but in this hall, we can also see the music.'

It seemed a reasonable explanation. I had been to discos where psychedelic colours and reflections seemed to accompany the music.

My mouth felt dry. 'You can have a drink, if you want one,' she observed. I wondered what had happened. I was thirsty, but yet I didn't want a drink.

'Ah, well,' I said to myself. 'I'll soon be in my hotel and I'll order something.'

And that was strange, too. I knew I had to get back. I had a string of appointments, but the more I wandered about this place, the less hurry I felt to return.

We passed a group of young people standing about. Some faces seemed familiar. Some even looked like my old grandparents, but that was not possible. They had died years ago. One of them smiled at me; I could have sworn it was Uncle John. He was a character, very jolly, always laughing, fond of the bottle. One day they found him flat on his back clutching a bottle in his hand. He had fallen, his head had hit a stone wall and he had died instantly.

The young woman also smiled. I think she knew what was passing through my mind, but she said nothing. We walked on, looking at the buildings and the lawns and flowers. What a nice place, I thought.

As we passed one spot, she told me it was a clothing shop and I might like to try on some clothes. The woman herself wore a simple long white gown, like a nurse might wear in a hospital. Was she a nurse of some kind, I wondered?

'All right, let's have a look,' I replied, 'but then I really must go.' So into the shop we went.

What a strange place. No manager, no one serving. 'Oh, you just try on anything you fancy. If you like it, you can take it with you. They don't worry about money here.'

Well, that was a turn-up for the book. I needed some new clothes, never had time to do much shopping. Tried on a few suits, but didn't really like them. Then saw a long gown like the one the woman had on.

'Go on,' she said, watching me. 'Put it on. Bet it'll suit you.'

I must say I felt a bit of an idiot. I'd never worn anything like it before. It was long and straight and very soft blue in colour. I pulled it over my head and let it slowly fall down around and about me. It felt soft. It also seemed to glow, very quietly, not only outside of me, but also inside. I felt really good. I knew I couldn't go to my appointments dressed like this, but it did feel good, and the appointments felt a bit less urgent now. Maybe the people wouldn't mind waiting for me.

'Would you like to see how you look?' The young woman smiled. She was nice. I wondered if I had seen her somewhere before. She was friendly, at ease, and really interested in me, in a nice sort of way.

'All right,' I said. 'Let's see what I look like.'

She took my hand again and placed me before a long mirror. I looked at myself. Was that me? I looked years younger, as if I was about twenty years old. I also stood up straight. There was no sign of the slight bend to the side usual with me after an accident I had had. I just stared and stared. This was me as a young man, not a middle-aged businessman. All the wrinkles and furrows had disappeared from my face. My skin seemed smooth and bright.

'Keep looking,' she said. 'Tell me what you see.'

I didn't know what to say, just spluttered out a tumble of words.

'Why, this is me, years ago. What has happened? And look, I'm standing up straight. I haven't done that for about ten years. And now look, there seem to be colours coming out from the long gown all around me, as if I was on fire, but not on fire. What on earth is happening? Where am I? Who are you? Where are we?'

She stood quietly, still smiling.

'Well,' she replied at last, 'I can tell you one thing. You certainly aren't on Earth. You're in a much better place. You recognised those people smiling at you, but you couldn't believe your eyes, couldn't admit what you saw. These things take time. And you didn't mind my holding your hand because, years ago, we had held hands in the same way. You didn't object because something told you it was all perfectly normal and all right. And now you're wondering where you are. Where do you think you are?'

'I don't know,' I answered, 'but I know I don't want to leave in a hurry.'

We walked on, again passing the group who had smiled at me.

'Hello there,' said Uncle John. 'Don't you recognise me?'

'Yes, but you've been dead for years,' I replied.

'Dead right!' he laughed. 'There are some others you know here, waiting to say hello to you.' I looked around. Gracious, there were Grandma and Grandpa, but they didn't look like old folk. They looked almost as young as I did.

'Hello, young 'un,' they seemed to say together. 'Welcome to your new home.' New home! It burst on me like a thunderstorm. My new home! I looked at them, smiling, at Uncle John. He was smiling. At the young woman. She was smiling. She wanted to explain something. I could see it in her eyes.

'We just couldn't let you carry on as you had been. You were only fifty years old, but you were rushing about the country, busy, busy, you never took any care of yourself. You had to see the company make a profit. You had to keep selling, keep visiting, keep working. And you brought it all on yourself. We tried to warn you, but we couldn't get through to you properly. You never relaxed. Your last journey, you were so exhausted that you fell asleep, and you never woke up again, at least not on Earth.'

She stopped. I thought about what she had said.

'Where am I then, in heaven?'

'Not quite,' she replied, 'but not too far away. Now you'll have the chance to relax. Now you can give yourself a chance to do things you always wanted to do, but couldn't find the time. We don't have time here, so you have all the time in the world.'

It sounded crazy, but somehow I knew what she meant.

I just looked and looked and nodded and nodded and walked and walked with her wherever she led me. I, too, was smiling.

## The Mission

### A Metaphysical Fantasy
(2003)

*This is a fantasy. I tried to imagine the state of our planet and its inhabitants in the year 2050 through the eyes of one, namely Brother David, who left Earth in 2030, not so far ahead. I also tried to find some redemptive element that created hope for the future.*

*Take with you words and return unto the Lord* – Hosea

*Nation shall not lift up sword against nation. Neither shall they learn war any more* – Micah

*Purify our hearts to serve You in truth* – Hebrew prayer

I had left Planet Earth many years ago. My development since then had been considerable, and now I was privileged to be present at a gathering of Shining Beings. I say 'to be present', but since my evolution had not reached their level, it was necessary for me to be shielded from the light they emanated.

I was aware of their deliberations but I could only see them by reflected and filtered light.

They were different from me. Although I retained form, reminiscent of the most buoyant period of my earthly days, they were pulsations of light, adopting forms as and when they wished.

I wondered why I was privileged to be allowed near them. The year, according to the Christian reckonings on Earth, was 2050, although other cultures, other religions, had other reckonings. I had had a long life as an Earth being, a male, who lived in the European area, but who had travelled widely around the planet. I was much closer to its daily reality than those with whom I was now assembled.

When I had left Earth some twenty years before, the events taking place there were frightening. The advance of science was seemingly unstoppable, irrespective of consequences, far ahead of moral and social development. The human population was also advancing, having grown four-fold in a century.

During my Earth-life I had studied the evolution of the physical world. I had marvelled at the expanding mind of man, most of the great discoveries, evolution, the nature of the atom, the cell, of unseen yet powerful forces, the advance in surgery, tissue retention and use, organ transplants, changes in the very processes of reproduction, all these, mainly the product of European and United States endeavours, had given man greater control over himself and his environment.

Yet alongside this, man could still not control his animal inheritance, which constantly burst out in physical lust, violence, terrorism, genocide, racial and tribal wars, and in the spread of pestilence and disease.

Even the moralistic religions history had thrown up were unable to stem the flow of hatred. Sometimes they added to the problem.

While still on Earth I had tried to indicate paths to reverse this trend, but I was one tiny voice.

Whilst pondering these thoughts, a voice suddenly entered my consciousness, and filled me with the following words: 'You are wondering, Brother David, why you are here with us. I, Ruah, speaking for my colleagues, will tell you. First, I must assure you that you will not suffer by your presence here. I know your level is not our level, but you have attained highly, and the light we shed will not fall directly on you. You will see and hear us only indirectly, shaded and guarded from the strength of our emanations. You will be able to converse with us in the usual manner, by the dialogue of thought forces that pass between us.'

I was amazed that I was in such company. I had spent some time on Earth, not only in my last life there, but also since passing on to my present higher realm. The expression 'thought forces' was familiar to me. Even in my Earth time I had become familiar with the means of communication by thought. An old book, published as long ago as 1911, had described the process. I had been involved in direct voice sittings in which the vibrations of thought had been converted into human sounds and words.

The teachings of many, notably Oliver Lodge, had described the evolution of mind and spirit over millions of years alongside the physical evolution described earlier by Darwin and Wallace. And in my new world, links were made and developed by thought and mind rather than by physical sounds, although that method was always available.

My mind returned to what Ruah had just told me.

'Why have you honoured me to be among you?' I enquired. The reply was not something I had anticipated. 'We, thirty-six of us, are coming together to consider a major intervention in human evolution. We have watched similar evolutions among human-type beings on other planets, those still undiscovered by Earth men and women, despite all their scientific advances.

On these other planets we have been pleased to see a comparable moral evolution, so that peace and harmony reign, and progress to higher spheres and levels, always learning and seeking, has not been disfigured by what we have seen on planet Earth.

'Your presence can be of help to us. You are frequently involved in the affairs of their continents and societies and individuals, and we seek the benefit of your experience.'

Politely, I sent to them a thought.

'You all have far greater power and influence than me. I admit I am much involved with the human species, but you could gather so speedily yourselves all that you wish to know.'

Ruah responded without pause, ahead of me.

'Brother David, we, as you correctly say, do have the qualities that could garner all we wish to know rapidly, but our past experience based on the varied human mental development, has been disturbing.

'You see, whenever one of us plays any role in human history, human society immediately creates of us a God. You and I know that we are all emanations of the infinite force of Love called God, all of us at different strengths and potencies, but human development has been such that it cannot desist from creating us into Gods, involving a type of worship and adoration totally out of place, unbecoming and illusory.'

Within myself, hearing the echoes of these words, I knew how right Ruah was. I knew how the Hebrews had created a God out of their experiences, how the Japanese had done likewise, and how they both believed their groups were especially favoured by the Gods they had created.

I knew how peoples of old had created Gods out of rivers and mountains, how Egyptians had worshipped animals and birds, and how even the Greeks and Romans, with their advancing knowledge, had yet created statues as Gods, even raised men to the level of Gods.

I knew how the Indians, a people filled with special knowledge and a love of religion, had created many Gods, of fertility and destruction, of love and power, and had given them physical form. I knew, too, that they had gone too far in believing souls can pass on and return in animal form.

I had witnessed how the Chinese, and other gifted people, had made Gods of their ancestors, but had also sought ways of moderation.

I knew, too, that an inspired Hebrew had been erected into a God, or part-God, by non-Hebrews, how that had led to an institution based on fixed immutable ideas that had held back the advance of knowledge for a thousand years while inflicting horrible deeds in the name of that very God.

I saw the same development in the sands of Arabia where another man was erected into the unique messenger of God's last word, as if any last word is possible – and how that belief had fired people to spread their ideas by sword and conquest.

I saw the great hold all these ideas had on the minds of their followers, giving them the security and comfort of answers to all questions, but also closing down entry into their minds of higher thoughts, which would have led to peaceful advancement.

I had watched also the advance of the Gods of material success and seen the misuse and degradation of both body and mind, especially in Western countries, where the gratification of the physical senses had become the dominating ambition among millions.

These thoughts passed through my mind as the words of Ruah echoed within me. And Ruah, of course, knew immediately all that I had been thinking.

'You are right, David. You see whenever one of us influenced or inspired men and women among Earth beings, we were transformed by them into Gods. You know, and we know, what havoc that has created among the human kind, as they are perverting their knowledge, corrupting their minds, and souls, destroying their planet, and are close to destroying themselves. So we are now assembled to consider a decision, a course, we never believed we would ever have to consider.'

'And what is that?' I asked, still wondering why I had been asked to be present and involved.

'The decision,' Ruah replied, 'is whether the time has come to limit the amount of free will that has been granted to Earth man. It is a decision we have never had to consider with the occupants of other planets. We know free will is already limited by parentage, by indoctrination when young, by the words and pictures that pour out incessantly into their eyes and ears, but, despite all this, they still have enough of an element of free will to enable them to rise above themselves and advance towards their potential.'

'But how can I help?' I enquired. 'In terms of time I have been a voyager from the Earth world only during these last twenty years.'

'Time does not matter,' came the reply. I could see, by reflection and in a shaded manner, the pulsating lights of those assembled, sometimes taking physical form, sometimes emanating in rose, white and gold lights. At times they were pure thoughts, at other times visible to me as separate beings taking human form.

Ruah continued: 'We want you to return to the Earth sphere, not as a human, but sufficiently reduced in vibration to be able to make contact with men and women there, also the animals, who inhabit that globe. We want you to assess the forces that are afoot and whether the human population of Earth is capable of saving itself from total destruction. This is a mission of great importance. You have been chosen because you experienced on Earth, and in Earth form, those years, in Earth terms, from 2000 to 2030, when so much changed so speedily. Also, you yourself have advanced much since you came to our spheres. Will you accept this mission?'

I could see the flashing lights of the thirty-six, however dimly, confirming what Ruah had said, and urging me, in the exercise of my own freedom of will, to accept the task ahead. It was never comfortable for me to leave the care and light that surrounded me in my present abode and descend to the thickness and mental and spiritual darkness that enveloped so many parts of the Earth planet. It was not an inviting prospect, but, of course, it was a duty that had to be performed. I wished to help Ruah and those shining beings, as well as to help those I had left behind on the planet, especially those who were striving for moral and spiritual advancement.

'I will accept your mission,' I announced, 'and will indicate to you when I can report, so that you can raise me again to this level, however briefly.'

I perceived a flashing of lights, and somehow heard within myself, a message of hope and of encouragement that clearly had emanated from Ruah and from those around him. I had agreed to undertake a difficult task, but I knew that what I reported could have momentous consequences.

The more I thought about it, the more I realised the responsibility I bore for the future of Earth's residents. I knew that the exercise of free will was the most significant aspect of human individuality. This contrasted powerfully with the solely instinctive, almost predestined, behaviour of most of the group forms of life, from insects to birds, and the majority of animals. Perhaps only some dolphins and few domesticated and cherished animals were of such a nature as to escape for a period from total immersion in the dominance of group attachment and had achieved a modest measure of individuality.

The contrast was also vital between the human breed, in which the mind has developed so significantly over hundreds of thousands of years, with the very machines that man, in his growing scientific wisdom, has created, for man was not only created, over aeons of time, but was also a creator himself.

In my earlier Earth years, I had watched the creation of a kind of lesser, automatic beings named robots. With advanced computer knowledge, these beings were endowed with aspects of brain-power that enabled them to perform all manner of functions. A host of writers had described their development, from H.G. Wells to Isaac Asimov, sometimes positing ideas of robots acquiring human emotions. But the robotic revolution forecast in the twentieth century did not materialise quite as foreseen, partly due to the enormous expansion of the human population itself.

I understood well the deep concern of those who had authorised my mission. Any diminution of human free will would convert Earth men and women into beings somewhat similar to the group behaviour of the ants and the bees, dominated by their reproductive processes, or to the automatic, indoctrinated mechanistic behaviour of the robot, all immersed in material activity, devoid of the moral and spiritual elements that had made such advances within limited sections of the human species.

I pondered yet again why I had been chosen for this task. Possibly it was because I had been part of the turbulent human world for many decades until my translation to the world of the spirit in 2030. Possibly also because since that year I had had the opportunity of making contact with and observing the uneven development of those among whom I had once dwelt. And yet possibly also because the written and spoken word, as well as the unspoken yet recorded thought, had played a prominent role in the latter part of my earthly life.

To make contact with Earth from my present abode presented no difficulty. During the last quarter of the twentieth century and the first quarter of the twenty-first century I had had many opportunities to make contact from Earth with those in my present realms. This had taken place through sensitively charged people known as mediums. I had read extensively in this field, and realised that this form of contact had been the real basis of all the major religions, a fact still unacknowledged by their institutions and leaders.

I learned, too, from my experience then, confirmed by my post-Earth lessons, that there were not two worlds, as often described by spiritualistic adherents, but many, many worlds, many worlds in the world of the spirit, many worlds within our planetary and galactic neighbours, and especially, as I was later to note in my Report, many worlds within the single orb of planet Earth itself.

To make earthly contact was therefore no problem. Since 2030 I had been there frequently, albeit undetected and unobserved by human beings, except where special contact was made, or where I had impressed myself on those whom I loved and cared for and wished to help, although my ability to assist was limited always by the law of free will affecting the human race.

Nor was there any other impediment to my observation of Earth. When science, so developed among the ancient Greeks, Indians, Arabs and Chinese, finally escaped the dead hand of clericalism, especially in the continent of Europe about 500 years ago, the advances made had been phenomenal. The scientists, unlike the clerics of all organised religions, knew that there was no last Word, of God or of science. Each generation built on the discoveries of its predecessor.

I had been fascinated to see that this burst of new knowledge had taken place notably in Europe and in the United States, itself largely an emanation of Europe. This was not so surprising since the idea of human rights, of individual rights, of novel forms of democracy, had all arisen in Europe and the United States, and had thus enabled science to flourish.

When on Earth, I had studied and studied this amazing advance, the wonders of medicine and surgery, the understanding of the human body and its parts, the constituents, chemical and electrical, of the atom and of the cell, of heredity and the genetic processes in all species and forms of life, of the non-material forces that needed matter with which to express themselves – gravity, electricity, electro-magnetism, light, cohesion. I learned of dimensions of light and sound that existed which Earth humans could only measure by machines, of the nascent exploration of space, with the revelation of Earth's insignificant role as but a speck of dust within a single galaxy. Indeed, I learned that there were indeed many more things in heaven and earth than man, mortal man, and immortal man, could ever comprehend.

My studies extended, too, to the controversial, seemingly illogical, ideas of the new scientists of the twentieth century, confirmed in the twenty-first century and by my own personal experience. The more the scientists studied, the more there was to study. There grew a kind of theology in science, but, unlike religion, the dogmas of one scientific movement gave way to new dogmas. They were ever-changing, from gravity to relativity, from spontaneous generation to bacteria to the double helix, from precision to the notions of uncertainty, non-locality, even to phenomena that exceeded the speed of light.

I knew the scientists were heading in the right direction. They themselves were not to know it, but it was a spiritual direction. Some of them would have been shocked, appalled, at this knowledge, so immersed were they in the inherited materialistic doctrines of the nineteenth century. In fact, they were heading irrevocably towards the deepest insights of those mystical elements of old religions, which but a few could perceive.

For me, leaving aside these ideas, and to depart from the assembly in which I had just been charged with a crucial mission, required but a single thought. To translate myself from thence to Earth simply needed a further thought that operated instantaneously, faster than the speed of light or sound or any other phenomenon. I lived in a world of thought forces, which had none of the constrictions of earthly men and women, or indeed more advanced men and women on other inhabited planets.

Being something of a sentimentalist, I occasionally looked at the comprehensive records we maintained of human endeavour and thought, all of which were immediately available to me in my normal abode. The words of an ancient poet registered with me:

*The heavens declare the glory of God*
*The skies proclaim his handiwork*
*Day after day they pour forth speech*
*Night after night they display knowledge*
*There is no speech or language*
*Where their voice is not heard*
*Their voice goes out into all the earth*
*Their words to the ends of the world.*

Of course, people of that age had no real understanding at all of what the inspired poet had divined. It just sounded good to them. But the poet had perceived a scientific fact that no speech or language was necessary where knowledge was available instinctively in worlds beyond the terrestrial sphere.

We spoke by thought. We lived in a world of thought. We created by thought. And so, by thought, I embarked on my survey of the state of the human race on Earth. What I saw and perceived, because I could penetrate beneath the outward physical reality into the thoughts and feelings of men and women, disturbed me greatly. There were some elements of hope, but the planet was wracked by inherited forces competing with newer efforts. I perceived not one world there but many worlds, trying to live alongside each other, even though each was based on different values, different experiences, different histories.

To be honest, since 2030, I had been deeply involved in many new and exciting interests available to me. I could now attempt many things I had wished to do when on Earth. Of course, I had kept an eye on those I loved, and watched with pleasure the development of younger members of my Earth family, occasionally influencing them in different directions, but never affecting their own freedom of choice.

I had watched, too, the uneven progress of the general human family. Deep divisions continued to exist, and many could never acknowledge that they were members of one family. Science had expanded enormously, again in Europe but particularly in the United States. The scientific and industrial revolutions had begun in England in the 1700s and grown beyond all recognition. Space travel and exploration had expanded, but the most notable advances had rested on the computer and its offspring. Every young child, in the developed countries, could operate the most sophisticated machines. The worlds of the internet, virtual reality, information technology, burst onto the scene in the last half of the twentieth century, and blossomed thereafter.

This had helped notably in medical diagnosis and treatment. Parallel to the study of quantum physics, all doctors had learned the process of radionics and radiesthesia, a fringe programme in my youth, but now the daily pattern in the medical world, as a method of assessing health.

Yet I knew that progress was not universal. Even as Chadwick, Rutherford and Einstein were making their momentous discoveries in one part of Earth, in another part people were still eating their fellow men. Such was the paradox of human development. Even while solutions were being found for all manner of diseases, such as smallpox, tuberculosis and polio, men in Germany were committing the greatest crime recorded in civilised history, the premeditated, scientific annihilation of millions of their fellow creatures.

That same people had used poison gas in World War I, used since only by Arabs on Kurds and fellow Arabs, while the horror of germ warfare was being prepared. In fact, due to leakages of germ and atomic material, vast areas of Earth had been declared 'no-man's land', into which entry was forbidden.

I wondered what I would find among the religions. Long before I had passed to happier climes, some of them were beginning to talk to one another peacefully, instead of murdering each other as they had done for centuries. I knew that in the century in which I had been born, women, for the first time, were beginning to share in equal rights, but only fitfully, and only in more advanced parts of Earth. The aggression that had helped human beings to survive, and the male dominance that had typified the general animal kingdom, still influenced many societies and many minds.

To us, in our world, and especially to Ruah and his companions, Earth was a dark place, which gave off an atmosphere of tension and dark thoughts. However, I had been entrusted with a task and I prepared to embark on my mission. I wondered whether I should, through some sensitive, divulge my presence, but decided this would not be wise. Yet for the Shining Ones even to consider interceding in human affairs in the manner they had discussed, was an indication that I could expect to find some ugly facets of human development.

I was not mistaken in these dire expectations. It was worse than I had imagined. I found societies in all continents where minds and bodies had been perverted. I had known killings had not lessened, that since the war that ended in 1945, there had been another fifty wars, some going on for years, during my earthly lifetime. Millions of people, adults and children, had been slaughtered, sacrificed, especially in Africa and Asia. Whole peoples had been uprooted. In many cities no one could walk safely. Disease was rampant. Some fanatics who took the lives of others were actually termed 'martyrs', a dreadful perversion of the term.

Some governments, at a loss to know how to cope, had impressed on the foreheads of offenders initials, which could not be removed but which could be seen by everyone. The letter A stood for Aids, a terrible affliction, the letter C stood for Corruption, the letter V for Violent, the letter D stood for Drug Addict, the letter K stood for Killer.

It was a terrible thing to be so marked, and those who walked with such letters imprinted on their heads were treated like the lepers of ancient days. It was a desperate remedy for a desperate situation.

There was endless noise everywhere. Machines of every kind created noise, in the home and in the streets, from new forms of radios, television and mechanical instruments of communication that destroyed quiet and privacy, and the noise contributed to mass illness, as well as to rioting and public disturbance.

Those in charge did not know how to beat back the forces of crime that surged everywhere. Prisons were full. In some countries, where the taking of life was a crime, the punishment was to take the life of the criminal. They still did not understand that no one had the right to take the life of anyone.

I saw plentiful food in the developed countries and mass hunger in more backward countries, as had happened in my day. I saw many families and marriages, disintegrate. While marriage as such did not exist in my present world, the spiritual identity of souls and the love between them bound them closely. On Earth, marriage had been a natural, human invention to give security to the man, the woman, and especially to the children. It had developed in all societies, independently, and had been of value. It distressed me to see so many who disregarded its human and social benefits.

In the western parts of the United States especially, and in a few European and Asian countries, the advance of science proceeded relentlessly. Every year I saw startling advances and new processes. It was impressive. So was the massive range of products available in shops in the richer countries.

But amongst them all, hardly anyone paused for a while to ask the truly fundamental questions. What is a human being? What is a human being made of? Why are human beings on planet Earth? How did human beings get there and develop there? What was the purpose of human life, if purpose it had? What would happen to human beings after physical death?

These were not questions that many asked. They were too busy with other things. The material world had become the be-all and end-all to them, confirmed by perennial indoctrination through the media of the day.

A few did ask these questions, though not necessarily the formal religious functionaries. These matters, as in the past, were more often considered in what were known in the West as Eastern countries.

I saw small groups only, trying to get to grips with answers and with the increasing degradation of the natural world. Rivers, seas and land continued to be poisoned by all manner of death-giving chemicals. Even the air in many places, full of chemicals, could not be breathed safely. Efforts had been made to solve these problems, but with only partial success.

Although nations were coming together in regional groupings, deep antagonism and old resentments and hatreds still affected them, whilst the world body, the United Nations, was rent by propaganda, disunity and conflicting national ambitions.

The more I looked, the more despairing I became that the human race had either the will or the strength to evolve to a higher level of existence, but instead seemed likely to condemn itself to a gradual process of self-destruction.

I sent a mental message to Ruah that all was not well, but that I wanted more time. He flashed back his approval of my request.

Wherever I looked I saw auras of darkness, and stained dismal colours. Here and there gleamed an occasional brightness, which betokened feelings and thoughts of love and co-operation, but not often was this to be found.

In my present form of existence I did not need sleep. Twenty years before I had left behind all my aches and pains, all my pills and medicines. In my new world I was free as a bird to go and come as I wished. Occasionally, I would sit in a London park watching the people. It was the nearest I got to what Earth people called resting, not that I needed any rest.

Once, whilst so engaged on my mission, a strange message began to form in my mind. It was not from Ruah or from any level beyond Earth. It was from somewhere on Earth itself. I was astonished. Who could contact me in such a manner? Surely only one who was acutely sensitive to the world of the spirit could attempt this.

Could my utter despair with the course of human life have imprinted itself on some human who wished to make contact with me, some being more advanced than his or her contemporaries, who was able to penetrate to my vibrational level?

No one had been able to do this previously. My presence was, I believed, unknown to the human race. The message persisted: 'Come, do not despair.' Extraordinary! I responded, though not expecting a response: 'Who are you? Where are you?'

To my amazement, my questions were answered. I was given details I had requested, and, in a flash, I found myself standing alone in a warm but dusty spot in the heart of India. What was to follow was even more exciting, uplifting, incredible. What I perceived then was to become a single ray of hope amidst the moral darkness that had so far surrounded me.

I looked round. I saw a city of several thousand people, with homes separated by gardens, trees and fields. I saw no tall buildings. Everything seemed to be in balance, in proportion to the human size. People were working in the fields, growing crops. Animals grazed. A few central buildings seemed larger than the rest. I learned later that these were schools and colleges for all ages, as learning never ceased, and also included hospitals, music and artistic centres and meeting places. The air was clearer. There seemed a sense of purpose about the place. To some extent I was reminded of the scenes I had encountered when first I ceased to be an Earth resident some twenty years before.

My mind was full of questions as a figure approached. I wondered if he could see me. I made an effort to lower my vibrations to Earth level.

'There is no need to do that,' I heard in my mind. The figure – a man – was draped in some toga-like garment; it was simple, white, covering most of his body. He stopped close to me and sat on a stone. I wondered whether with his particular gift he could also see me. The answer came at once. 'Yes, I can see you as well as you can see me. You are surprised at what you see here?'

'I am,' I replied. 'I have traversed your planet, seen such anguish and suffering and degradation, so much violence of expression and action, that really I wondered what had happened to the people I had left behind. As you had somehow understood, I was beginning to despair when your message reached me.'

The figure nodded and was silent for a while. Then he spoke. 'Normally when we have visitors, we invite them to share our meals with us, but this I know I cannot do with you.' I nodded. I had long since ceased to have need of food or drink.

He continued. 'But what I can share with you is the story of our city. My name is Tikvah. I am one of those who lead and direct this place, which we call the Earth Rescue Centre. What you see is a new development in human social evolution, a blueprint, we like to think, and hope, of a new beginning for our brothers and sisters. What you see is still but an experiment. We may succeed, we may not, but the people living here have come from all parts of the world to take part in this experiment, to learn our methods, and then to return to their countries and establish similar centres.'

I was intrigued, fascinated. Here we were, on Earth, me from my level, he, Tikvah, from his, yet conversing, mind to mind, in pictures, in thoughts, in words. It was almost unbelievable.

'Tell me more: how did you begin, when did you begin, why did you begin?'

The figure remained seated. In the distance people were walking, working.

'I will explain,' he began. 'It is really quite simple. Throughout the last three or four thousand years, as we evolved into conscious history, groups of like-minded people have come together, often just to learn, but sometimes to create new patterns for society. I need only mention a few names and you will understand. Plato, Socrates, the Judean prophets, Buddha, Confucius, Jesus and later small groups in many parts of the world, inspired often by these figures of history, seeking to create a new type of man in society.

'When the atomic arms race began in the second half of the last century and man looked as if he was about to destroy himself, small groups of scientists and thinkers met and worked for peaceful solutions and for the lessening of fear, the fear that actuated the policies of all governments.

'There was hope that the international bodies founded after the end of the second terrible Earth war in 1945 could achieve much, but they had no power or strength, and were undermined by the same fears as the national governments.

'Yet groups still met, especially scientists, doctors, ecologists, all trying their best to raise the level of human behaviour and thought. This continued well into the twenty-first century, but had little effect, and so, remorselessly, man drifted on his downward path.

'About ten years ago something happened. A group of us held a meeting – I was a scientist – and, to while away a moment we watched an old film of an imagined space world. For some reason all those films used to portray space beings as enemies, as aliens, intent on war and violence, were really just projecting man's own mental states onto the galaxy, and in fact were so wrong.

'In one film we observed two men about to strike each other when a space being of a more advanced level was present. By the force of thought only, that advanced being prevented the violence, and the combatants stood there, transfixed, arms raised aloft, unable to move until released by a further thought from the advanced being.

'When the film ceased, we spoke together eagerly. We realised that to achieve our objective of peace on earth we had to study the reality and the practical application of thought forces. Year after year we met privately and deepened our studies, our experiences, and especially forms of mental development and self-discipline.'

Tikvah was so eloquent that I almost apologised for interrupting him. 'Does that explain your ability to contact me, by thought, though I was thousands of miles away?'

'That is correct,' came the reply. 'Let me explain.' He continued: 'As we met, we scientists and thinkers, we were able to learn of the amazing development of spiritual and mental forces discovered in the previous two centuries. Scientists had worked on the assumption that all that existed was matter and motion, yet their science came to a dead-end, postulating, however, there was a "something else" which existed, but which was not provable by strictly scientific means. It was a mystery that still eluded them.

'The non-scientists took a different view. They agreed as to the existence of matter and motion, but theorised that reality also included mind and spirit.

'Both sections discounted the literal explanations of man's creation and development given in the various holy books of the religions as legends and myths, but both decided to work together to discover those forces of mind and spirit, if that were possible.

'This involved an enormous amount of study, research, and especially of practical self-discipline. Eventually there emerged from our ranks a few highly developed beings who, by taking thought, could negate the effect of gravity, and create material objects where none previously existed, and could even affect the thought processes of others, in the manner we had seen on the film.

'We realised that we had discovered the most powerful force in human history. It was vital that, unlike other forces, things like gunpowder, guns, aerial flight and atomic fusion, it was not to be abused, and so we held our meetings in secret, in private.

'We knew, however, that this secrecy could not last for long. Others would become aware of our discoveries, and would try to use their forces to control people's minds for political and commercial purposes.

'Yet we wanted to help the millions who lived on Earth, perhaps nine billion souls, all at different levels of understanding and moral and social evolution.'

Tikvah paused. He raised his eyes and looked in my direction, as though he could actually see me.

'We then decided that meetings alone were not enough. We had to establish a model society that could become an example to the world. We debated where to establish such a society. We knew that most of the world's main moralistic religions had emanated from the Jewish and Indian peoples, but the Jewish state was still beset by problems and was small, whereas India had plenty of land and a long tradition of special cities and places inspired by advanced beings, like the heroic Mahatma Gandhi for example.

'So we created our own small world here, a world different from everything around it, a world using the power of thought forces, alongside more conventional human resources. It was the start of a new adventure, which we hoped would give a fresh start to a declining world.

'We drew up some general objectives, five of them, to which we hoped to find solutions:

1. How to adjust the whole of economic, social and religious life to our newly discovered reality.
2. How to relate to our Earth environment and other forms of Earth life.
3. How to relate to phenomena and beings in our solar system and galaxy.
4. How to raise the level of man in terms of behaviour and thought.
5. How to understand further the nature of God.

'All the many human organisations around us were busy issuing what they termed "mission statements". No one had a mission statement comparable to ours. Our mission was in fact to work for the salvation of man, as simple as that.

'This meant we had to change in the most radical fashion all the assumptions and patterns that existed in most places on Earth.'

He paused. He sensed that I was about to ask him another question, but, as I was about to do so, a different message flashed within me. It was Ruah, seeking to know whether I was ready to report on the state of Earth and its inhabitants. I asked for more time – Earth time. This was agreed. I asked Tikvah my question.

'You had made a profound discovery, perhaps the greatest in human history. How were you going to prevent its misuse by the ruling powers on Earth with their spying systems, their information-seeking satellites, their vast intelligence agencies, equipped with every kind of scientific device?'

His reply came at once.

'What we had discovered was beyond the boundaries of normal science, beyond the imagination of most authorities that were in control. They had no means of understanding the source and nature of our forces, however hard they tried. So we went ahead and set up our permanent Centre here in India, with a few hundred persons who came to us from many societies. We had to establish a kind of programme or standard of behaviour and existence and these, after much discussion, we set out in a Code. May I explain to you a few of the provisions of that First Code?'

The Code included the following:
1. Each of us is entitled to complete freedom of thought and expression, but each of us has a duty to think thoughts and express words of the highest level so as to raise the moral climate of our community.
2. Each of us has a duty to respect the thoughts, expressions and bodies of one another.
3. Each of us has a duty to work at providing the means to maintain a healthy community.
4. No act of violence is to be committed by any member against any other member and especially not against any child.
5. The family is to be the basis of our society wherever this is possible.
6. There is to be complete equality in every respect between all members of the Centre.

'These were just some of the points we included in our First Code, to which all members freely assented after full discussion, much as the

Constitution of the United States emerged after lengthy debate. But we also decided on patterns not found in any other society, which reflected our new world outlook. Let me explain.'

Again I nodded. Tikvah continued:

'We changed much that had previously been thought normal in human society. For example, take religion. It was obvious there could be only one world religion.' (Ruah and others on lesser levels had often mentioned this, perplexed and sorrowful at the religious separation and hostility that prevailed on our planet.)

'So what we have done is to establish a single religious building. Into it we have installed all the insignia and labels and artefacts of all the main world religions. This became the Religious Centre. There would be no separate holy book. We took the main sections of all the so-called holy books and incorporated them in one volume we called The Book of Religion. There were to be no priests of any kind, no religious functionaries of any kind. Man needed no intermediary between him and God, has never needed any.

'Each member could then use the Book and the Centre as he or she wished, or not at all.

'We taught in our schools extensively, using all the immense knowledge of our members, but history we taught as world history, without the national and group bias all former histories had contained. This meant looking with new eyes at all that had transpired in human affairs.

'We studied nature intensely. We also had daily periods for breathing exercises and meditation.

'We established an Information Room involving the media, including television, radio and all the highly developed audio-visual forms, as well as newspapers. But we agreed that no individual could use the Information Room more than once a week, to prevent the continual daily indoctrination and conditioning that afflicted the rest of the world.

'We abolished money, and hence all the professions and occupations that were based on money disappeared. We produced food and clothing and homes and goods ourselves, using the best scientific brains available to us.'

I stopped Tikvah at that point. I told him that he and his friends were creating a world here on planet Earth similar in many ways to my own world beyond. He nodded. He explained that they had studied our worlds from the many messages that had been received from us, and that they wanted to create conditions here below as close to those above so as to lessen the shock to people when they left their physical bodies.

I now knew how wonderfully these people had developed thought forces through a few of their most sensitive individuals, but wondered if they had attained our level, where no one could lie without it becoming immediately apparent to everyone through his or her aura colours.

Again Tikvah had garnered my thoughts. 'Indeed,' he responded. 'This is perhaps our greatest advance of all. We look around the world, see political leaders and others making statements that they know are untruths, which we can scientifically establish as untruths. Were we to extend our comments worldwide we could create chaos within governments.

'However, we are keen to set an example to others. Because no one here can lie and not be immediately perceived to be doing so, and because of the moral level of our society, we have been able to dispense with the folly of prisons, the external control of police forces, and the great panoply of lawyers, judges and courts. They have all disappeared.

'A wrongdoer here is seen as such by all concerned and judgement then comes from within that person.'

I marvelled that, here on Earth, amidst all the lies and violence, wars and killings, hunger and disease I had witnessed, there yet could be found such a group of people whose patterns of life and experiences reflected so much of those of my own world, and were so far in advance of the world around them.

When Tikvah and I had finished our conversation, and I had seen the city, its people, its houses, its fields, its study centres, I marvelled anew that such a place could have arisen. It renewed in me hope for this planet's men and women.

Tikvah invited me to return whenever I wished. They were continuing to develop their thought forces and sending out good thoughts throughout the world to help afflicted mankind. The task they had undertaken was tremendous, to reverse the whole trend of greed and selfishness, corruption and disease, that pervaded so many lands.

However I remembered that I had work to do, a mission to undertake. In a flash I had left Earth and returned to Ruah and the wise ones. As before, I was shielded from the light they emanated. I described in great detail the decline of the human species and all its afflictions: the failure to control people's immense physical desires and the urge to gratify all their senses, their institutionalised violence, their divisions on grounds of colour, race, gender, belief, their overwhelming noise that made Earth a planet of noise, and the likelihood that humans' own destruction would be linked to the progressive destruction of the planet, its species, forests and seas. The aggression that had enabled man to survive was still so imprinted on his complex brain that, despite all the messengers of peace and moderation sent to guide him from our spheres, that aggression remained potent and was leading mankind to disaster.

'So you believe we should intervene and limit their free will, before they destroy themselves and quite possibly, the peace-loving inhabitants of other planets?' asked Ruah.

'I would have said yes,' I replied, 'until I saw a small ray of hope arise in India, in a tiny society, whose inhabitants have accepted our teachings and who have developed the forces of mind and thought to a level far above that of the humans who surround them.'

'But they are merely a handful among proliferating billions,' responded Ruah. 'What influence can they have, so few amidst so many?'

'There is hope there,' I responded. 'From that small Centre, which they call Earth Rescue Centre, men and women imbued with their spirit will create similar Centres in other lands. It is just possible that they may touch the inmost souls of many, so that the merest soul flicker can quicken and glow among them more and more.'

I added many details about what I had observed. Although shaded and partially concealed, I could perceive the pulsating lights and occasional forms of those who deliberated. I managed to discern certain words and phrases. 'There is no compulsion in religion.' 'Love your neighbour as yourself.' 'Love one another as I have loved you.' 'The Noble Path is the way, overcoming all desiring.' 'Nation shall not lift up sword against nation, nor will they learn war any more.' 'For the Lord has come to test you.' 'Know thyself.' And many more words I had heard before in other tones but here they were, together. I was transfixed, as Ruah spoke to me, mind to mind, thought to thought.

'Your Report is acceptable to us. We will give Man a further chance. We will not limit his free will further. He may just save himself and his world. We will not interfere. We will respect his freedom. Only he can judge himself and save himself. It may be, by his efforts and the example you have described, he will raise the level of his thoughts, and overcome the animal within him.'

Thus my mission was at an end. I retired, thankfully, and returned to my accustomed level, among those with whom I could relax, but thoughts of Tikvah returned to me again and again. I hoped and prayed that he and his friends might succeed in their own daunting but awe-inspiring mission.

Ruah *means spirit in Hebrew, whilst* Tikvah *means hope. Hebrew legend has it that there are thirty-six illustrious spirits on earth helping mankind.*

# AUBREY ROSE

## THE DUNBLANE TRAGEDY

*In the last decades we have seen dreadful acts done by individuals in possession of a gun. When that individual is unbalanced, obsessed, or full of hate, the consequences are dreadful. An American soldier gunned down a host of other servicemen. Someone in England's beautiful Lake District went on a rampage, destroying innocent life after life. In July 2011 the same horror destroyed many young people in Norway. What is so horrifying about the story here described is the murder of innocent children, cut off from life so brutally. What follows is an extract from* Journey into Immortality.

In March 1996 a terrible tragedy took place. An obsessed, some might say possessed, individual murdered sixteen children and a teacher in a school in Dunblane, Scotland. The country mourned, but no one more than the devastated parents, cruelly parted from their deeply-loved children.

A week or two later my wife and I spent a few days in a pleasant East Anglian hotel. In the middle of the night I awoke. Normally I am a sound sleeper. All was dark, still, silent. My wife lay fast asleep. I was told by some inner voice to get up and write. I objected. It was warm and comfortable in bed. The prompting persisted, becoming more urgent and insistent, as did my repeated objections, but eventually I got up.

I began to write as if in a dream, largely unaware of the words flowing from my pen. I finished, lay down and immediately fell asleep again. Next morning, when I read what I had written, and understood the meaning of the words, I burst into tears. What I had written was as follows:

**A Child Asks**
*I miss my mummy and daddy.*
I know, and they miss you.
*Where am I now?*
You are being cared for. We are helping you.
*Can I see my mummy and daddy?*
You will, dear, in time.
*Will they see me?*
They will see you, in time.
*Why did that man do bad things?*
Because he was ill, unhappy.
*Why was he unhappy?*

Because no one loved him and he loved no one.
*Does he not have a mummy and daddy like I have?*
He does.
*Do they love him like mine?*
They are far away from him.
*What will happen to him?*
We will care for him also.
*Will he see me?*
He will, and every time he sees you he will cry and cry.
And every time he sees your friends who are with you,
He will cry and cry, for a long time.
*Why did he take me away from my mummy and daddy?*
He does not know, but he will cry whenever he sees you,
And he will weep whenever he sees your mummy and daddy.
*My mummy and daddy are crying also. Can you help them like you are helping me?*
I will help them, child, I will help them. One day they will know you are well, and with me.
*Please help them.*
I will, I will, I will.
*Thank you. You are my friend also, my new friend.*
*Please tell my mummy and daddy I am with you.*
I will, I will, I will.

Sadly, there have been so many more Dunblanes in the world, as crazed or politically obsessed and racially or religiously conditioned individuals have committed similar blasphemies in Tasmania, Israel, and elsewhere, spreading universal grief. I say 'blasphemy' because the only real blasphemy is that committed against life, removing this precious gift. The same madness has affected groups of people who destroyed themselves, again obsessed by religious perversion and conditioning, in Texas, California and Switzerland, comparable with the mass self-murder in Guyana years before. If only those involved realised the effect of their actions on others here and the rescue efforts for them from those active in the world of the spirit.

The world has still so much to learn. It still has to grow up and put away childish things that pervert, corrupt, and eventually destroy life, human life, and also our living planet and its inhabitants.

My hope is that this book may encourage others to look at themselves and the world around them with a wider perception, to seek out their own truths as, through the influence of my son, I have tried to do.

AUBREY ROSE

## ARTICLES BY MICHAEL EVANS

*This gentleman passed on aged ninety early in 2011. I include three articles by him as a token of my regard and as a form of tribute to him. He worked long and hard in the field of the rescue of departed souls who had found no resting place. Attending his rescue circle in Exeter I was fascinated and impressed by the calm, careful way he described to agitated souls their condition and what they should do and believe. It was a therapy between worlds, across time and space.*

*In the first piece, 'What Have Spiritualists Done for Society', Michael points out the contribution made by notable individuals, including scientists, to mankind, all those mentioned having a belief in Spiritualism. One so included is Air Chief Marshal Lord Dowding, head of RAF Fighter Command at the time of the 1940 Battle of Britain.*

*The second article, 'Alfred Russel Wallace, Scientist and Spiritualist', confirms the sterling contribution of Wallace to the theory of evolution by natural selection but as part of a wider conception. The third article is 'The Scientist's Dilemma'. Evans wrote touchingly to the editor of our leading scientific journal as follows: 'I have little hope that you will publish this article but I felt I must give you the opportunity, should you be so open-minded.'*

*Such courtesy is typical of this respected and respectful man. The article was never published. I hope Michael is happy now that it appears here. Perhaps one day scientists will do what Michael Evans advised and make a thorough investigation of the claims of spiritualists.*

### WHAT HAVE SPIRITUALISTS DONE FOR SOCIETY?

Obviously the great gift of Spiritualism to the world is the evidence that we all survive death, and communication with those who have passed on is a fact.

However, to a materialist, this is not impressive or even interesting. Yet a materialist would be impressed if he knew even a little of the contribution that Spiritualists have made to many aspects of life in the past and also in our life today.

To take one example. During the American Civil War, President Abraham Lincoln, that most revered of American Presidents, accepted mediumship and attended seances in the White House. The military situation at one time was desperate. His troops were demoralised and it looked as if the slave-owning states of the South would win the war and the United States would be broken up. A spirit message through a medium told the President he must do two things: first, he must take an open carriage and, along with his wife and children in full view, he must drive along the whole of the front line where his soldiers faced the enemy. This would give them the confidence to fight on. Secondly, he must make a proclamation that if his armies were the victors then all slaves in America would be given their freedom. He carried out both of these instructions. The North won the war and the slaves were freed, ending one of the most cruel and barbarous treatments of human beings in Western civilisation.

In the scientific field, Sir William Crookes, who was President of most of the scientific societies of his day, as well as the Society for Psychic Research, made many tests with mediums and announced that he was fully convinced by the evidence that there was indeed a life after death. When his wife died he saw and held her fully materialised body.

Sir William was a man who innovated in many fields. He developed the extreme vacuum which led to our present type of electric light bulb, later devised by Thomas Alva Edison, an American Spiritualist, who also invented the phonograph, the forerunner of the record player, the mimeograph, the first office duplicator and a system for distributing the electric power on which our homes nowadays so generally depend. This distribution of electric power literally changed an entire civilisation, freeing mankind for the first time from endless backbreaking toil and bringing manufactured goods into the poorest homes. The modern factory producing millions of items from cars to aircraft, from refrigerators to vacuum cleaners, is entirely dependent on electric power which both drives and controls the sophisticated machinery which produces the goods.

Millions of people now left the land to become factory workers, earning wages with which they could now buy the products of a vast modern economy.

William Crookes also invented the cathode ray tube, that vital part of our televisions and our computer monitors on which we see the images on the screen. He discovered the metal thallium and perfected a method of obtaining silver and gold from the crude ores. He was an authority on sanitation, especially the disposal of sewage, and he invented the Crookes lens, which protects our eyes from the harmful effects of ultraviolet rays – our sun glasses.

Another famous scientist was Sir Oliver Lodge. He was Professor of Physics at Liverpool University and then Principal of Birmingham

University. He was President of the Physical Society and the British Association for the Advancement of Science. He developed the first successful transmission and reception of radio signals and sold his patent to Signor Marconi for fifty pounds. Marconi, who was also a secret Spiritualist, went on to make a transmission across the Atlantic and founded a vast, worldwide industry.

Oliver Lodge and his son developed the spark plug on which our petrol engines still depend today, and he invented an early vacuum cleaner of a different pattern from the one we use nowadays. He investigated famous mediums and proclaimed himself converted to complete acceptance of the evidence for communication between the two worlds. When his son Raymond was killed in the Great War, he wrote the book *Raymond*, about the communications he received from him and the book was a bestseller.

John Logie Baird, the Scottish inventor of television, whose system was adopted in England and Germany in 1926, believed in communication from the Spirit world and stated that he had communication and advice through a medium from Thomas Alva Edison, the pioneer of electrical power.

Interestingly enough, the messages came in Morse code, which was evidential because Edison started out in life as a telegraph operator on the American railroad system, which used the Morse code. Baird invented black and white transmissions first, then colour and finally 3-D television which, so far, has never been successfully adopted on a large scale.

Nikola Tesla, who devised alternating current, which we use universally today in our houses, had psychic experiences all his life. His many inventions appeared visually in front of him, but he refused to ascribe them to the Spirit world, always seeking a scientific explanation for them until, after staying with William Crookes, whom he greatly admired, his mother died and appeared to him in a dream when he began to say that 'perhaps it could be true'.

In the literary field, as most people know, Sir Arthur Conan Doyle, creator of the Sherlock Holmes stories, was a convinced believer and toured the world lecturing about the New Revelation of Spiritualism. He was also a doctor, an eye specialist, a champion boxer, played cricket for the MCC and was the man who introduced skiing from Norway into Switzerland and founded a new tourist industry there. When my wife and I were staying in Switzerland one autumn, we found the hotel preparing to close, with the staff moving to another hotel in the mountains for the skiing season. In this way they had a year-long continuous season for their tourist trade.

Alfred Russel Wallace was a famous biologist who, independently from Darwin, conceived the idea of evolution through natural selection as the 'origin of the species'. This opposed the Church's teaching that God created every single living creature from elephants to fleas in one act at the beginning of the world. Wallace wrote to Darwin, who had already thought of the idea, and they published a joint paper which caused terrific controversy in 1858. It was denounced by the Church, but evolution is now generally accepted by modern churchmen and scientists. Wallace was a convinced Spiritualist who published a book, *On Miracles and Modern Spiritualism*, in 1874 and lectured in Exeter on Spiritualism in 1886. In our circle we were thrilled when he came through to us with the most wonderful evidence, which took eighteen months to be proved conclusively. The first day he came through the medium George Pratt, was the same day that I had borrowed the above-mentioned book from the Exeter City Library.

How was it then that a small group of Spiritualists had such an effect upon our modern world? I think the answer is that all the scientists and inventors of the past are still working, and when we are judged fit to receive a new discovery without doing too much damage with it, it is passed down to us, sometimes telepathically, sometimes in dreams and sometimes through mediumistic communications. In my book *Billy Grows Up In Spirit*, dictated by Billy himself, he says '... you see it's with us before it's with you. Computers and television were with us long before they were with you'.

Spiritualists have, therefore, been responsible for the development of much that is in daily use in work and homes across the world. The electric power that comes into our homes, the radio broadcasts that we listen to, with the recent development into portable and mobile phones, the electric light we switch on, the screens that we watch on our television sets and computer monitors, all based on the cathode ray tube, the television itself, the sewage and drainage system connected to our toilets, the spark plug which powers our cars and the sun glasses which protect our eyes, were all developed or improved by Spiritualists – and the detective stories we read or watch on television, all stem from the ground-breaking *Adventures of Sherlock Holmes*, which made Conan Doyle the highest paid writer in the world.

Is this all then that Spiritualists have done which affects us all today? By no means! In World War II, Hitler was told by his generals and admirals that they could not guarantee a successful invasion of Britain unless they had complete control of the air. They planned five attacks between Lyme Bay and Brighton. Hermann Goering, head of the Luftwaffe, said this mastery of the air could be achieved in four days. So the whole fate of these islands rested on our Royal Air Force.

Two Spiritualists were in key positions and Winston Churchill was consulting the medium Bertha Harris regularly.

Sir Archibald Sinclair was the Minister for Air – he later performed the ceremony at the opening of the new Exeter Spiritualist Church – and Air Chief Marshal Lord Dowding had developed Britain's air defences and was Commander-in-Chief of Fighter Command during the Battle of Britain. Both of these were Spiritualists and Hugh Dowding actually sat in a rescue circle which was giving help and counsel to those of his beloved aircrew who had passed over. He later wrote the book *Many Mansions* in which he described his beliefs. He recently returned through medium Colin Fry at the Noah's Ark circle and sounded in fine form and very good humour.

So, in addition to the literary, scientific and technical advances that Spiritualists have contributed to our life today, our very freedom to write, to read and to live our lives as we wish, we owe to brave, clever and spiritual people who publicly braved the prejudice, scorn and opposition of their day to tell the world the truth – there is no death.

Can we do any less?

## ALFRED RUSSEL WALLACE
### Scientist and Spiritualist

One day, in our circle, Harry, a trance medium, saw a vision of a three-masted sailing ship in full sail. As he watched, it caught fire and sank beneath the waves. We had no idea what this meant.

Some time later, I borrowed a book from the Exeter City Library, *On Miracles and Modern Spiritualism* by Alfred Russel Wallace, first published in 1874. I already knew that Wallace had given a lecture on Spiritualism in Exeter in the 1880s. At our very next meeting, the great man spoke to us himself, saying:

'I used to try and interest people in this subject. Your healing is progressing very well but others are concerned with that.' He said that he wanted to speak of the search for higher things, the consciousness of man, or as you would call it, the super-consciousness. He asked: 'Why are you searching for these things? Is it for your own ego or is it to help? In your meditation do you get the upliftment from it, and a more caring attitude to mankind, or do you keep it to yourselves? The mind of man will develop and more and more will be revealed.'

One lady (not a medium) could always tell when he was with us, because she could smell his leather gaiters and Harris tweed jacket!

Some months later, we watched a programme on BBC2 about Alfred Russel Wallace. It explained, among other things, that when Wallace returned from exploring the natural history of Brazil, the sailing ship caught fire, his collection of rare specimens was lost, and that he and other survivors were only rescued after ten days adrift in a leaking lifeboat. We now saw the meaning of the vision that Harry had seen.

When he died in 1913, Wallace was, perhaps, the most famous scientist alive, the last of the great Victorian thinkers – Huxley, Malthus, Darwin, Kelvin, Lister, etc. He is forever associated with Charles Darwin, and the presentation of their joint papers to the Linnaean Society in 1858 on *Evolution through Natural Selection*. These papers, which were based on brilliant observations of nature, by two of the greatest students of natural history ever known, exploded the Biblical account of everything having been created originally by God, never afterwards to be changed. They showed how living things had changed and evolved over time and that man's body, itself, was descended from an early branch of the ape family.

These epoch-making discoveries outraged the Churches, but the ideas eventually won the acceptance of nearly all educated people, including many churchmen.

Wallace was the founder of many later sub-branches of science, such as, evolutionary theory, ethnology, zoogeography, bio-diversity and ethology. He also started the use of statistics in medicine and the rational studies of the planets. He was a Spiritualist, a Socialist and a supporter of the emancipation of women – a very unpopular idea in a male-dominated world.

In one important respect, Wallace's ideas differed from Darwin's theory of evolution. He felt there was something especially different about the evolution of mankind, compared to the evolution of plants and animals. He did not think that the blind forces of 'natural selection' and the 'survival of the fittest' could have produced such traits as the loss of protective hair and musical, artistic and mathematical ability and concepts such as 'Love your neighbour as yourself'. He felt that, in some way, an unseen force guided human evolution, and, being a convinced Spiritualist, he felt that this force might well be the Spirit world.

Nearly all Wallace's ideas won acceptance except this one, the idea of spirit influence in evolution. Materialist scientists, who had just removed God from their studies, shunned this idea like the plague, although they praised his ground-breaking research in Brazil and his sixty fact-finding expeditions to the Malay archipelago.

Wallace's idea that the Spirit world might be the guiding hand behind both the creation and evolution of Nature has received recent confirmation from the work of Dr Michael Newton, the author of two popular books, *Journey of Souls* and *Destiny of Souls*. Having found a method of intense hypnotism which enables his clients to access memories of many past lives, both on earth and in the Spirit world, he has heard from people, who as spirits remember learning to create rocks and simple plants out of energy in special 'practice worlds'. When Dr Newton said: 'I thought Nature did that', the spirit, Nenthum, said: 'What do you think Nature is?' One of the most momentous and meaningful remarks ever made! If accepted, this remark could revise our whole concept of nature and the universe! Nenthum also implied that the 'Big Bang', and all that followed from it, was caused by 'The Old Ones' who work with the 'Source'.

When the startled Dr Newton said to an advanced spirit: 'Let me understand something. Do you just go to a physical world and build a mountain while someone like Hyanth concentrates on life forms, such as a tree?'

Spirit: 'No, we work with physical worlds which are forming and we set in motion the geologic forces which will build a mountain. My structural projects don't have to have life. Also Hyanth doesn't create a forest of adult trees on worlds suitable for life. Her people would design the cells which might eventually grow into the trees they want.'

Some of Dr Newton's clients say there are billions of planets on millions of galaxies where life could exist.

Is there other testimony to the fact that there is a spiritual influence on evolution and a spiritual cause of all existence? Even materialists who deny the existence of Spirit must admit that in the something called 'life' there appears to be a tremendous force to survive, multiply, vary and advance to more highly developed forms, yet they are still unable to say what this force is.

The writer, mystic and friend of Dr Raynor Johnson, Ambrose Pratt, came back through the writing medium Miss G. Cummins, to say: 'I am one of many souls who work at the breath of life in regard to birds to be born each spring. The old pattern has to be conserved and there has to be a collective drive in regard to the launching of the young of each species every spring. Another time I shall tell you of this creative work.' Ambrose Pratt had been a prime mover in the movement to preserve Australian wildlife when he was on earth. He said that his aspiration was to become, eventually, one of the Divine Hierarchy of souls who maintain and conserve the material universe.

On his return through the medium Grace Cooke, Conan Doyle commented on the nature spirits he could now see, who care for living things. He said: 'How wonderful it is to see little fairy creatures, busily carrying life force and sustenance to the plants. Lacking this fairy aid your plants would soon wither and die. Without plant life, man would soon die, likewise. Without the major powers, controlled by lords of nature, by the devas, your physical world would fall into chaos!'

Perhaps the reader is disbelieving? I must admit that I, too, would have laughed at the idea of 'fairies', outside of Shakespeare's plays, but, as often happens, one has to have one's own experience to be convinced. One afternoon in our rescue circle, we were helping a lost one who spoke sweetly through a trance medium. Incredibly, by her answers, we realised we were talking to the spirit of a 'dead' fairy, whose work had been to succour green plants, and who was still doing the same in her next dimension. She was saddened that humans were destroying so much that they had cared for, for so long. We reunited her with some of her old group who had passed and she thanked us in a sweet, gentle voice for she had been lonely after passing. The medium did not believe in fairies and was surprised at what she had transmitted. About a week later, another medium told me that my deceased wife was 'delighted that I had found out about the fairies'.

Geraldine Cummins was perhaps the most distinguished 'writing medium' of her day. These extracts from her family scripts bear on the question of creation:

'Do you know what Hilda's and Harold's task will be at some far distant date? To look after the life behind all the flowers that spring up, grow and die on your earth! Guardian Angels of the flowers!'

Hilda later wrote herself: 'Harold and I are making beautiful plants, shrubs and trees in this world after death, so that, sometime, we shall be fit to become Guardian Spirits of plants, shrubs and trees that grow on earth – as we advance into the Greater Life, we become more and more part of the Divine Creative Spirit. The Divine Creative Spirit is behind the birth and growth of everything on earth.'

Our first major teacher, the Tibetan, said that: 'Mankind, as a whole, are undergoing evolutionary development in order that they may become conscious creators in matter.'

Two modern scientific theories seem to possibly relate to this question. One is the Anthropic Principle, which finds that of all possible universes, this one seems peculiarly designed to support life. The other one is the Gaia Hypothesis that the earth is a living spiritual being and all life-forms are its children. Many people like the Gaia idea but as a whole, the scientific community looks askance at such ideas. They still prefer the orthodox model, which holds that mind is a product of the brain, and when the body dies all consciousness ceases – there is no life after death. It will be a bit of a shock for most of them when they pass – not 'out' as they expect, but 'over' to a world they dismissed as fantasy.

To me, it looks as if Wallace was indeed correct, and modern scientists are exploring the hidden secrets of a universe which was created, under God, by spiritual beings whose very existence scientists dismissed from their calculations. Once passed, however, they may eventually become part of that Divine Hierarchy themselves.

If scientists were to accept Wallace's idea, it would cause as big an upset in the scientific world as his original idea of evolution through natural selection did in the churches in 1858.

## THE SCIENTIST'S DILEMMA

One can sympathise with the dilemma that scientists find themselves in with regard to Spiritualism, a dilemma that has existed since the nineteenth century. If the fact were admitted that even one person had genuinely received a message from a dead person via a medium then the scientific world-view would have to be greatly enlarged. The matter and energy which science says makes up the known universe cannot be all there is. There must be another realm outside it, inhabited by conscious beings that were once humans on earth.

In the nineteenth century, when scientists of the top rank such as Sir William Crookes, Sir Oliver Lodge and Alfred Russel Wallace proclaimed their conviction of the truth of the phenomena of Spiritualism, they were widely abused for their ridiculous claims. Spiritualist phenomena, like miracles, were obviously contrary to the known laws of science and could not possibly be true and every effort was made to prevent them publishing their views in scientific journals. The same objections were made to mesmerism but hypnotism is widely accepted now and recently demonstrated on television.

Wallace replied that all facts and theories should be looked at impartially and without prejudice. If the phenomena occurred, as they had satisfied themselves they did, then a theory should be sought which best explained them, and Spiritualism appeared to be such a theory.

He quoted Humboldt who said: 'A presumptuous scepticism that rejects facts without an examination of their truth, is, in some respects, more injurious than unquestioning credulity.'

The acceptance of this theory of Spiritualism appeared to have such startling implications that many could not face them and every possible argument was put forward against the truth of the phenomena. These included deliberate fraud, imposture, gullibility of the observers, mental aberration of the said scientists and, in Sir William Crookes's case, alleged infatuation with the female medium.

After centuries of fear of persecution by the Church, scientists had at last got rid of God as creator of the whole completed range of living things with the theory of evolution by natural selection, put forward jointly by Darwin and Wallace, and they had no desire to reintroduce the Deity, yet these invisible, intangible spirits of the dead said there was a Divine Being at the head of a Hierarchy of ever wiser and wiser Spirits.

No agreement was reached. The believers never retracted their views. William Crookes insisted to the end that he had seen his dead wife and had held her materialised, living body in his arms long after her death.

Any new discoveries have had to face the criticism that they conflicted with the known laws of nature, or the edicts of God, but in the end they have won general acceptance. Why then has Spiritualism completely failed to win the acceptance of the scientific community when, from my own experience, many of the facts on which it is based are true.

It took nothing but fact after fact to convince me, a hardened agnostic, but after conversing with over seven hundred separate spirits, all recorded on tape, and having a book dictated to me by a former principal of a university college, and having speech with Alfred Russel Wallace himself, I have to declare myself a knower, rather than a believer, until contrary evidence appears that this is all a gigantic worldwide conspiracy specially arranged to deceive me, a simple soul, who desires nothing but to discover truth.

At least the Victorian detractors did attack these leading thinkers for their ridiculous credulity although they devoted little time to checking the facts for themselves, considering the momentous implications of a life after death in an unknown realm. May I suggest that modern scientists have a better way of dealing with this awkward evidence – they simply do not look at it! There are good reasons for this, I feel. They have no desire to attract similar abuse; there is no professional advancement to be obtained from research into such a subject and no grants are available. A student doing a PhD in anthropology by studying the work of my group had to face innumerable hurdles before she finished her work. But, above all this, there is the question of repeatability, and the experimenter effect. Wallace found, and others have confirmed, that the entrance of a determined sceptic can affect both the sensitive medium and the subtle energies involved in the experiment; thus the sceptic can satisfy himself that the phenomenon does not exist and make no more trials.

The interest among the public in this subject supports several television shows, and their advertisers, each week, such as 'The Sixth Sense', and the site about the medium Helen Duncan, imprisoned in World War II for revealing that HMS Barham was sunk before the news was released or even known, has had 60,000,000 hits. One can ignore programmes on television where editing may be going on, but when such effects occur in one's own living room among a group of friends over a period of eighteen years, one cannot doubt the evidence of one's senses.

# PART IV

## MORE VOICES

What I have written in previous parts of this book, especially Part II, can in no way do justice to the individuals named. I have scarcely touched the surface of each story. There is of course no substitute for reading their own books in full: but the least I can do is to illustrate some of their thoughts and ideas by quoting a few of their actual words. Inevitably I have limited myself to just a few main points.

AUBREY ROSE

## THE WORLD OF LESLIE FLINT

Leslie Flint's own account of his life was first published under the title *Voices in the Dark* in 1971. I was involved in updating the story some years later and writing the introduction. The original description states: 'The story that follows is of extraordinary interest because Leslie Flint, as a medium, has the rare gift of Independent Direct Voice, and recorded on tapes are literally hundreds of voices of the dead who have come to speak to him and his sitters at public and private séances throughout his long and brilliant career.' Indeed Jim Ellis had a vast quantity of tapes, many hundreds.

During his lifetime Leslie was tested by every means known to psychical research, with his lips sealed, with electrical devices attached to his throat, in his own home and outside, and still the voices came, a host of famous communicators, as well as ordinary people trying to contact living friends and relatives. Leslie Flint wrote: *Sometimes those who speak from beyond the grave achieve only a whisper. At other times they speak clearly and fluently in voices recognisably their own during their life.*

As a youngster Leslie was fascinated by the film 'The Four Horsemen of the Apocalypse' starring Rudolph Valentino, a film he later invited me to see. In 1926 Valentino died. Leslie wrote: *How could I guess that far in the future I would be more friendly with Valentino dead than I could ever have been had he lived.*

Indeed, in Hollywood, in Valentino's own home, the film star was one of the voices who spoke to Leslie. Flint's awareness of his mediumship developed. He became clairvoyant.

*I could see and describe the spirit people who gathered around us. I could even hold intelligent conversations with some of the spirit entities who were able to manifest through my mediumship and I can still do so today.*

Eventually he gave up his former career and decided: *I would give all my life, all my gifts and all my devotion to serving my fellow-man and to proving through my mediumship the glorious comforting truth of man's survival of his bodily death.*

In his book he mentioned, and I confirm, that: *Sometimes I and my sitters would wait in the darkness of the séance room for an hour and nothing at all would happen. There is no question of any medium being able to 'call up the dead'. Indeed the facts are quite otherwise.*

So many famous souls spoke through Leslie, including members of the British Royal Family. Edith Cavell stated: 'You must love your brother whether he be an enemy or not. Try to love and forgive, not to hate.'

Leslie wrote: *I think I can safely say I am the most tested medium this country has ever produced.*

Though he was tested by scientists, universities, doubters, nothing faked or false could be found.

*Literally thousands of different voices of discarnate persons have been tape-recorded for posterity, speaking in different dialects, in foreign languages, unknown to me and even in languages no longer spoken on this earth.*

On the subject of animals, Leslie wrote: *I am convinced that the love we give to our animals on this side of life lifts them on to a higher plane of existence than that which many other forms of life achieve and that when we die we shall find them waiting to greet us.*

He spoke not only about animals or the many who spoke from beyond this world. From years of experience he stated: *Angels, guides, spirit helpers, call them what you like, were once men and women of all races and creeds who lived on earth.*

At one session came the voice of Professor Charles Richet, an eminent French physiologist, who stated that every living being has a substance known as ectoplasm, which is a life force, and Leslie confirmed that: *A physical medium like myself has a great deal more of it than most people.*

It is, of course, the ectoplasm emanating from Leslie that creates the voicebox into which thought becomes sound. (I mention Professor Richet again later.) Leslie said that he never doubted *the reality of my voices nor questioned the integrity of my spirit helpers.*

One striking message came from a Doctor Frank, who was killed because he would not co-operate in the horrific surgical experiments carried out at Dachau concentration camp by the Nazis. The doctor stated: 'There is no death. We live and we try constantly to inspire you. I ask you, I beg of you, I plead with you, to do all in your power to bring this truth to all humanity.'

Many people spoke through Leslie, many world-famous souls, but also beings who had left earth unready, still filled with hate, often as the result of murders caused by such earthbound revengeful entities. By contrast, many beautiful glowing words came through Leslie, words far more eloquent than could ever have originated from Flint himself, a largely uneducated man. Yet he hoped that scientists might one day discover a means of direct communication between the two worlds.

He concluded his book with the words: *I have used my rare and strange gift as honestly, as selflessly and as devotedly as I have been able.*

Leslie passed on in 1992, to join all those who had communicated through him. He has had no equal since.

## Sir Oliver Lodge and Raymond Smith

I sat with Raymond Smith while Oliver Lodge spoke through him, as he did almost daily for a period. A vast amount of material was thus assembled, particularly in Oliver's three books previously mentioned. All I can do here is to include but some of the wise words of this noted and brilliant scientist. I quote as many as I can in order to do justice to him.

*The quality of your prayer determines the level of consciousness it reaches.*

*Prayer is thought.*

*From the world of mind, greetings. Physical life on this speck of dust within God's creation is rather like that of a caterpillar on the leaf of the cabbage. Earth is his cabbage leaf.*

*It is thought that we try to send from our world to yours and not language.*

*There is not one spirit world but an infinite number of levels of consciousness.*

*As you progress spiritually you find yourself in the environment which best suits your state of mind.*

*There is law and order even within the sub-atomic particles of one atom.*

*Great souls no longer need shape or form, they are light.*

*The universe consists of matter, motion, mind and spirit.*

*One day will come the blending of scientific and religious thought.*

*That great infinite mind that, for want of a better word, we all call God.*

*Man in his innate vanity seems to delude himself that God created the universe so that this one planet, Earth, could support life.*

Lodge refers to a plan for each life but how that plan is put into effect 'depends on the free will of each individual'.

*We drink the cup of forgetfulness with each rebirth.* An echo of Wordsworth.

*Reincarnation only takes place when the time is right.*
*I therefore implore you to listen constantly to the thoughts that are given from invisible dimensions instead of putting the emphasis on the personality of the transmitter.*

*An understanding of God and creation lies far beyond our spiritual grasp.*
An echo of Einstein and Darwin.

*Your prayers are heard by those who do God's work.*

*Healing – the greatest of all gifts.*

*The power of the mind is so great; you are all spiritual beings.*

*I still try to help many with their scientific work.*

*Learn and experience as many lessons as possible whilst incarnate.*

*Ask, and you shall receive, contains a greater philosophy than mankind appreciates.*

*In my world I can communicate with those in my level of consciousness without even uttering a word.*

Lodge also confirms how thought becomes sound in an Independent Direct Voice medium.

*Your mind is you. You are not your body. The mind determines what every cell in your body should do. The human body is a shadow of the real self – the mind.*
How might this relate to my words on cancer?

*Mediumship functions through the right hemisphere of the physical brain.*

*Religion has been responsible for more murder, violence, wars and torture than any other organised society.*

*It is the desire and work of the group assembled here to try to blend religion and science, for superstition still prevails in both.*

*It is time that all religions combined into one universal philosophy.*
Echoed by all those who communicated.

*Religion has failed in encouraging man to explore our world.*

*Superstitions in many holy books must be replaced by knowledge, facts and truth, though amongst the many false teachings within the books of religion lie many truths.*

*The medium Jesus.*

*The theory of natural selection without any intelligence to guide it is absurd.*

*There was no beginning. There is no end.*

*Scientists have to widen the horizon of their experiments to include forces that do not obey the laws of physics.*

*There are parallel universes that correspond to the development of the mind.*

*Earth is the prison of the soul – our world is a world of freedom.*

*In the beginning was a thought.*

*No singular religion is correct – not even Spiritualism.*

*All of my scientific work did not make me any wiser or more spiritual than the ordinary man.*

*In my life, it was my desire to blend both science and religion.*

*Search with an open mind.*

All these words came to Raymond Smith from Oliver Lodge. June, Raymond's wife, also talks with Oliver, and recorded over 400 taped hours of such talks.

*Some healers can dematerialise diseased parts of the body – any external or internal incisions heal immediately.*
This was my own experience, as previously described.

*Only when religions put away the tool of fear and use the tools of science will the knowledge of survival be substantiated.*

*We are all on an infinite journey in search of God. God is love.*
Not Lodge's message, but from the group around him.

*There is no such thing as coincidence.*
From Franz Anton Mesmer, of the group.

*Earthly life is a school of learning.*

*The spirit joins the body at the moment of conception.*
Relevant in the abortion debate.

*Tribes of the past accepted communication with our worlds as natural.*

*Love continues to become even greater in our world.*

*The forces of the mind are far superior to anything material. The latter is temporary, the former permanent.*

*Ladies are more sensitive, intuitive and emotional than men. Most men are insensitive and behave more like animals.*

*Religions have been born out of the fear of the unknown.*

*You are a form of energy.*

*The subliminal self contains experiences gathered during other incarnations.*
I have referred very little to past-life regressions or previous incarnations but there is a vast array of literature on these subjects.

*Dreaming is just as important as waking.*

*Have confidence and faith in yourself rather than in others.*

*Mind can affect matter at a distance.*
As I found through my own experience with distant or absent healing.

*Life's computer [is] called a brain.*

*My friends and I live in a non-matter world that seems more substantial than the earthly world of matter.*

*Brain, a complex piece of matter, is used by what is called mind.*

*Brain and mind – soul are two separate entities.*

*Darwin's theory of evolution – much of it is true, yet at the same time some guiding intelligence formulated that theory, Darwin just discovered part of it.*

*Both science and religion still close their minds to reality and truth.*

*Mind has no gender.*

Lodge's group includes Franz Mesmer, Charles Richet, Sister Mary, Phillippe Armand Chastenet, and Mentor the Teacher. There is so much I would wish to quote but conclude this section with two significant messages from Oliver Lodge:

'Every cell of your body is servant to the organ of which it is part, and all organs are servants of the brain. The brain is the servant of you, your spirit, your celestial being. In the same sense we are all servants of that infinite intelligence God, we are parts of his/her/it.

'The actions of any living creature are stimulated not by atoms but by the energy which exists in the space between the atoms. In the case of life, that energy is called mind.

'The atheist must feel that everything in creation just happened by chance, by the law of natural selection. For everything within creation to have just happened by chance has the same mathematical possibility as throwing millions of bricks in the air and expecting them to fall in the form of some wonderful cathedral. The religious fanatic wants to make God a personality, hence the many religions in your world worshipping different representations of God – different images.'

# BEYOND THE RAINBOW

*Above* Lord Dowding
*Above left* Sir Oliver Lodge
*Left* Leslie Flint

AUBREY ROSE

BEYOND THE RAINBOW

*Top* Raymond Smith
*Above* Douglas Conacher
*Right* Nan McKenzie

*Facing page* Sai Baba

# AUBREY ROSE

*Top left* Elizabeth Farrell
*Top right* Harry Edwards
*Above* Vera Chesno and Irène
*Right* Irène Noah

## SIR ARTHUR CONAN DOYLE

I make no excuse for writing further about Arthur Conan Doyle even though I never met him during his lifetime. I did live for a time around the corner from 221B Baker Street, home of celebrated sleuth Sherlock Holmes, but that's as far as it goes. So what follows is not unlike other parts of this book. Nor could I have met him. He passed away in 1930 at the age of seventy-one when I was but four years old, an innocent East End child. His world was not my world. In fact they could not have been more different. He had an Irish background, an education in Scotland, a medical practice in Portsmouth and a shining career of notable achievement.

This man, larger than life, wrote forty full length books, several plays, histories, famous stories like Brigadier Gerard, Silver Blaze, and above all, he was the creator of the immortal logician Mr Sherlock Holmes. That isn't all. He was, as already mentioned, a boxer, a notable cricketer, a pioneer motorist, keen golfer, billiards expert, introducer of ski-ing into Switzerland, and heaven knows what else. This was a man for all seasons. He might have finished up as a member of the Cabinet, the House of Lords, full of honour, distinction and public acclaim. This was a true success story, the highest-paid short-story writer, ten shillings a word, in those non-inflationary days.

And yet, all this took second place to his investigation of the world of the spirit. It was the daily death of the finest young men in the horror of the First World War trenches that impelled him into this field. He had investigated in a leisurely way haunted houses, poltergeists, and so on, but, with the surge of heartbreak and family loss around him, he came alive, as perhaps only he could, to the reality of this other world. In fact he says so:

'I suddenly seemed to see that this subject with which I had so long dallied was not merely the study of a force outside the rules of science but that it was really something tremendous, a breaking down of the walls between two worlds, a direct undeniable message from beyond, a call of hope and guidance for the human race at the time of its deepest affliction.'

He had climbed a mountain and could perceive vistas denied to those who dwelt in the valley.

True to his wholehearted self, he threw himself, body, mind and soul, into a lifetime crusade to bring the good news to as many as possible of those enveloped in a totally materialistic world. He helped to found organisations in Britain, advancing the cause of Spiritualism. For eleven years he moved heaven and earth lecturing through Australia, South Africa, America, Britain. Although a doctor himself, he ignored all medical advice. He never spared himself, until he succumbed to the inevitable end of his life here.

Once he was caught up in the cause of the spirit, his life became a mission, a crusade. He was determined to convince the world that man survived death, that consciousness continued at different levels, and that we mortals on this planet could communicate with those who had passed on. This belief became his passion. I could go off along tangents and byways to explore this many-sided individual, but I limit myself to his link with the medium Grace Cook.

This lady, the ninth child in her family, lost her mother when she was a mere seven years old. The mother was able, however, to continue to communicate with her husband, and Grace grew up convinced of survival and communication in a family sympathetic to these views. By the time she was eighteen she was speaking in Spiritualist churches as a psychic and clairvoyant. This became her life, her mission, some years after Conan Doyle had left the earth. She travelled all over Britain exercising her undoubted gifts, aided by a guide known as White Eagle.

To digress for a moment, it is interesting how many guides seem to be of non-Western background, more often coming from Tibetan, Indian, Chinese, or Native American nations. I recall that when I sought help for my son, David, from famous healer Ted Fricker, his guide was an African. Maurice Barbanell, when in trance, echoed the wondrous words of Silver Birch. For some reason White Eagle told Grace Cook she would be known to him as Minesta, meaning 'mother'. Grace became friendly with the Stead family and through them made contact with the Conan Doyles, who invited her to their house near Crowborough in Surrey.

This was in 1930. Grace was due to go but the visit was cancelled as Conan Doyle was on his deathbed and passed on in that very year. However, a link of significance had been made and the lives of the two became interwoven, forming a link between two worlds. From the world of the spirit came a series of messages of great importance from Arthur through the mediumship of Grace.

I have read those messages, again and again, covering well over a hundred pages, words of great eloquence and perception, indeed of inspiration. I could fill this book with quotations, so impressive do I find them. White Eagle referred to Conan Doyle as 'Nobleheart' and gradually Doyle manages to speak through the medium: *I am here, I am here. You must forgive my emotion.*

*It is marvellous to speak with you all again. You do not, you cannot, understand what all this means. I have come back. I have passed through some wonderful experiences. I see a mission before me.*

He refers to God as *the creative essence*. He continues, *I see myself. I see certain things in which I was mistaken. No man can have the entire truth. Survival of the human soul is a proven fact, is unquestionable.* And, like so many other communicators, he confirms that the spirit world is a world of thought. Indeed thought is more powerful than action.

He dwells on the truth that the kingdom of heaven is within. Man must not live for himself, not for his good name, nor to acquire personal power or property, nor for success, but to contribute to the common good. In giving all, he receives all. Then, and only then, will he enter the kingdom of heaven.

There are many echoes of Jesus in Conan Doyle's words. Through Grace he talks on many subjects – mediumship, communication, levels above levels, the ether, the 'Summerland', the astral, mental and celestial planes, previous lives, evolution, the effect of the nature of a person's life here on his place there, of interplanetary life, of the power of thought on material objects (*vide* Sai Baba), of there being only one universal religion, even his prophecy that 'a race of men will evolve considerably in advance of humanity of today'. He explains the relationship between good and evil, of balance, of worlds that astronomers cannot perceive, not worlds of physical matter. He seems to have a regard for the teachings of Jesus and Buddha and speaks hardly at all of other religions. Having been a doctor, however, he speaks at length and in detail about disease and healing and the deep causes of physical ill-health.

He considers the nations of the world that subsist on suspicion and fear and the dominance of materialism, even in the orthodox churches. He emphasises the need for a common brotherhood among men and nations in order to avert their eventual destruction, and calls for a change of values. He foresaw the great suffering that lay ahead for mankind because of its fear, its materialism, and its values. And, of course, within but a few years came World War II, with the curse of brutality to be seen everywhere – the sheer horror of the Holocaust, the march of death from continent to continent. Yet Conan Doyle offers a hope for the future.

This remarkable man passed on in 1930. In 1931 and 1932 he poured out his messages, couched in that earnest, enthusiastic, eloquent manner that typified the whole of his earthly life. His words are contained in 110 pages of Ivan Cooke's *The Return of Arthur Conan Doyle*. Come on, you scientists,

Humanists, atheists, do you think Cooke made it all up? Read it for yourself, the words of a man who had lived life to the full in his seventy-one years.

I first met ACD, as he was often called, in 1980. I kept meeting him (in words) in 1981, 1991, 1999, 2000, 2004, and finally 2011. On each occasion I wrote my reaction over all the pages containing his messages. I could never have done that with the new technological reading wonders. The gist of all my comments was the inspiration I received from the words I read and absorbed year after year. Let me share some of these with you. His first words from beyond:

*Thank God! God bless you. I am here – I am here! I have come back.*
Indeed he had.

*I have passed through some wonderful experiences.*

*No man can have the whole truth.*

*Survival of the human soul is a proven fact, is unquestionable.*

*One of the first things a man is faced with on his escape from Earth life is a world of his own thought.*

Indeed, repeated so often is:
*Thought is more powerful than action.*

What has struck me through all the 110 pages is the similarity to the words of Sai Baba, of Jesus, and of Buddha. He often refers to the last two but rarely mentions any other religion or religious figure. How often does he repeat the phrase: *The kingdom of heaven is within.*

As with Sai Baba, I compare Conan Doyle's words with those of Jesus. Again the heart, love, matters.

*So long as a man remains enmeshed in intellectual pride he can never find the truth.*
He refers to: *The prison house of arrogance.*

*Man must live not for himself but to contribute to the common good. In giving all he receives all.*

Time and again he indicates how difficult it is to explain his world to us:
*It is extremely difficult to explain to a finite mind the actual facts concerning the mental state of the individual soul after the change of death.*

He indicates that the new life depends on the *arrival's mentality* and *his attitude during his former life towards his fellows.*

Again, like Jesus and other faiths, Conan Doyle emphasises purity of spirit although he comments that mankind *is only just awakening to the value of spiritual life.* He does not want people to grieve too much as *the spirit is continually being held back by those who mourn its passing.*

Personally, I have found that despite the loss of a much-loved wife and son, I have been uplifted by the knowledge that they live still. Indeed, we have spoken together since their passing.

I am fascinated by Conan Doyle's progress in the world of the spirit. In early communications he states:

*I am only the spokesman for greater ones than I, and when my mission is finished I shall leave this earth and advance. I am under the direction of the wise ones. I now come back to reveal a finer life, a nobler path than had ever dawned in my earthly conception. Man must be taught the truth concerning his life after death.*

This statement turned my mind to my story, The Mission.

Conan Doyle comments on the aura around individuals: *Each man bears around with him a complete record of all that has happened to himself. He finds himself in an unspeakably beautiful heaven world, so different from what I once anticipated.*

Interestingly he refers to a Second Death, that second awakening, arousing in him *the wonder, the infinitude, the allness of God's love for me and for all men.*

Real love permeates all his words, the love of which Jesus spoke. The contrast is in the lower astral plane, which consists of *burning and persistent desire.* This reminded me of Buddha's teaching, that one must try to conquer desire, the cause of suffering. This implies choice, free will. ACD confirms that *man's own free will is ever operative,* though it is also linked to destiny.

I was happy to read Conan Doyle's comment on the wonderful mysticism of parts of the Bible, such as the story of Jacob's Ladder. Again, he emphasises that *everything depends on his material and spiritual quality at the time of his release.* Death-bed rituals and words mean nothing.

He describes different levels – astral, mental, celestial – and the place called 'Summerland', written about by brilliant, creative Michael Bentine, whose own book, *The Door Marked Summer,* is so inspiring. Conan Doyle details these spheres or levels in the beyond. He mentions the third mental plane where there is even an absence of form, as envisaged in The Mission.

He is definite about the source of our creativity. From the second mental plane *springs all the creative urge or activity which takes an ultimate form on earth as art, literature, music, religion, science.* Scientists, please note. I think

Einstein might well have agreed. Certainly, Alfred Russel Wallace would agree. He was a great scientist and convinced Spiritualist. I do wish that one day we could get rid of the 'ists' and 'isms'. Wallace would approve Conan Doyle's statement that: *Within us all lies an inmost centre of our being, a divine birthplace of man's spirit, which even to reach, much less to comprehend, is beyond all intellectual striving or attainment.*

Didn't Baba say the same, as did Einstein?

I was by now so carried away by Conan Doyle's eloquence and glowing words that I wrote in the margin of his book: 'The words and teachings of Conan Doyle are tremendous, needing to be read and re-read. It reveals to what extent our modern age is deeply enmeshed in materialism, in material thought and material emotion.'

I wrote these words in 1980. My enthusiasm has not abated, nor have my views changed one iota.

Conan Doyle confirmed something Baba, Jesus and indeed Elisha, could do, and that is, to influence material objects. With Jesus it was the story of the loaves and fishes, and the wine at Cana. With Baba, it was the many objects he created. Conan Doyle confirms that: *Man can control the elements and create at will by filling his consciousness with the universal creative life force. This leads to control of all the material elements around them.*

This effort of spiritual willpower affects the vibrations and influences physical atoms. Baba, there in India, by this power, can fill whole containers here in England with his sacred ash called *vibhuti*, and, amazingly, has continued to do so after his passing physically from Earth in 2011. This I have seen with my own eyes.

It is much the same with absent or distant healing, which Harry Edwards practised. Often this process is linked to colours, about which Conan Doyle speaks at length, detailing the appropriate colour for each specific illness.

Again and again he looks beyond individual creeds and speaks of the gospel of universalism. He speaks of the all-pervading life-force governing plant life, animal life and human life. Behind every manifestation broods the great world of spiritual reality. His comments on free will and destiny are instructive.

*Destiny stands for a range of physical experiences through which man must and will pass in the course of his mortal life. Free-will choice lies in his own reaction spiritually to the conditions which largely rule his ordinary physical life.*

As I read on, buoyed up by the writer's eloquence, I was reminded of the beauty and poetry of the Psalms.

But amidst the increasing horrors and turbulence of our planet, Doyle prophesies:

*A great new continent will emerge where there is now but a waste of ocean and there will be an equivalent subsidence of level whilst a race of men will evolve considerably in advance of the humanity of today.*

He also refers to inhabitants of other planets. Indeed he looks forward to brotherhood between nations leading on to an *interplanetary brotherhood born of interplanetary communication*. He adds: *Planets of an ethereal substance are even now within the radius of the solar system but they are invisible to the eye of man or to his most powerful telescope.*' Sadly he acknowledges that: 'Earth is the darkest planet of the system.

Also sadly, as I write, I realise that I cannot do justice to all that Conan Doyle has to say: his analysis of good and evil, complementary to each other; the materialism of the orthodox churches, *deifying the Nazarene*, a church *overridden by creed and dogma*; the fact that there is no vicarious atonement; and his detailed teachings on illness and disease, which usually arise from lack of harmony between psychic and physical bodies, as well as discussions of the process of healing.

Conan Doyle summarises twelve psychic centres in the body alongside precise approaches to specific illnesses. As I re-read his writings, I recall similar words and treatments by Harry Edwards. There is often a spiritual cause of illness and of healing linked to spiritual efforts.

Again and again, Conan Doyle seeks *a common brotherhood*, overcoming the *havoc through materialism, death through materialism. Each soul must lose itself in order to find itself – let all sense of self fall away. Only one true religion exists, only one reality behind all forms – the religion of true brotherhood is love whilst forms and ceremonies, creeds and dogmas avail nothing without the living spirit.*

Let me end with a quotation, which embodies a sublime vision, pure in outlook, inspiring and uplifting. These are Arthur Conan Doyle's words from his present abode:

*It is profoundly difficult to express spiritual realities with words fitted only to describe material and physical conditions. Nevertheless, I would hold out to all people a hope beautiful and true beyond compare. I would assure them of the progress to be won by man's constant desire for beauty, love and wisdom. I would describe a life perfect in its power to express all the higher feelings and attributes which lie hidden in the depths of man's nature. Not one soul, whether it be of a white, a black, a yellow or a red man, but finds provision made for it in the vast universe of spirit. I would paint such a picture of the heaven world, were I able, that it must satisfy every desire and fire the imagination of every living soul on earth. Were the words mine I would show a world of spirit ever evolving, opening to new vista after vista of beauty. As one attains one sees fresh heights beyond. The air grows finer, brighter. Exultation fills one's being, nerving one to fresh effort and attainment.*

These eloquent words confirm the hope for the future, a hope reflected in all those with whom I have come into contact and whose thoughts I have tried to describe briefly but, I hope, faithfully.

## SAI BABA

The guru's full name is Sri Sathya Sai Baba. Many books describe his life teachings and manifestations. My friend Ruth wears a gold ring he produced out of mid-air (something from nothing) but his teachings, although linked to the Indian sub-continent and its faiths, have a universal quality. I must confess I had never heard of him until a group of his followers landed in my home in the 1990s. I quote here a few of his thoughts, but do also consider the titles of books about him. In *Seeking Divinity*, Dr John Hislop quotes these words by 'his hero' Sai Baba:

*We shall be judged not by the creed we profess but by the work, the industry, the sacrifice, the honesty and purity of character. Realise the heaven within you. The sole purpose of spiritual disciplines is the purification of the mind and the heart.*

One of Howard Murphet's books is called *Sai Baba – Man of Miracles*. In it I read that 1926, the year of Sai Baba's birth, was called Akshaya, meaning the 'never declining, ever-full year'. This I found encouraging as it is also the year of my own birth. In fact, we were both born in the same month. The books describe many 'miracles', healings, objects created magically by Sai Baba, his materialisation elsewhere, his over-shadowing. When presented with a piece of rock, Baba said: 'Beyond your molecules and observe God is in the rock.' He spoke of the complacent, all-knowing attitude of many men of science, deploring their ignorance of ancient wisdom.

And yet many men of science, physicists, geologists, even nuclear scientists, have confirmed the quite extraordinary nature and power of this man. The quality they describe takes us beyond the description of healer or medium, although both are applicable to him. So many find a god-like element in this being, who seems beyond space and time. There is a God-man tradition in India, as elsewhere, for example in Greek and Roman times; but here we have an accumulation of evidence that is powerful, evidence confirmed by highly qualified independent observers, including an Indian Prime Minister.

Many years ago an article of mine was published nationally. It described a beautiful garden at the centre of which rose a kind of temple. Many paths led to the central point, each path representing a religious faith. They all met together. It was symbolic of different paths to the same truth. I was happy to find that a similar construction exists in Sai Baba's ashram. He does not wish anyone to leave his or her faith. 'If you are a Christian, then be a better

Christian', he states, and so on with other faiths. He teaches no new religion, only the overwhelming power of love.

He makes a powerful impact on many, not merely on ordinary people. The book *Inspired Medicine* is a testimony by eighteen leading medical practitioners of note as to the truth of Sai Baba's teachings and healing power. How often are the incurable cured? His abilities are reminiscent of those of Harry Edwards but are even more remarkable. One doctor quotes Sai Baba as saying 'any incurable disease can be cured with love'. Indeed, there are frequent comparisons between the words of Baba and Jesus. This analysis is set out in some detail in *Sathya Sai Baba*, a work by Peggy Mason and Ron Lang.

For example:

Jesus – *Blessed are the pure in heart, for they shall see God.*

Baba – *The pure heart sees beyond the intellect, it becomes inspired.*

Jesus – *Search not for the mote in your neighbour's eye, but look to the beam in your own.*

Baba – *Instead of seeing faults in others, search for those in yourself.*

Jesus – *Judge not that ye be not judged.*

Baba – *Do not judge others, for when another is judged you are yourself condemned.*

These are but a few examples of many similarities in the teachings of Jesus and Sai Baba.

Reincarnation has been a feature of both Christianity and the Indian traditions, but was expunged from Christianity in the sixth century. It remains very much part of Baba's life, he himself being a reincarnation of a previous teacher (Shirdi Baba). He once stated: *The good fortune that has brought you face to face with me is something for which you must thank your merit won through previous lives.*

He himself owned nothing but created all manner of practical institutions, hospitals, schools, welfare bodies. Like Jesus he was concerned at the world's obsession with wealth. He comments: *The rich must sacrifice their wants so that the poor may secure their needs.* In words that could have emerged from Jesus, Baba states: *I have come to repair the ancient highway to God. I have not come on behalf of any sect or creed or religion. I have come to light the lamp of love in the hearts of all humanity.*

At the same time he believes in effective action, stating: *Hands that help are holier than lips that pray.*

There is one aspect of his outlook that appeals to me especially. Much of my life has been involved in the field of human rights, individual rights, group rights, and society's rights, for indeed society also has human rights. Sai Baba created a school and set out his views on 'education in human values'. He believes the prime purpose of education should be directed to the development of character.

But he also comments: *Men today are concerned solely about their rights and have no regard for their duties, obligations and responsibilities.*

This is one comment I really applaud, as I do the rest of his teaching on education. He even refers to the teaching profession as: *The noblest, the most difficult and the most important.*

He devotes many words to the responsibility of parents. He concludes that: *Education is for life, not merely a living.*

My friend, Ruth Grant, in her fascinating account of contact with Sai Baba, *From Bitter Came Sweet,* reflects on many of Sai Baba's sayings.

These include:

*The Lord will accept a heart without words but he will not accept words without a heart.*

*Love is selflessness, self is lovelessness.*

*Education without character, science without compassion and commerce without morality are useless and dangerous.*

The pithiest and most direct of Baba's teachings are:

*Help ever – hurt never. Love all – serve all*

In March 2013, I attended a service in a temple devoted to Sai Baba. This was in London. I was impressed by the feeling of peace and reverence. But what impressed me even more was that, despite his passing from our material world, Sai Baba was still sending to this temple large quantities of *vibhuti*, or sacred ash, which I inspected. There is no question or doubt about this. Those in charge are of the highest integrity.

Thus there is contact from world to world just as with Leslie Flint, Oliver Lodge and many others. It is a form of contact, perhaps by the power of the mind, which can affect our material world. In a way it is akin to the distant healing of Harry Edwards.

We do not know what lies ahead of us if this pattern expands. It may prove the saving grace of our ever-violent, turbulent planet.

I must conclude here or else I will be carried away with the story of this remarkable being. I have included him even though his life transcends in some ways the other accounts in this section, but it does describe rare patterns of healing that are quite beyond the understanding of the worlds of medicine and science. I would love scientists and humanists, atheists and agnostics, to read the books mentioned, a few among many, and give their explanations of the phenomena set out in such detail.

## Douglas Conacher

You have probably never heard of Douglas Conacher. Amongst a galaxy of famous names, each eminent in his own field, we now have the ordinary, average man, yet one who blossomed into something extraordinary. He was a publisher, mainly of books on orthodox religion and philosophy. Deeply religious, he was a devout member of the Church of England. His publishing business was situated in the shadow of St Paul's Cathedral. The books he published and read never entered the occult, psychic or Spiritualist stream. A biography of Douglas would be short indeed. Born in Scotland, married for the first time in 1937, at the age of fifty-eight, to Eira, then aged thirty-nine. There were no children but these two were a devoted couple until Douglas passed on in 1958 after serious illness. This could be the life story of myriads of ordinary souls – birth, adulthood, marriage, death. Yet after his death, Douglas came alive in a splendid and spectacular way.

Leslie Flint was involved. From 1965 to 1967 Eira sat with Leslie. Douglas had discovered a new, exciting and exhilarating world and poured forth his reactions profusely, simply, so that Eira was able to publish two books of his words. I have been equally excited by what I read in both *Chapters of Experience* (1973) and *There Is Life After Death* (1978). I have read, re-read, and read yet again all Douglas had to say and I covered the pages with endless comments. For a short time I was in touch with Eira before she too passed on. This lovely, loving couple are now together.

But I have a problem, as I have had with Oliver Lodge and with Leslie Flint. How can I summarise a host of wonderful words set out in 280 pages and do justice to Douglas? I will try, and hope he forgives me for my brevity. Indeed I hope Eira does too. She declared, whilst here, that her sittings with Leslie brought her great joy, confirming: 'Life took on a new radiance, a new realisation of its purpose and splendour dawned on me'.

She hoped that these talks would help 'to bring a clearer realisation of the eternal nature of life'.

So Eira sat there with Leslie in the dark recesses of the room while the tape recorder whirled away, embodying the voices of Douglas and Leslie's alter ego, Mickey, as well as Eira. In direct voice, Leslie could also join in but rarely did. Of course, it is Douglas's thoughts that are converted into sound. He refers repeatedly to thought forces. His world is: *a thought world, a world created by thought forces. Remember that thought forces are living things and very powerful. We can transport ourselves from one place to another by thought.*

I pondered on this world of thought, on Harry Edwards being able to heal people miles away from him, on Sai Baba's creation of material objects by thought, of my own personal experience of absent healing. Douglas adds: *It is possible here to communicate entirely by the power of thought.*

Indeed: *A person is no more or less than his own thoughts.*

He confirms: *What really counts here is the state of mind and character built up through the earthly years.*

The element of reincarnation is frequently raised by Douglas: *Man must not confine his consciousness to one physical earthly existence. One life on earth can only skim the surface of experience. A new experience will provide different conditions to those when you are on Earth before.*

In my investigations and researches, how often have people talked to me of 'old souls'? Douglas confirms that most of the great teachers and prophets of old were old souls, who returned for a particular purpose. How often psychics referred to our son David, who passed on aged twenty-one in 1978, as an old soul. Indeed, from Douglas's world, David confirmed that he came for a purpose and was now on a high level. His poetry, painting and music were sufficient testimony. Douglas describes his many incarnations, at times with Eira, in ancient Egypt, Karnak, England of old, Crusades, medieval Padua, the French Revolution, even as a Jew at the time of Jesus, and he 'provides considerable detail. On the other hand he concludes: *I do not think I shall ever incarnate again. Life never ceases to be wonderful. I have never known such peace and calm.*

There is considerable description of group souls: *A group may consist of hundreds of people who have interwoven together during different periods of time.*

He refers to Eira and himself as 'twin souls', of the same group and: *There are thousands upon thousands of these group souls going through experience essential to them in the same vibratory condition of life.*

Vibrations are significant in explaining so much. Incidentally Irène Noah, Vera's daughter, informed me that she and I were twin souls, possibly even sister and brother at some stage. Who knows?

Douglas mentioned that he had been involved in 'rescue' work, helping the confused, the victims of violence, who knew not where they were. Shades of Michael Evans...

Douglas refers too to 'reception stations', helping recent arrivals to adjust, needed for many since, although: *I did not take very long to adjust, for others it was different since fear is very predominant with the majority of people before they* pass over. This includes: *Fear that unless they have fallen in with certain religious beliefs they will be punished.*

Indeed: *They have to rid themselves of a lot of earthly thoughts.*

Although Douglas describes in considerable detail his world, the scene, the flowers, buildings, books, records of past events, animals who survive through love, the continued creativity in music, in colour, in words, of those pre-eminent in their earth life, there are certain themes he returns to again and again: *Beings from other worlds, or other planets, are going to make themselves known very soon. Then I think the earth is going to change.*

These beings, *far more advanced than ours*, will herald *the salvation of the earth.* He has high regard for the role of science, which will confirm both survival and communication, so that, as some modern scientists may concur: *Many of the religions, if not all the religions as you know religion today, will be non-existent. Man has some shocks coming.*

Douglas finds it hard not to talk about religion and religious figures, perhaps not surprising in view of his earthly work. He refers to St Francis, whom he has met and who had 'great spiritual experiences'. People with long histories fascinated him: *I have talked to many ancients over here, Chinese and Egyptians from whom I have learned a great deal. Thousands of years ago in ancient China and in ancient Egypt they had discovered certain things which today have yet to be rediscovered. The ancient Chinese had a tremendous philosophy, they had a tremendous power. They had a wonderful form of communication between our world and yours.*

But it is about Jesus and Christianity that Douglas expounds at length. I can but summarise his thoughts, most inadequately, I am afraid: *Jesus of Nazareth, a man of utter simplicity and humility who had no desire for position. He was born under normal circumstances, in the ordinary way.* No virgin birth, according to Douglas.

*The Church has built around Jesus something that he himself was not concerned with. They have built religion around him. Jesus had little or no time for religion. He had no time for power and position. Christ did not pretend to be God. People have learned to worship Jesus, but Jesus was the last person who desired worship. He only wanted people to see in him the simplicity of a way of life which would release them from pain and sorrow.*

*Christ was not the beginning and the end. He was a follower of other great prophets and seers. Christ was a great teacher, a great prophet, a great realiser of the truths of eternal life, and he imparted those truths to his disciples. He was in constant communication with the so-called dead. He was a great instrument or a great medium, a medium for truth in many, many ways which the church has denied and feared. The Christian church – all denominations – has made of the truth of Christ, the teachings of Christ, one enormous maze.*

Here is a former keen Church of England member now looking afresh at that church. Current Church of England members must be drawing a deep breath. But Douglas does not stop there. He feels the church *paints a picture which is so much of a myth and fairytale. And we do not have to be reminded of the terrible things that have happened in the name of Christianity.*

Douglas confirms there is no heaven or hell, no miracles, in fact *Christ was a man the same as any other human being but he had the power of the spirit so strongly within himself. I have always felt this, that Jesus was all the greater, more wonderful, for being just a man, like other men, born like other men, rather than being a demi-god or part of a god.*

To Douglas the idea of the Trinity makes no sense. He wants us to realise *that all great teachers and prophets have the same message.*

He believes that *the truth, as Christ taught it, has been overshadowed by pomp and ceremony, by creed and dogma, by material conception – even of heaven. It is all so pathetic and very sad.*

Thus Douglas looks with fresh eyes at what many have done to Jesus. In fact he wants us to widen our vision and *to have our minds free, unshackled, we must never feel that we know all the answers. Truth must be all-embracing, always open to change.*

There is such sincerity, eloquence, fervour, in the words of this fine being. I cannot do justice to all that he says. I look at my comments, scrawled over the pages in 1992, 1993, 1994, 1998, 1999, 2005, 2006, 2007, 2012 and 2014, all inspired by the truths expounded from his present world. I can do no better than to set down my 1992 comments:

'So eloquent and so honest and so excited by the expanding universe of his mind and of his new experiences. His language has dignity and simplicity and he shows the ability to change in the light of new experiences.

'There is a truth greater than any individual religion, any single philosophy, that we have to spread gradually, to overcome the encrusted barnacles of creed and mind that inhabits so many, many corners of this world.'

I added in 1999: 'I hope Douglas and Eira are together progressing in joy and in harmony. We are all indebted to them for their efforts. Bless them.'

I just hope they feel I have done some form of justice to their thoughts and memories, however brief and inadequate.

## Virène – Mother and Daughter

In the summer of 2009, at a simple ceremony, I presented Ron Huldai, the Mayor of Tel-Aviv, with a book that had come to me via Vera Chesno and her daughter Irène Noah. He was delighted with this account of his city's development since its foundation at a meeting on sand dunes in 1909.

It appeared that Vera, active in France and England in the early 1930s, had been asked to go to Egypt to encourage attendance at a trade fair in Tel-Aviv. She did so, having her first experience of camel riding in the process, and attended a celebratory dinner in that city. Next to her sat a man whom she had not met previously. They were both silent, until they realised that they had the Russian language in common. In due course they became great friends. He was Meir Dizengoff, the main historic figure in the development of that city and its first mayor. He presented Vera with a book illustrating over twenty years of civic growth, endorsing it with a dedication and personal signature.

When Vera departed this world in 1985, the book descended to her daughter Irène, after which it passed to me. I had the pleasure of seeing it placed in the municipal archives of that vibrant metropolis, to the delight of the mayor.

This story is typical of events in Vera's life. She was gifted, in languages, in music, in her vivacious personality. She was also a woman of courage. As I have mentioned earlier, I edited her life story, which was written when she was in her nineties. I was amazed at the sheer, unstoppable determination of this woman. Nothing was more remarkable than her survival in France during the horrible years of the World War II and her protection of Irène, her beloved daughter and only child. (More on this is given in Part II.)

As I write, in the comfort of peacetime and in civilised, peace-loving Britain, it is almost impossible to project one's imagination into the world of Nazi oppression and Vichy complicity that turned every day for nigh on five years into a day of peril. No wonder, after 1945, that Vera had health problems. No wonder, either, that Irène suffered throughout her life, especially in her last thirteen years, from acute illnesses arising from stress and malnutrition. Both women were victims of the debased, sub-human Nazi mentality that led to 40,000,000 deaths in Europe.

I met Irène, almost accidentally, in 1995 and we remained in touch for ten years. Vera had passed from this realm in 1985 but I first met her at the beginning of 2003. From then until the summer of 2005 I was in regular touch with her, almost weekly, sometimes daily.

In the early morn, when all in my home were asleep, I would ring Irène; we would speak and then, medium that she was, there came through her the voice of Vera, and not only Vera, but others too. On occasions these included my mother, my son David, and a Dr Reinhardt, a medical man, who had passed on at the end of the nineteenth century. Another who spoke was Paul, who had been like a husband to Irène for years – they were a couple closely attached to one another.

A word about Paul: he was a German, not a Jew. He came from a village, married, had a family, became prominent as an engineer and factory owner, and was publicly honoured for his achievements. He came to England, met Irène, and never returned home. He said that he and Irène had once long ago been man and wife, when he was in fact not a German but a rabbi.

Paul told me that he felt he had been a Jew named Solomon and he wished to renew that status. So he and Irène had created a small synagogue at the top of their house in Hove, East Sussex. Irène took me there. It was touching. She and Paul threw themselves into local Jewish life, even editing the *Jewish Newsletter* for the south coast.

As ill health took its toll on Paul, Irène nursed him as he grew frailer until he passed on. At my first contact with Vera, Paul spoke too, and I told him that Irène loved him. Vera said Irène and I had been twins together in the past, and that my current link had in fact rescued her daughter from being 'marooned on a desert island'!

Vera's bubbling, dynamic personality emerged clearly during our conversations. She spoke at first in Russian and we always said goodbye in Russian – *Dosvidaniya* – whilst Paul said *Auf wiedersehen*.

David also spoke to me, in complimentary terms. They all wanted me to concentrate on my writing, not to be diverted, not to be a 'bee' going from flower to flower, but to be single-minded, and to take care of my health.

These themes continued throughout my two years of contact. 'Don't get involved in politics, in organisations', I was told. 'Don't comment adversely on any religion.' They felt I had some kind of a mission. I had to complete something my son could not finish. He looked to me to fulfil what he had wanted to undertake himself.

I was delighted that some words came from my mother. We exchanged compliments. She had been a wonderful mother. I was intrigued that there was a group there including Vera, Paul, Dr Reinhardt, David and my mother. I asked about other members of the family. Vera explained that people of a similar quality or mentality came together. She said: 'It takes two to tango', meaning that people had to have sufficient in common to be together in one group. People would come together if they had a common perception and understanding. Vera explained that 'to make a fire, or a soup, you need the right ingredients'. Her words.

As with Eira and Douglas Conacher, as with Leslie Flint and Raymond Smith and others, how can I summarise here nearly two years of communication? That I had to take care of my health was a common theme. I was likened to a chariot: 'See to it that a wheel doesn't come off.' I should be single-minded: 'You don't build a roof first. You build the foundations first.'

Vera explained too that behind her group there was a larger group. She inferred the existence of level upon level. I was very much the concern of the Great Maggid Dow Baer of the eighteenth century, and even of my esteemed Rabbi Nachman. This was often mentioned.

Somehow I seemed to be linked to the eighteenth century. There was the famous Maggid, or teacher. Here, too, were Shneur Zalman, a great ancestor of Vera, and also Levi Yitzchak, another leading light, ancestor of my friend Ruth. What can I say about all these links? Who knows about past lives, something that had never concerned me?

The group discussed the book I was then writing. Vera advised what should go in and what should be left out. They implied that the title *The Rainbow Never Ends* had come from them.

We discussed at length the cassette of songs Irène wished to sing, albeit in the last year of her life. She had studied singing, had performed publicly. She always claimed that singing, like laughter, was good for one's health. So, with the help of keyboard expert Steve, Irène sang six love songs in six languages (as mentioned in Part II), while I spoke the continuity words. We had great fun, and it lifted Irène's spirit as she fought desperately the permanent Multiple Chemical Sensitivity syndrome (MCS) that confined her perpetually to her home.

Their concern for my health continued, so I tried to limit my activities. Reinhardt advised me to learn how to master the cells in my body. Apparently he had been both surgeon and psychiatrist and had passed on at the age of fifty from tuberculosis.

What at least was comforting, were Vera's words – 'we will guide and help you' – and indeed I felt that to be the case. (Vera, incidentally, was impressed with our daughter Esther.) I have been lucky to have had such guidance. I have had health problems, entailing trials and tests, but I am so grateful for all the help as I approach my 90th year. Vera added that these teachers of old were cheerful and advised us to act likewise.

I made this note in January 2005 – 'It is amazing how Vera listens in, then intervenes, and then Irène talks. It all seems so natural, except of course, that when Vera talks Irène cannot as Vera uses Irène's voice box. Vera always starts off in Russian but easily switches to English.'

I had been doing healing but they wanted me to reduce this: 'you are to heal souls' were the words I heard. Quite an undertaking!

Incidentally, Vera stated that 'Sheila is a lovely person and ideal for you'. She certainly was. I noted Reinhardt's comment too – 'don't eat too much, take care'. Irène, in her studies, had noted heart attacks following meals that were too big.

Irène was a radionics/radiesthesia expert and kept an eye on me that way. This led to Vera's advice to 'be like a snail drawing back its horns. Go slow. Look after the machinery'. She knew how tempted I was to go here and there and get involved. There was an amusing moment when Reinhardt referred to his 'clucking', in order to limit my many activities. I replied that clucking led to the laying of an egg. He responded '*Sie sind wirklich ein Doktor*'!

At times Vera mentioned that they, from their world, do orchestrate events, meetings, here. I said I hoped that did not limit free will. It did not, but they did suggest ideas to me.

From June to August 2005 Irène declined in health. It was sad to see this brilliant woman worsen, hardly able to eat anything and reduced to a bag of bones, but looked after so attentively by Steve.

There was no hope, and on 9th October 2005 she passed from us to join her mother and her beloved Paul. They were now all together, surrounded by a loving, caring group. I have not since been in touch with Vera or Irène, but arranged a memorial meeting soon after her passing and also an Irène Noah Day in October 2010, five years later, when we spoke and sung her praises. I hope she and Vera were with us and approved. Mother and daughter, Vera and Irène – *Virène* – an inseparable duo, were now permanently reunited, in joy and happiness, free at last from the pains of this world, whilst I here, was so privileged to have been close to these wonderful souls.

## JESUS

I first made contact with Alan Ross in 2009. The next year he sent me three quite remarkable books. One was called *The New Testament of Spiritualism*. I have explained how it came into being. If its contents, over 500 pages, are true then it is the most revolutionary book ever written. My comment inside the front cover reads: 'What a unique and extraordinary book. I don't know what to make of it.'

The back cover includes the following: '*The New Testament of Spiritualism* is a collection of 166 channelled messages received through the means of automatic writings. These extraordinary spirit communications originate from spirits inhabiting all levels of the spirit world. In this book you will read eye-opening accounts from Jesus of The New Testament, The Gospel, authors and a great array of spirits from throughout history'.

Ross lists the famous communicators, though I notice that hardly any emanate from India, China and the Far East or even the Moslem or Sikh traditions. There are thirty-eight contributions from Jesus himself.

Alan Ross goes on to say: 'Their purpose is to correct the errors of the Bible. The teachings contained in this book expel many of the myths and superstitions created by the early church to protect its interest and to control the people in their beliefs through religious rites and dogmas.'

Somewhat proudly he adds: 'Gain insights not to be found elsewhere. The book is an epoch-making revelation from the Spirit world.'

By this time the average person would have closed the book, heaved a sigh of resignation, and passed on to something more practical and immediate. That would be a pity. The book is worth looking at, whether you place any credence on its contents or not. Over ninety pages emanate from Jesus. Devout Christians, raised on the Creed and the 39 Articles, would find their blood pressure rising as they peruse the remarks stated as coming from Jesus.

A few examples: *As to my sitting on the right hand of this throne, this is not true. The great law of compensation is as you sow so shall you reap.*

Jesus is quite explicit: *I am not God, and no part of the Godhead.* As to the many mansions in his Father's house, *no one else can build these mansions for you, only your own soul development.*

Jesus then refers to his family: *I was born in Bethlehem and when I was a few days old my parents took me to Egypt. The murder of the innocents is substantially correct.*

Jesus had four brothers and three sisters, all born in Egypt. His father was a carpenter and the family lived in a Jewish community near Cairo.

*The Bible account of my being begotten and all the attending circumstances are not true.*

Jesus urges: *You must have more faith and pray more.*

He refers to his name Jeshua, calling it *a common Hebrew name*. Some of the New Testament stories, such as walking on water are not true, whilst the account of the woman taken in adultery is correct. He emphasises again and again: *I was a man as other men are men, only I had become filled with the Divine Love.*

He teaches personal responsibility and calls it a 'false doctrine' that *he that believeth on the Lord Jesus Christ shall be saved.*

He refers to his brother *James who loved me very much. Jesus was a Hebrew,* he declared. He never came to found a new religion – God was always existent – a being without beginning, the idea of which the finite mind cannot grasp. He refers to change eternal as the law of the universe, but there is also design in creation.

I could quote endlessly. It is fascinating. For example: *The soul of man is the real man. The soul's home is in the spirit body.*

The words on healing would certainly appeal to Harry Edwards: *Faith sets in motion healing forces and energies. Faith permits the healer and the sick person to make contact with the spiritual forces.*

Healing will thus never arise from cold intellect. He also makes reference to spheres and levels, so often mentioned by others.

Jesus looks beyond his own Jewish world. He explains the stories about Abraham and Moses. In fact – *There will be a religion of the future and a comprehensive and final one founded upon the truths you are now receiving for it will be inclusive of all the other religions.*

I can see Sai Baba and Oliver Lodge nodding in approval. But Jesus also nods approval of the Hebrew prophets who *contributed to the elevation of the spiritual concepts of the nation and gave the people and their leaders a deeper insight into the real nature of God.*

Who cannot but feel inspired by the beating of swords into ploughshares, when men will learn war no more. What a wonderful vision. When, oh when, will man learn war no more!

The last message from Jesus is signed by him as *Your brother and friend.*

The reader can discount all of this, but would that be wise? I have touched on only a few salient points. There is a wonderful spirit of love that emerges from Jesus's words. No wonder a religion was created around him.

My friend Alan Ross also produced for me a much smaller book, a mere 110 pages. I read it in one go. My comment at the end reads: 'Gives so much food for thought. Church dogmas are rejected. Much is clarified. Extraordinary!' The book is entitled: *The Genuine Jesus – A Channelled Autobiography.*

Again, my namesake in initials makes no modest claim on the back cover – 'Rarely does a book come along with the power to dispel archaic man-made beliefs and superstitions and replace them with logic and truth from the spiritual world.'

I believe Alan Ross is completely genuine in what he says, and he has therefore brought to our attention 'this breath of fresh air', as one critic describes it. As to the actual words expressed, 'no one can doubt their sincerity', adds another critic.

The sections of the work are Birth and Youth, The Ministry, The Last Week, The Reappearance, The Second Coming, The Teachings. Alan Ross states: 'All of the material in this book originated from Jesus apart from a few minor items.' He adds: 'In *The Genuine Jesus* there are concepts about his life and teachings that, to my knowledge, are not to be found elsewhere.'

I have quoted much, but add a few more extracts from this personal account by Jesus himself: *My name in Hebrew is Jeshua ben Joseph for I was named after Joshua ben Nun, who followed Moses. My mother's name was Miriam. The story of the angel telling her of the birth of a child by the Holy Spirit is fake.*

This myth apparently arose from the early Christian compilers seeking support as a means to convert their pagan compatriots: virgin birth was popular among the ancient religions, even in Buddhism.

*Joseph was a devout Pharisee, legally married to my mother.*

I have always admired the Pharisees, who received a terrible press in the Gospels. Jesus describes the move to Egypt and life there. As he grew: *I became convinced of my mission.* Jesus describes his relationship with his 'cousin', John the Baptist, who, incidentally, was also a Pharisee.

Jesus comments on baptism: *It is a man's creation and means nothing more to God than an outward ceremony.* He was never: *Tempted by the devil, because there is no devil or Satan or any Lucifer.* He repeats again: *I never entertained the idea of establishing a new religion.*

He refers to his relationship to Peter, Nicodemus, the son of Gurion, the Pharisees, the process of healing, the story of Lazarus, the transfiguration, even the miracles which were never performed by him but by God working through him. He comments on institutionalised Christianity as a kind of power structure for the priestly class. *Judas was not a bad man as he has been depicted. In fact his betrayal was really an act that grew out of his love for me and belief in the greatness of my powers.* Poor Judas – the traitor's name unjustified, according to Jesus, for 2000 years. He confirms the love and support of his brother James.

Jesus's version of what happened on the Cross is not as described in the Gospels. In fact later on he refers to how: *The Bible became filled with fake doctrines and teachings. I am not a saviour but I was simply performing my mission.*

I am sure by now any devout Christian would say 'enough is enough' so I will not add to Jesus's comments on the Resurrection, on Peter and Paul. Let me end with some positive words of Jesus: *As now written, the Bible is a grand book and does preserve a number of my sayings and teachings. However it is not the true mouthpiece of God in many particulars. God's truths are simple. Any religion that cannot be understood by the ordinary exercise of the mental faculties cannot be a true religion. The Bible was compiled from many writings.*

He adds, too, that: *There would be a religion of the future inclusive of all the other religions. Truths are so many, so great and so deep that mankind has acquired only a smattering of them.* Acceptance without question of particular dogmas and creeds of the churches, *is the major reason why mankind has not progressed further.* He adds what Conacher and Lodge and others have stated: *Life on earth is just a fleeting shadow of the spirit life,* but also: *Prayer is most important. Whenever the opportunity presents itself, one should pray. No mediator is needed or the prayers or ceremonies of priests or preachers.*

I just pray I have accurately reflected the words set out in the two books I have mentioned – and done justice, however small, to the great world figure of Jesus.

# PART V

## RELIGIOUS RITUALS:
## WHAT THEY DO AND DON'T DO

It is really quite fascinating to look at the rituals that accompany religious practice and belief. Years and years ago, one of the rituals was to sacrifice human beings to appease the gods. Then animals were substituted for humans, possibly as part of the Abraham-Isaac story. Animals are still sacrificed but most religions have put such customs behind them.

I now present you with just a few more examples. You can think of others, I have no doubt. Food and clothes or coverings of some sort play quite a role, as do water and wine.

The importance attached to ritual intrigues me; I am at heart a non-ritualist, as my Mastership of a Masonic Lodge long ago confirms. But clearly to many people ritual is of crucial, symbolic even profound importance. Here are a few examples.

Alongside the benefits and positive aspects of religion and religious practices, and they can be substantial in times of both happiness or distress, I have been vastly intrigued at the manifold and varied customs that adorn each faith.

Perhaps nothing is more obvious than what covers the body. In my own tradition there are men whose heads are rarely uncovered, as is common with women in a different faith. Some followers uncover their heads on entering a building to pray, whilst others do just the opposite. Some remove their shoes, others do not.

In praying, some kneel, some sit, some prostrate themselves, some stand, some sway, some bow, some wear special garments or objects on or even under their normal clothes, while still others wear special head coverings, often to denote pilgrimages they have made or groups to which they belong.

I recall chairing an important interfaith gathering when suddenly one of the platform speakers looked at his watch, got up, and ignoring both me and the audience, walked outside to pray; he later returned, totally unapologetic for his abrupt exit. The power of habit!

Similarly, whilst on a plane journey, I saw a dozen men stand up and begin praying and swaying in unison. Heaven knows what the pilot thought – no doubt he was wondering what on earth was happening at the back of the plane. The group's single-mindedness took no account, gave no thought, as to the effect on other travellers or, indeed, of the safety of the flight.

Some people pray with their eyes tightly closed, some cover their heads, some rock to and fro, some pray in silence, whilst yet others raise their voices to high heaven. There are also so many different customs and rituals regarding birth, marriage and death; on circumcision in two faiths and baptism in others; as well as the belief in the power of contact with water, deemed by some to be 'holy' to the point of total immersion. Millions have their sins washed away, they believe, by a dip in the River Ganges whilst others discard their sins on the sea coast.

Marriage ceremonies vary enormously, although I have observed that in Hinduism and Judaism, two faiths normally unconnected, the bride walks many times round the bridegroom. The poor fellow must feel giddy! In some faiths, death is marked by speedy burial – probably linked to climate conditions – or in others by delayed burial. Sometimes coffins are used to house the body, or it is cremated, or even exposed to the elements. Some abhor cremation because they think the body will be resurrected, as the ancient Egyptians believed.

Some places of worship are filled with statues, representations of people, even of animals, whilst other temples expressly forbid this. Most religious followers are devotees of light in one form or another, perhaps as candles or electric light, whilst incense also plays a role. Sometimes men and women sit together, though often they sit separately. Certain faiths have strict rules prohibiting the consumption of particular foods, including the manner of their preparation, and such bans can apply to alcohol, too – yet others make the taking of certain foods and alcohol an essential part of their rituals.

Many faiths include the obligation or recommendation to visit places deemed 'holy'. There are many books describing sacred places, indeed books themselves are so often regarded as holy and sacred. Some rivers, some buildings, some mountains are designated 'holy'.

Beards are universally popular, even obligatory, for men of course. Some have side curls, some never shave, whilst beards in some descend way down. Beards are often regarded by their wearers as symbols of authority and standing.

Some pray facing a certain city or a particular building or monument, reverenced as holy places for what has occurred there or for who lived or was buried there.

There is no end to the examples of these practices, so often regarded as more important than the essential moral teachings of the faiths concerned. I have said nothing about the role of the human voice, of prayer leaders and choirs, of musical instruments, nor have I described the significance of communal as opposed to individual prayers, or even, in some doctrines, the importance of silence.

Thus, the variety and strength of custom, particularly group custom, is immense. To many religious adherents, a breach of any of these requirements is almost equated with sin. But truly, they are, from the viewpoint of the spiritual world, of little consequence. It is a fascinating panorama. Perhaps variety is truly the spice of religious life.

## The Failure of Religion

Have our present world religions been a failure? Adherents of each major religion would deny that they have. They would dispute whether a distinctive revelation of universal truth could in any way be termed a failure. Rather they would say that men and women have failed to live up to the highest aims of the faith. God has not failed, man has.

They would add that each religion, particularly their own, has inspired great acts of devotion, help, healing and care for the less fortunate. How could these acts be part of a 'failure'? There is an element of truth in such assertions. There have been good people, and good acts, recorded in the history of religions, and of non-religions. There have also been high moral teachings and exemplary lives led by various individuals, which have been based on religious faith.

Yet the question remains as to whether the religions have been an unmixed blessing in terms of the advancement of our species. A glance at the past histories of all the major faiths, perhaps with the exception of Buddhism, and to a lesser extent Hinduism and Jainism, as well as Bahai, reveals a monstrous history of murder, torture, genocide, slavery and persecution. In the name of religion there has been conquest and rapine, as well as the subjugation of many indigenous peoples. There has been an enslavement of freedom of thought, of enquiry and of expression. Some of the books on the list in the appendices to this book give great detail of the crimes of religious institutions, not excluding those that have occurred in recent times.

A single hopeful sign is that the last fifty years have seen the rise of an interfaith movement, a beginning of dialogue, necessarily superficial rather than fundamental, between leading representatives of the faiths. This is new and welcome.

At the same time, since the end of World War II, there have been well over fifty wars in the world, some continuing for years. The spirit of mutual hostility is abroad. Often it is ethnic, racial, tribal, in character, though frequently underlying conflicts of religious allegiance are at work, even subconsciously, in all continents. The resulting violence is appalling. In 2015 I have only to mention the word Syria.

There is no need to elaborate on the misdeeds of the past. The Roman Catholic Church is beginning to express contrition. Other religions and religious bodies would do well to follow suit. But today, in the first decades of this twenty-first century, the world scene of violence and hatred presents a sorry picture that the religions have not only been unable to prevent, but to which they have contributed in no small measure.

I have mentioned tribal aggressions, such as those in Rwanda where neither skin colour nor religion may be factors. Has religion been able to prevent the unbelievably large mass murders there, or in Cambodia? Did Christian Europe prevent the horror of the Holocaust? Did Shintoist Japan hold back the appalling treatment of fellow humans in World War II? Were Buddhist monks able to avert the endless Sri Lankan conflict or the persecution in Burma?

Was the Muslim faith able to prevent a million or more innocent souls dying in the Iran-Iraq war, or, more recently, the descent into the dark ages in Afghanistan? Was Gandhi's wonderful example a bar to his own assassination by a Hindu?

Did the Ten Commandments of Judaism inhibit Dr Baruch Goldstein from mowing down worshippers in a mosque or a young indoctrinated Jewish zealot from murdering Yitzhak Rabin, Israel's Prime Minister, just as a Moslem fanatic assassinated Egypt's Anwar Sadat.

The ongoing confrontations of Northern Ireland – no colour question there – is a blasphemy on the teachings of Jesus, under whose banner the separate parties contend. The Sudan presents a similarly unedifying spectacle of persecution and slavery based on religious and ethnic differences. Has religion influenced positively the problems of East Timor, Nigeria, Sierra Leone, the Balkans, the struggle of the Kurds, the attitude towards the ethnic Chinese in Indonesia? Did the teachings of Confucius and Lao-Tze, high-principled and urging moderation, influence the Communist ideologies which caused the death of millions in the 1960s and 1970s, perhaps forty million souls? Similarly the inheritance of Tolstoy and the Orthodox Church did not deter the Soviets from a similar mass murder in the 1930s, including the starvation of 7,000,000 Ukrainians. So the atheists have nothing to be proud about either, following the abject failure of the 'non-religions'.

There is no end to this litany of human disaster, both past and present. Will this be the inheritance of the so-called millennium years, and continue in the same way?

Once it burst the bounds of priestly constriction, approximately 500 years ago, science – the progressive revelation of God and his creation – has made enormous strides, unparalleled in history. It may, in time, give us an entirely new conception of the nature of man, of matter, and of his universe. Such an advance may have the force of a new revelation, which, hopefully, will raise man, his society, his thoughts, from the murky depths of current all-consuming materialism.

On the other hand, science has provided martial man with the weapons of self-annihilation and of destruction of nature, on this planet and beyond. In many ways we are engaged in a race against time, against ourselves, a race for survival of the species, in spite of the population explosion and environmental degradation.

Tentative ideas about a global ethic and interfaith development are expressed, yet these are but surface activities. There is already a global ethic in the Ten Commandments, the Sermon on the Mount, the ancient Hindu and Buddhist scriptures, and so on. There is no harm in seeking a common code of universal application but it will make little impact, first, on the mass of people, who tend not to think about these things, and secondly on those who believe that their religious way is the only way, the true way, the exclusive way.

If I were to set out a global programme of faith that might help man to survive – although I would probably be instantly dismissed or condemned by the vast majority – it would include the following, my Articles of Human Survival:

1. At the heart of being is the Eternal God of Love and of Mind, whom we cannot define or see, yet who is the mainspring of what is.
2. We human beings are the apex of physical evolution on this planet Earth, which is one of a number of planets in our solar system, nine defined, others not yet confirmed. The solar system is one of many in our galaxy, and our galaxy is one of many galaxies in what we call space. We are not the only forms of creation, nor even the most highly evolved, in those spheres. We should have some humility.
3. As science will discover, matter is illusory in the traditional sense, and we are physical expressions of a spiritual essence. That essence, that spark of God, is inextinguishable. We survive the death of our bodies.
4. Our future lives, beyond this Earth, depend on our behaviour while here. That behaviour, for good or ill, depends on the moral quality of our thoughts, actions and motives. We make for ourselves our own future.
5. No one died to save our souls or the world. There was no vicarious sacrifice to redeem us. Nothing is at second-hand; only we can condition our own future. No confession of sin on a deathbed is of any significance. We have direct contact with God, if we try, if we

seek, if we allow it to take place. The idea of Adam's fall from grace requiring later redemption is an illusionary legend.

6. There is a moral law. Enough prophets have indicated this and many have suffered for their attachment to the moral law. That law seeks the good of all, their progress and health. There is no virtue or merit in poverty. Taking life is the only blasphemy. There are no other blasphemies. No war is ever holy, nor is any killing. No one taking the life of another can be termed a martyr.

7. Enslaving the mind is as grievous as enslaving the body. Man can only progress through freedom of the mind, the spirit, and the body. All forms of slavery are against the law. Unequal treatment of men and women is against the law. The progress of man is through the enlargement of mind, of thought, of free enquiry and expression, as well as the enlargement of sympathy and understanding for, and care of, fellow-man, nature, and fellow-creatures.

8. No one religion, one faith, one philosophy, contains all truth. All contain elements of truth. All have arisen responsive to the needs of their time and area, and the stage of human development where they arose. Different human societies have always been, and remain, at different stages of development. The more advanced should assist those less advanced.

9. While certain places and buildings have taken on specific characters from past history and usage, there are no holy places, holy buildings, holy books. The only thing that is holy is life itself and its forms of expression.

10. Throughout recorded history, especially in the older civilisations, there has been contact between our world and the spiritual world. The scriptures of all peoples are full of such references. That contact has developed immensely in the last 150 years, and will develop further in the years ahead, directly and without the need of intermediaries. It is the widespread acceptance of this relationship that will open up the minds and hearts of men and women to the true characters and natures, the true purpose of their existence, and will bring about the revolution in human thought and behaviour that can save mankind from self-abasement and self-destruction.

The recognition and acceptance of these ten points, challenging, revolutionary to some, and probably horrifying to many, is in my view the only path to peace on this increasingly turbulent planet.

## Scientific Recognition:
## The Key To Spiritual Progress

Like Michael Evans, and others, I would urge scientists to examine fairly and honestly the claims of Spiritualists. Few have done so. The Church of England appointed a body to do this. The resulting report confirmed the claims made but the Church hierarchy was too frightened to publish it. Surely the scientists can do better than the Church. After all, like me as a lawyer, they are trained to study evidence, hard, real evidence. If a group of them did so, they are likely to reach the same conclusion as the religious group, but would not be afraid to make public their findings. At least that is my hope.

I first had any real awareness of what one might call the world of the spirit when my elder son fell ill in December 1976. The whole world of mediums, guides, materialisation, direct voice, healing, was largely a closed book to me. I, like many others, grew up against a background of a specific religious tradition, as opposed to an anti-religious, or secular tradition.

For well over a third of a century, I have been able to probe into this spiritual world. I have met noted mediums and healers, read the works that have illuminated this subject over the last century and a half, and experienced the processes of both healing and communication.

My conclusions, set out in *Journey into Immortality*, confirmed the survival of the soul when the physical body perished, of the reality of spiritual worlds, and of the links, in different forms, between those worlds and our own.

Had it not been for the catalyst of my son's illness and my burning desire to help him overcome the affliction of cancer, I wonder whether I would have ever arrived at these conclusions. Perhaps, instead, I would have acknowledged some passing interest in these phenomena, yet continued to live on the basis of a particularistic, received, religious wisdom.

My own experience, I believe, is a reflection of the very real problem of those who are active within the general field of Spiritualism. If they have a truth, how can they share that truth with the world in a way that will convince that world? They are asking people whose lives are dominated by material things, whether in rich or poor countries, to project themselves beyond what is self-evident to their senses. Some people may respond but the majority will have great difficulty in doing so.

In addition, current religious practices and beliefs have been sanctified by generations of indoctrination, ritual and authority. Some groups even have an identity largely because of their religion. To ask those in authority to accept as part of their faith and fundamental belief systems the tenets taught by spiritual guides such as Silver Birch and White Eagle is just not a realistic expectation.

The reasons for this are clear, at least to me. Religious bodies depend on authority – the church, temple, mosque or synagogue, and their hierarchy of religious leaders. The teaching of Spiritualist guides, with their universalism, could undermine that authority. An example is the Church of England's refusal to publish its 1939 report on Spiritualism. More recently in Pakistan a man was sentenced to death for describing himself as a prophet: how dare he! Fear provokes fundamentalism. Indoctrination destroys reason and justice.

Thus, despite some reformist tendencies in religions, the particular always gains an ascendancy over the general, the old over the new. It is more comfortable.

The same applies to those raised in a world of Marxism or other forms of secular materialism, which includes a number of university scientists. The world of the spirit is, to them, irrelevant, unprovable, distracting, far too vapid an idea on which to waste time.

Thus for 150 years the Spiritualist movement has found it difficult to make a real impact, despite the wonderful work done in healing, the revelations of communication, and the heroism of many of its adherents.

Since 1945 we have seen the growth of interfaith activities. This is new. It is mainly a western European or North American development. In Asia and Africa, wars between the religions continue but it is a hopeful sign that prominent figures in the various faiths are talking, rather than slaughtering, one another.

This change in attitude may represent only one low rung on the ladder from the specific up towards a more universal view, but it is certainly to be encouraged. It is unlikely that the truths enunciated from the world of the spirit will make a noticeable mark in the interfaith pattern. There are still such things as deep-rooted vested interests.

A few years ago, over a thousand religious leaders from all the faiths assembled in New York to expand this inter-religious dialogue. I did not anticipate much light emerging, but, if it did, all to the good. The hope that the teachings, ideas and truths that have pervaded Spiritualism will permeate these religions is unlikely ever to be fulfilled. When Luther replaced the Pope, the same sense of authority and dogma continued, though in a different guise, accompanied by unbridled racism.

It is my firm view that if there is to be any substantial progress in the march of spiritual perception it will take place through the avenue of science and the scientific method. Science is the wonder boy of modern times. It has revolutionised human life. Compare our daily life with that of some of the tribal and indigenous peoples of Asia, Australasia and South America. The contrast is enormous in every way, and almost always the result of the expansion and application of scientific knowledge – whether in medicine, sanitation, travel, production of food, provision of clean water, leisure, or the process of learning and education.

It is as if we are inhabitants of separate planets, First World and Third World, but we come from the same background and we inhabit the same planet. The difference is the application of science and its subsequent impact. All peoples are at different stages of development, for various reasons, but the pace of change is accentuating the pressures on everyone.

The onward march of science has been based on doubts about received wisdom, on continued investigation and the recording of experience, on the steady development of knowledge from rung to rung, looking forward all the time. By contrast, the pattern of established religions has been based on certainty, on catechisms, on slogans, on authority, but above all, on looking back at some defining event in the past: hence, not only the conflicts, but also the scientific martyrs, Copernicus, Bruno, Galileo. Sometimes, as in Hinduism, scientific enquiry has been incorporated into its early teachings, but in practice the faith has invariably been hierarchical and humanly divisive.

Yet one of the reasons the main religions have survived is that they contain an extra element lacking in the surge of scientific discovery: namely, a moral element. This was perhaps recognised by Albert Einstein when he said: 'Science without religion is lame – religion without science is blind.'

The moral element is fundamental to society. Man is a social being. In all religions, except perhaps Buddhism, moral guidance is linked to God and rewards and punishments, usually of a sentient kind, in the hereafter.

To an extent, it seems to me, spiritual teachings and modern science have something in common. Physicist Richard Feynman states: 'None of the entities that appear in fundamental physical theory today are accessible to the senses. Even more, there are phenomena that apparently are not in any way amenable to explanation in terms of things, even invisible things, that move in the space and time defined by the laboratory.'

Modern science (and all real science is modern, the result of progress made in the last 500 years) is based on change, on a developing process of discovery. In quasi-Biblical language we could almost express it thus: 'These are the generations of Newton, these are the generations of Planck and Maxwell and Mendel, these are the generations of Einstein and Bohr and Heisenberg and Schrodinger, these are the generations of Crick and Watson, and Feynman and Gell-Mann, these are the generations of the principles of uncertainty, of probability, of quantum mechanics, of big bangs and black holes, of unimaginable immensity of outer space and inner space.'

We reach the point where the prominent astronomer, Sir James Hopwood Jeans, ponders: 'The more I look at the universe, the more it looks to me like a great idea.'

Yet I doubt whether the immensely brave and intensely gifted Stephen Hawking would go along with that, believing that there is no future life and that no God created the universe. Yet, Sai Baba states: 'Spontaneous creation gave rise to something out of nothing!'

Modern science is engaged on a journey of discovery, based on theory and proof, on continual doubt and continual learning. So Richard Feynman (1918-1988), Nobel prize-winner, can say: 'The scientist has a lot of experience with ignorance and doubt and uncertainty. We take it for granted that it is perfectly consistent to be unsure that it is possible to live and not know.'

This makes it so clear why scientists, knowing that knowledge constantly unfolds, cannot accept the claims of religions that knowledge was given in the past, set in stone, and cannot change and develop. Thus to them, theories are never 'holy', not even those of Newton or Einstein. They are all part of a developing process, not far from the undogmatic, non-creedal approach of the Spiritualist guides.

It is therefore opportune for the Spiritualist world, which lays down no final doctrine and applauds the test of reason, to enter into a dialogue with the world of science. It is that route rather than the way of the religious institutions themselves that can lead to a wider acceptance of the universal laws and discoveries of the spiritual world. Both groups are on a voyage of discovery; both are involved in worlds beyond man's immediate senses, and, in my view, they are beginning to converge.

The scientist, the Spiritualist, even the ancient Psalmist, all have something in common. They are all seekers, and all have faith in something intangible ahead of them. The Psalmist may call that something God; the Spiritualist, the Great Creator or Great Spirit; whilst the scientist pursues the levels of reality that can explain more and more the world that lives in us and the world in which we live.

To expand the bridgehead of the spirit in our world, it is also necessary to penetrate the world of science. This means respecting the scepticism and doubts of scientists, but presenting to them the vast array of evidence that has accumulated over the last 150 years for examination using proper scientific method.

Assembling and presenting such evidence should now be the concerted aim of Spiritualists and Spiritualist organisations. That is quite an undertaking, but it should be possible to bring together a group of twenty or so persons who could prepare an outline of a programme, utilising links to organisations and individuals in different countries, their endeavours financed by these interested parties.

If the dialogue produced a positive result, it could have a substantial effect, not only on science and the standing of Spiritualism, but also on the main religious bodies, and may well affect the nature of any future relationship between them.

What I have set out is, of course, a personal view which others are perfectly entitled to call into question, but if my suggestion is taken up it could represent the biggest challenge, as well as the biggest opportunity, for the forces of modern Spiritualism.

# A FINAL WORD

I turn now to the doubters, particularly the scientists, but also to the orthodox in the religions. I have presented, all too briefly, a body of evidence which covers years, countries, individuals. I believe that an impartial court of justice would find some substance in that evidence. After all, as I have emphasised throughout, my professional life has been largely based on the assessment of evidence.

However, I have great respect for men and women of science. They are at the heart of human progress in modern times. Their discoveries in the fields of health, sanitation, food, transport, and many others, have been enormous, transforming modern society. So how might they look at what I have set before them in the preceding pages? Those who remain sceptical – and scepticism is healthy – might express the following views.

First, they could argue that the evidence I produce is insufficient for a definite view to be taken. Secondly, they could assert that the perspective and the experiences that I describe are not really factual but are all subjective, and that opposing opinions are not ventilated. Thirdly, it could be said that much of the evidence really comes from my own mind, my own biased assessment, a kind of self-indoctrination and internal motivation.

A fourth objection might be that, whatever the evidence, no reassessment of the basic tenets of science is necessary as to the nature of matter, of human beings, of evolution, or of the composition of the universe, galaxies, nebulae and the elements of time, space, mass, motion and energy.

Indeed scientists, particularly anthropologists and archaeologists, may find it difficult to reconcile the development of man – Neolithic, Neanderthal, Bronze and Iron Age man, homo sapiens – with the non-material spiritual element I have described. If there is any substance to my evidence, when and how did the soul element enter into material man? That must puzzle and perplex open-minded scientists. Oliver Lodge in his three books provides an answer to this question. I often wonder whether the reality of the spiritual world is just another stage in the process of evolution.

The main question remains, however. Are scientists and others prepared to consider seriously the evidence I have presented?

I can appreciate the attitude of some that there is no need to investigate what I have put forward, although I do regard that as an obscurantist and totally unscientific approach. After all, science has always progressed through change, a new discovery amending a previous, strongly-held truth, with each visionary in effect standing on a predecessor's shoulders. All such paradigm shifts follow calm, impartial assessment of newly available evidence.

I am also aware of how hard it is for any body, whether scientific, religious, or secular, whose stance is based on long-held dogma, to change course. The story of Pasteur is illustrative, as is the study of the cancerous consequences of smoking, first proposed as long ago as 1911 yet not universally accepted by doctors until well over half a century later. The Theory of Evolution, despite Darwin and Wallace, is still frowned upon, even rejected, in certain quarters. And indeed, in the same way, the main religions may find it objectionable to have to renounce or amend beliefs cherished and sanctified by time, ritual and prayer. However, I estimate that the men and women of science will show more understanding of this process than the scions of religious orthodoxy.

I would in fact have dealt in detail with the specific creeds and beliefs of the faiths except that those who communicated adjured me to avoid any such reflection or criticism. If the faiths are to change then they will have to change from within. Some will find this painful, as internal disputes and tensions already indicate, particularly as to the status and role of women.

But the main strength of religion over the Humanists and secularists, is that it opens up a dimension beyond that of mere matter. All the religions are but steps on a pathway that lead beyond the tangible world. Interestingly, words boldly displayed in the Sai Baba temple state: 'Honour every religion. All are on the pathway to the one God.' Indeed, most religions possess teachings of great wisdom, perception and consolation.

Thus religion has something in common with the advance of science, for scientists now agree with Oliver Lodge that matter, as commonly understood, is itself an illusion. Incidentally, Douglas Conacher states: 'A body has solidarity because it happens to be in complete vibration and harmony with the material matter in which we exist.' Perhaps one day, therefore, the twin paths of science and religion may find a common meeting-place and thus mutual understanding.

Even though many people may agree with the truth of my words about the world of the spirit, it is most unlikely that the pattern of their lives will change, either in terms of the religious practices of some or, conversely, the anti-religious stance of others.

The force of habit, especially communal habit, is immensely powerful, particularly if introduced into the mind at an early age. It takes a free and brave spirit to depart from conventionally accepted patterns.

The group ritual, almost theatrical performances of established religions, have far greater attraction and impact than the more cerebral and less colourful services of Spiritualist or Humanist gatherings. Even an experienced film or stage director could not better the drama of the election of a new Pope in Rome, right down to the release of white smoke. The same comment could apply to the various rituals of most other religions, all of which give satisfaction to their adherents.

The process of change, based on the acceptance of the teachings of those such as Lodge, Conan Doyle and others, will be very slow unless unexpected factors or discoveries come to light which change universal direction and beliefs – perhaps, for example, a direct link between us and those who have passed on.

Many people, too, have a vested, sometimes a material, interest in maintaining the status quo. This is especially so in religions but possibly also in the anti-religions. However, mankind will continue to evolve despite all the pain that evolution brings.

A study of history shows a constant battle between man as a free, spiritual being and man as an animal, so well described by the sixteenth century medical philosopher, Paracelsus. But these patterns are usually beyond the daily concerns and understanding of millions, if not billions, of the worldwide population.

The average man and woman, in much of the world, especially in parts of Africa and Asia, still cannot easily aspire to the world of the Spirit, so obsessed are they (and understandably so) with the simple, urgent need to find food, shelter, medical help and the means of staying alive in the face of constant violence, corruption, disease, hunger and persecution.

To a much lesser extent, this applies to people in more developed societies too, because they tend to be intoxicated with the attractions of new technologies. I cannot see, therefore, the emergence of a new Shakespeare, Rembrandt, or Mozart. Incidentally, it is confirmed that the plays of Shakespeare were written by ... one William Shakespeare!

One thing I have learned is that knowledge of the truth of healing and survival beyond death, as well as communication between two worlds, does not automatically improve the spiritual or moral qualities of people. Such knowledge should have a marked effect on behaviour but that is not always the case. In fact, I have had to use my abilities and experience as a lawyer to solve rifts and antagonisms between members of organisations, often of spiritualistic and healing backgrounds, who should know better.

At times I have noted more positive examples of high standards and personal dedication among followers of established religions and non-religions, which only proves that we are still just human. We have a long way to go. I pray that this tortured and rapidly expanding mass of mankind can change course and raise itself to a new level.

As I have said, I do appreciate what an immense challenge the world of the spirit is to scientists and to many among the religious orthodox. I have no doubt also that the contents of this book will come as a surprise, possibly a shock, to a number of people. After all, what I am suggesting amounts to an entire rethink as to the basis of a solely material concept of reality, as well as a disavowal of so much sanctified by centuries of devoted belief in established religious dogmas.

No wonder, therefore, that I have heard materialists speak with contempt of spiritual claims I have outlined. For example, they might praise Alfred Russel Wallace as an inspired founder of the doctrine of evolution through natural selection, yet pity him for his spiritualistic beliefs.

So I do understand scepticism, even cynicism, but the sceptics and cynics would be more respected if they examined carefully, scientifically, the claims made, and even the experiences, limited as they are, described in this book.

Finally, I am indeed aware of the conservatism of institutions, especially the religious ones, as, so often, they give a sense of security, purpose and identity to their adherents, as well as very real help. So I would advise that people who are happy with their current religious practices, rituals, fasts and feasts, should continue to follow those patterns. It would be far too disturbing to change, even if that were possible. The only proviso I make is that the religion concerned seeks peace and non-violence.

All I ask is that people consider what I have set down fairly, and relate my experiences and views to their own. Sudden change is not helpful but I hope readers will gradually, and with honesty, think about the things that I have described. Above all, a balance should be maintained between material needs and the world of the spirit.

I look, too, to the fair and open-minded scientist to delve into my evidence, bearing in mind that I have but skimmed the surface of a great and deep mine of information.

So there I leave it. I have had great joy in assembling and setting down my reactions, my experiences, my feelings, my thoughts. I hope, in a small way, my modest effort may contribute to a broader, more tolerant, more perceptive, view of the world around us, as well as the world within us.

# APPENDICES

## Author's Postscript

If you have waded through these many pages you may feel enough is enough. However, some learned folk, whom I greatly respect, have urged me to add a few extra items, which emerged from earlier years. So here goes.

In 1942 our family returned to London and to nightly bombing. We tried to sleep, under the stairs, in metal shelters in the house and garden, even on underground Tube platforms. My fearless father ignored the bombs. He kept to his normal bed nightly, and survived untroubled and unaffected.

In 1942 I attended a new school, Preston Manor, in Wembley, taking four subjects for the 'A' or Higher Schools examination, the passport to university. With the legal profession in mind, Latin was then essential. I knew barely a word of the language, but a dedicated headmaster gave me special attention so that, starting with *hic, haec, hoc*, by the end of twenty months I was zooming through Cicero, Virgil, Livy, *et al*.

In June 1944, a dozen of us sat in a windowless, dim, school air-raid shelter, challenged by the exam questions and the mayhem around us. Suddenly the engine of a V1 German missile, a flying bomb, cut out: it was on its murderous way down.

'Everyone under your desks.' We obeyed, and then heard an immense explosion but a mile away. 'Get up and resume your papers.' We duly got up and resumed.

It was then decided by my family that I should get away for a week, to the rural house of my sister, situated not far from William Penn's original home and Benjamin Disraeli's country seat.

In that land of peace and tranquillity I sat down, pen in hand, and set out my thoughts on religion. Those handwritten notes, pre-word-processor and computer days, emerged but recently from a pile of old papers.

I was urged to include the opus in this book, and the gallant publisher concurred. So I present to you now the thoughts of one bomb-free seventeen-year-old.

## My Religious Experiences
### by Aubrey Rosenberg

Perhaps it might appear somewhat presumptuous of a youth of seventeen and threequarters to write about his religious experiences, for his mind is comparatively immature, and is often swayed by passing ideas and short-lived enthusiasms. However I am sure that a detailed account of my religious thoughts and beliefs will help me to understand how I have reacted to my present religion, and will clear my mind of an unordered, complex mass of ideas. In addition, I realise the outstanding importance of attaining a clear idea of the value of various beliefs today, and, since I have plenty of time now, I shall set forward without further delay an account of my religious life.

I was born on November 1st 1926, in East London, the son of Jewish parents. Naturally, I was raised in the friendly atmosphere of a Jewish home, and was taught to respect all the ancient Jewish customs and institutions… including the old Rabbi. The division of the cutlery, the wearing of a hat, the fasts and feasts (there were many of the latter), the attendance at the synagogue on Friday evenings and Saturday mornings, the ban on the eating of 'trei.fa' food like bacon and eels; all these things I accepted unquestioningly and unconditionally. Ritual was extremely important, and the Jewish religion, full of signs and symbols, was to my mind, a set of 'dos and don'ts' regarding material things.

Another side of this fascinating religion was its extreme pliability. The rabbis and reverends were extremely clever men, and they adapted their religious principles to the new twentieth century form of life. By a rather subtle interpretation of the Mosaic Code, a new set of ethics grew. From my early youth it was continually hammered into my head that gambling, betting, playing cards, etcetera, were bad things to do (this was naturally quite right), and that on the Sabbath day one must not write, make fire, turn on the electric light, ride on any sort of vehicle, carry money about, go to pictures, dog meetings, games, places of amusement and so on and so on.

This was the law, and any violation of this most intolerant, puritanical system of ethics was not only a crime, but a moral sin.

My parents, however, were only lukewarm Jews. Like all other lukewarm Jews, who comprised ninety-nine percent of the people of our self-imposed ghetto, they 'never broke the Sabbath but for gain'. We went to the pictures on the Sabbath day, rode, carried money, lit fires, turned on electric lights and, in fact, were ghastly breakers of the Holy Tables. This was of course deprecated by the severe, austere 'firm' believers, who spent their Sabbath exhorting God to save the lost tribes of Israel, send the Messiah and work for the betterment of all mankind, especially the Jewish kind. Nevertheless, the Jewish way of life in the home was kept up, and we... the Chosen People... maintained our poor view of the un-Jewish masses.

I remember how, after the age of seven, I used to run to the synagogue on Friday evening, all excited and eager, and afraid that I might be late. Usually I was far too early. The performance never began until more than ten people were assembled in one place. The first ten in my synagogue were always old, tottering men with grey beards, hoary hair and new suits. On Friday evening these people regained their self-respect. They washed... an unusual event in the East End... and they combed what hair they had (although their heads were covered all right in the synagogue), and put on a clean suit of clothes. These people tried to look holy as well as feel holy.

Once ten people had assembled, the Cantor emerged from a back room with a silver and white headpiece, and a magnificent, long robe – white, mystic, wonderful. He always appeared seemingly by magic, and to my young and wondering mind, he seemed to glide in as if he had just come from Heaven. After the usual preliminaries, the service began and the Cantor and the 'flock' sang the prayers either individually or in unison. Throughout the service, clean-faced men were continually coming in and there was an unusual amount of talking and shouting. Perhaps my own eagerness in attending service was due to the distributing of wine by one of the officials to the young. It was indeed a powerful incentive to one to attend the synagogue on the Sabbath.

A point that always interested me about the service was the amount of money that changed hands by verbal declaration: to maintain his respect before the community, a man called to read a portion of the Law always donated some money to the synagogue's funds. On the Sabbath day many lights always seemed to be on, and I used to wonder who had switched them on, and somehow the service always seemed to me to be more of a 'social evening' than a religious ceremony. I remember vividly one day, when, in my eagerness to arrive at the synagogue on time, I forgot to take my cap with me. I ran into the Holy Place with a bare head, and the whole congregation turned towards me, full of moral, righteous indignation at this affront to their religion. The ever-present official stopped me, admonished me and sent me home. I was not allowed to pray because I had forgotten to bring my hat.

The Jewish Holidays were always a source of pleasure and profit to me. Apart from money gifts, I used to obtain sweets by wandering from synagogue to synagogue and collecting the gifts offered to regular young attendants by these establishments.

Thus my outlook on religion from the ages of one to fourteen can be described very briefly. I accepted the contemporary beliefs, customs, ritual and institutions blindly, and I converted what was really a religion of Sabbatical self-denial into one of enjoyment and pleasure. For the most part, our family were too occupied with this world to think much about the other place. Heaven to my father was a place where he could work at tailoring, without worrying about profit and bad machines; to my mother it was an enlarged house where she did no cooking or cleaning but had the housework done for her; and to me, Heaven was a field where I could play football for as long as I liked without having my mother worrying me about dinner, bruises and school. Hell was a place that was never mentioned, except as a term of abuse.

I maintained this attitude of mind for the first fourteen years of my life, and by the age of fifteen my beliefs had become frozen into a rigid set of dogmas that could not, should not, and must not, be criticised.

I ought not to ignore one incident, however, which increased my hatred of hypocrisy. At my 'Jewish Confirmation' at the age of thirteen, I read a portion of the Law in a 'house-synagogue'. As I read the piece, two of the senior rabbinical officials stood before me, dressed in long curls and shaking themselves violently, and occasionally glancing at the top of the room out of the corners of their eyes. They tried to act like holy mystics, and I knew then that they cared more about their rent and their stock of wine than about their religion. In fact, in my early life, my most strong impression of the so-called religious people was that they subordinated their beliefs and their faith to their own material interests. How I despised these hypocrites!

I have thus far described my 'religion'. It was the religion of average children. If their parents were Jews, they were Jews, if their parents were Christians, they were Christians, and if their parents were shallow atheists, they were more often than not violent atheists. My religion was a national one. It bound the Jews together. They lived amongst themselves and, in most cases, traded amongst themselves. They were a nation within a nation, these British Jews.

Unfortunately, they rarely questioned their religion and it proved a great help to them in their business. Some shops depended wholly on the religious for their profits. I accepted this religion and this way of life unconsciously, for I was not even a thinking creature by the age of fifteen.

II

For two-and-threequarter years after the age of fifteen, I wondered continually about religion. The seeds of scepticism, sown in my thirteenth year, blossomed forth once I began reasoning and thinking. As my mind grew, so my outlook changed. I investigated the Western religions. I saw what they had in common, and I even dared to question the basic assumptions of each and every religion. After I matriculated at the age of fifteen-and-a-half, I moved to a new school and a new house, where the environment was solely Christian. Surrounded by Christians, constantly hearing Christian services and hurt by the intolerance shown by my parents to 'Christ and his religion', I naturally became more interested in Christianity. I began to read the Gospels, and I discussed Christianity with my schoolmates.

I was attracted by the lonely figure of this most noble man. In the heat of my emotions, I found reasons to support my sympathy towards the Christian religion. I was not worried then about the Trinity, the miracles, the birth and the death, the Resurrection and the authenticity of the story. That I accepted as the whole truth unquestioningly, just as before I had blindly accepted the Jewish religion.

As the days went on, I saw in Jesus Christ all that was noble, all that was beautiful, and all that was good. My hatred for the Jewish priests and for the narrow dogmatism of Judaism increased, and somehow, if I believed in God – and I never questioned His existence then – nobody but Jesus could be my God. To my mind His moral teaching was perfect. His was not a narrow teaching. He taught something noble, something lofty. My Jewish Heaven disappeared, and a mystical, yet beautiful, Kingdom of God took its place. It was at this time that I was knocking furiously, and I thought the door had been opened to me. I was not one of these doubters who lived godless lives. About these godless people I once asked: 'What rock will they cling to when they are going down? They have only a straw, which will drown with them.'

No, I had found something beautiful, something true. I had never been sceptical of the existence of God; in fact I had never questioned His existence. All that had happened was a change in the nature of Him. Before, His had been a name to be revered and worshipped, but now He had become a splendid reality, to be loved and cherished. My enthusiasm for Christ grew daily. I sailed along joyfully, for I had not yet traversed the stormy seas of scepticism, nor passed through the rocky straits of doubt. I was at peace with religion, for, in my immature, emotional youth, I had discovered the greatest secret of time and space: God.

My parents were naturally alarmed and disgusted at my zeal for an alien belief. It was contrary to the Jewish tradition and to the Jewish way of life. However, for a few months I was a Christian. The religion appealed to my emotions and to my hatred of ritual and hypocrisy. At sixteen it was really easy to adopt the Christian religion. It meant a change in God, a change in belief. But it required nothing new in the way of action. For years I had been a Christian – or had attempted to be a Christian in my moral life unknowingly. I remember how I used to harangue my parents in the long evenings of the winter, night after night, on the virtues of Christ and Christianity. They suffered me patiently, but I am sure we all profited by my speeches and their tolerance.

My father was a confirmed atheist and had always been so. He never knew this for he had maintained his Judaism in spite of himself. The most characteristic thing about my father was his unreserved scepticism towards all things.

My mother was a different sort of person. Her belief had been deeply rooted by her parents and grandparents. She had never doubted about God… she still doesn't, and I praise her for her consistency and her acknowledgement of her own limitations. She was a fairly tolerant person; she had bourgeois aspirations – towards a respectable, comfortable existence for herself and her own. She was fond of noting that her family were honest and (mostly) educated people, and that she herself had travelled through Germany and Holland. But these minor lapses must not be considered as presenting the whole Mrs Rosenberg. She was a good, hard-working, intelligent woman. She was a good wife, mother, friend and businesswoman. She helped others, and she shared my hatred of the hypocritical priests and rabbis. Her religion was to do good, and to her, God was always a mysterious Man In Black somewhere in a mysterious universe.

For several weeks, I presented the character of Christ to my parents. After an hour's talk they were usually tired of Christ, but eventually they (mother especially) took on the side of Christ against the wicked Jewish Sanhedrin. My mother shared more broad-mindedness than I had expected. My father was, as usual, cynical: however my mother came to the conclusion that he was a fine man.

In this manner, therefore, I came to be a Christian. But my Christianity turned out to be only a passing phase. My enthusiasm wavered as my mind matured. I became confronted with doubts and further scepticism. The actions of so-called Christians disgusted me. If I began to lose my belief in the divinity of Christ, I never wavered in my high vision of Jesus the man. Slowly I lost my faith in the Gospel story, but more about that in the third part.

### III

Perhaps it was due to sixteen years of anti-Christian prejudice that I broke with my newly found religion. Perhaps it was due to new personal contacts, or to my reading of new books. In any case, all three facts had a hand in my break with Christianity.

It is indeed an unfortunate thing that a Christian convert immediately finds himself challenged by a decrepit old Church, with a set of irrational dogmas, the 39 Articles, by the Historical Failure of Christianity, by the unattractive history of Christ's Church itself, and by the demand to break with all the old, established Jewish customs affecting the home, health and personal relationships. There is an innate conservatism in every one of us, a desire to keep things as they are, and to distrust change. Some of us can see how dangerous this outlook is, how it might lead to extreme disaster, especially in our own world of new discoveries and new ideas; others, however can see no harm in it at all. As is the custom in Britain, a compromise between the two extremes of revolution and reaction is effected, with happy results.

This Christianity therefore to me represented the revolution in thought and action. The Judaism represented reaction. However, the changes necessary to make my action conform with my belief were too great. The belief was there, yet the action was not. All that is today considered Christian, e.g. the way in which the home is run and the observance of Sunday, were repulsive to me. I had been in 'Christian houses' and I thought the Jewish way of life much better. Thus, in my belief I was a Christian, and in my action, a Jew.

The Church and the disunity of the 'Christian army' also beset me with difficulties. From the beginning I was repelled by the Church of England. I had discovered Christ and believed in Him, but I despised all these things about Popes, Protestants and Catholics, baptisms, confirmations, bread, wine, choirboys, white collars and long faces. Thus I had to reconsider what

I had found so attractive in the religion, and I discovered that it was the morality and the beautiful character of Christ that had tempted me into this mass of complications and contradictions called Christianity.

I read and re-read the Gospels and I found the Sermon on the Mount and the character of Christ more and more beautiful. But I also found the chaff amidst the golden corn... at any rate it then appeared chaff to me. I found too the miracles, but I could not think of Christ as a miracle-man, a benevolent, loving, tribal witch-doctor.

After consideration, I realised that I could in no wise call myself a Christian, nor could I say that I had ever been a real Christian. The poetry of the Gospels had attracted me, but the writers had lost sight of facts in their wild and queer flights of fancy. The bread and wine, the 'moving of the stone', the ascent, descent and so on, the feeding of the many with so little, the sea-walking – all these things gradually filled me with disgust and amazement... amazement at my gullibility.

It was in this way that I broke with Christianity. I cannot say I was right, though I thought then (and I still do think) that I was. Christianity to me had become a passing phase, a momentary spasm of violent emotion. The change in my mind may well have been due to the immaturity and irresponsibility of youth, but I think that my reason revolted at the thought of the seemingly impossible 'miracles' of the New Testament.

At this stage of my development I was getting on for seventeen. At fifteen-and-a-half, I had discovered something new and wonderful... something thrilling... I discovered my mind... I discovered thought and reason.

I used my 'new mind' like a child with a new trainset. I thought and thought and thought, and gradually my outlook broadened and is still broadening. Like a train, my mind ran along narrow ways and broad ways... covering ground and gaining speed... branching off through mountains, through storms and through calms. I was excited by this mind; I could cover much more ground at a far greater speed.

The first 'station' where the train of thought had stopped was at Christianity. After refuelling and cleaning, it continued... and the old station faded far into the background.

Henceforth, my story will be one of doubt and certainty, of belief and disbelief. I become like a ship on a storm-tossed sea. I am the ship and the ship is still rolling, but the storm is less furious and there is great hope that the waters will soon be calm and the ship will continue in safety.

IV

(The paragraphs below describe my thoughts about religion in the last year. I consider it the most important of my life.)

With the break with Christianity a whole new world opened out before me. I have not given my reasons in full for discarding Christianity… that would require a separate chapter by itself. A detailed account of the controversial points of the religion is unnecessary here. One hundred authors can put forward one hundred arguments against Christianity, and another hundred can argue for it. By falling back on a defence of 'mystical faith', apologists can erect a sort of impregnable Maginot Line around the Christian terrain. But this argument paradoxically is not an argument, and it ends all argument. A prolonged discussion of controversial points can only be based on the acceptance of reason, as the discriminating factor between right and wrong. On what other basis is any argument carried on? However, the Christian apologists, with their 'believe, and you shall be saved', do not discuss; they state, indeed they demand, unconditional acceptance of their terms.

However, some of my reasons for leaving Christianity will unfold themselves in the course of this story. In any case, I began a new adventure (as yet unresolved) in the summer of 1943, when I was nearing the age of seventeen.

With the 'old tables' broken, I was in a state of unconscious agnosticism. The incentive (as believers), the incentive to do good, had gone, yet I found that my actions never changed in the slightest. The old morality remained, deeply rooted in my very being. However I never troubled then to believe in nothing. It was due to a large extent to personal contacts, to relations with H, that I renewed a flagging interest in religion. This youth had become a mentally-militant-atheist, an aggressive non-believer. Although I had left my religions far behind, I was still somewhat taken aback at this firm attitude of H.

His ideas were thought-provoking, and I, wishing to make use of all minds, including my own, began to read 'pernicious' literature.

I took an interest in the works of Shaw and read all his plays. His blasphemy was humorous and subtle and therefore not so shocking, and my mind was prepared and nurtured, through his works, for the more outspoken books on religion.

I read Shelley's *The Necessity of Atheism* with very little enthusiasm. I still wonder why a book that had a 'willing-to-believe' reader never impressed me very much. On a holiday in September 1943, I began reading Bradlaugh. His works had a stronger effect on my mind. Here was a militant atheist, who practised what he preached, and who found in non-belief a powerful incentive to do good. My irrational belief in 'something' gradually broke down before my own reason and that of Bradlaugh, Shaw, McCabe, H and others. I found the God with infinite characteristics just too much to swallow. Soon I believed I had discredited the basis of all revealed religions – God, the Lord, the Almighty – Loving, Merciful, Just, etcetera, etcetera.

To me, science appeared to be the hope for mankind. Religions began to seem like a collection of moral doctrines personified and adorned with myths and fanciful tales. Even my heritage of Biblical morality grew less valuable in my eyes. I remember clearly a conversation with L who showed me the inadequacy of the Ten Commandments. I remember how I fought for them, and how they went down one by one. Thank the stars he never turned to the Sermon on the Mount! However I would have fought for this moral code, and I would certainly have won, I'm sure of that.

I recall now that in the December of 1943, I experienced a short-lived spasm of a vague, mystical belief. It could not have lasted more than a day or two, and I still can't understand how it happened. I asked myself, 'Do you mean to say that all this world exists, with man and beast, with flower and tree, without any motive force, without any master hand?'. This question seemed to grow and grow in my mind until I could think of nothing else.

It spread right through me, and for a period my non-belief wavered. I realised that there must be 'Something'. After realising this, the word 'Something' changed into God, though I never resolved for myself the nature of this God. This was a most unsatisfying state of mind. I agreed on the existence of Something about whose nature I knew... or hoped to know... anything. It was not long before I returned to my atheism with an accompanying faith in the rational answer of future scientists to my question. It was the nature of matter that was causing me all this trouble. Soon, however, I learnt that scientists were investigating the nature of matter and that if a common source (believed to exist) of positive and negative electric charges could be discovered, all my troubles would vanish in a moment. I pinned my faith to science, and left the vague Something as a disconcerting memory. In retrospect, my return to atheism seems completely irrational. I should have pursued the idea of God to a satisfactory conclusion. However, it is wrong for me to criticise my past in the light of present knowledge. I am only trying to give an account of my religious experiences, not a criticism of them.

Thus I was now once more an 'infidel', a non-believer. The reaction against God hardened, and I entered upon a period (a short one, though) of extreme irreverence and blind intolerance. I abused God, Judaism, Christianity and the Bible, violently; I was 'over-inspired' by the fearless free thought of Thomas Paine and his original denunciation of Christian beliefs. His belief in God never for a moment disconcerted me. I admired Paine for his courage and his truthfulness. 'My religion is to do good' became my own adopted religion, and I continued in it, though with various amendments.

As I write, I realise how immature my mind was, and still is. I believed and disbelieved with the passion of an emotional youth. Youth always feels things immoderately. Youth is guilty of broad, all-embracing generalisations, which have little foundation in fact. Knowledge, reason and prolonged meditation have not yet tempered his eagerness and daring enthusiasm. Experience is the prerogative of critical adults, who break up heedlessly the cherished illusions of youth. Unconsciously, one feels a simpler and richer life in one's youth. To use that true but hackneyed phrase, youth is the 'voice of inexperience'; it is also the voice of a throbbing, pulsating desire for speed, for self-enjoyment, for love and for life.

At the beginning of 1944, I was therefore a youthful type of atheist. I revelled in the 'blasphemies' of Hyde Park orators, and laughed at the fanatical and illogical Christians who stood up preaching with much 'wailing and gnashing of teeth'. I began to read the works of the Rationalists. I still had only a basic knowledge of science, but I had a great faith in it. Perhaps I was an unconscious victim of the 'mal du siècle'. Through science the word became life. It seemed the answer to all my questions.

At the end of January 1944, despite the extreme atheism of H, and others, my views on religion underwent a gradual change. I realised that my atheism was the result of a violent reaction against all forms of orthodox religion. Leslie Stephen, Ernest Renan and other writers helped me to see beyond the range of my blind prejudices. I saw that I had no right to be an atheist. It was the fashion, it is true, among many young people, but I was determined to be completely true to myself. I had been a sincere atheist but I understood the immaturity, the limitations, the inexperience, and the weakness, of youth. It was time to reconsider my atheism.

I did not, however, reconsider all my past beliefs. I developed my atheism to what I thought was a more justified belief for a youth like myself. I made a compromise between a vague sort of belief in God and a belief in no God, in fact, I became what is known as an agnostic.

This new 'religion' came to something like this: I did not believe that there was a God or that there was not a God. I did not know. I was young and comparatively ignorant. I was not justified in placing my belief in the wonders of science without knowing more about science. My knowledge was still slight. My reasoning faculties had not properly matured yet, and I still lacked experience of life. I had never seen the Glory of God, I had never experienced God properly. My earnest prayers (and those of millions in this world) seemed to have – and did have – no effect. My knocking opened no doors. There seemed to be so much evil in the world, so much war and hatred, despite the coming of Christ. Prayer seemed a sort of self-satisfaction to the praying person.

It seemed to help, in adversity, if one believed in prayer. On the other hand, I could not give a rational explanation of the universe. I could not think of matter coming into existence, of the being of so many things, of the fairly ordered universe, without some motive force. Whether it was to be a force or a Force depended on my outlook on morality.

To me, morality seemed a changeable thing, like human nature. It seemed dependent on the material. Moral codes have been taught by many great teachers, such as Confucius, Buddha, Christ, Nietzsche, and others. Morality is the prerequisite of civilisation. Law is the attempt to force people to obey a certain moral code. I could therefore see no justification for believing that a certain moral code had been sent to earth from heaven. Much of our morality is indeed concerned with material things – money, the body, property, etcetera. How could this morality have any divine significance? I came to the conclusion, therefore, that morality belonged to man alone, and came to man alone. It was changeable and constantly changing. In this way my Force disappeared. In this way my agnosticism was strengthened. The enquiry into the sources of morality became a test for my belief in God's existence. The results were negative.

But morality had always been allied with religion. I had therefore to consider my own views on what was moral and what was not. I was an agnostic, but I had to consider carefully my attitude to the morality of each religion. Ritual I had discarded years before as it had filled me with disgust.

Thus, apart from discussing Nietzsche's influence on me (I shall touch on this later), I have brought my story right up to date. In the next chapter I shall give an account of my beliefs at the present. I am now seventeen-and-threequarters, and it is July 1944.

## V

If I were to be called anything today, I would be labelled as an agnostic. It is a simple faith, an inconclusive faith. It recognises our limitations and our small knowledge. If I were to say that there was a personal God, I might be just as mistaken as the ancients who believed unconditionally in the Ptolemaic Universe. If I believe I am either right or wrong – and how can I say what I am? – let it suffice that I recognise what I do not know. It has been asserted by some that atheism and agnosticism are one and the same. This is not true. Atheism denies the existence of God, whereas agnosticism does not. To my mind, atheists are wrong in asserting that there is no God. Past history ought to teach them how dangerous it is to assert things with insufficient proof. However, one thing atheism and agnosticism have in common is that they both ignore God with respect to ordinary life.

The moral beliefs of both Atheists and Agnostics derive from numerous sources. We understand how God is neglected and how man becomes all-important in these two faiths; we may also see how an act directed against man and man's progress becomes a sin; also we see how greatly the 'humanism' of atheists and agnostics is influenced by 'revealed' and 'inspired' moral teachings. In the main the humanists accept the New Testament morality. They revere truthfulness, to others and to oneself, they place great importance on the motive of an action or an utterance; they demand the neighbour-love of the Bible; the spreading of rational and ethical knowledge becomes a veritable mission (The Rationalist Press Association is a sort of missionary society); they support the maxim of 'do unto others as you would have others do unto you'; they demand the abolition of extreme inequality of income, the wiping out of poverty, the speeding up of the scientific war against pain and disease and pestilence. They abhor hypocrisy. If one believes, one should stand forth and say so.

If one doubts, one should state one's doubts. There is not much in this world that I hate more than hypocrisy in religion. To me it makes little difference if one is a Christian, a Jew, an agnostic or an atheist. I do not want to suppress all beliefs except my own. That is spiritual and mental dictatorship. That is base and abhorrent. What I do want to see though is a cleansing of the soul; I want every one to state plainly what his religion is; and above all, I want every man to act according to the teachings of his religion. (I am not thinking of the immoral religions like Shintoism, or Nazism, which is a sort of religion.) I respect a Christian who tries to imitate Christ in his actions more than an atheist or an agnostic who cares little about others and concentrates solely on his own well-being. The roots of modern humanism, and especially its political and economic sides, Socialism, are firmly rooted in the Christian moral and ethical teaching. Let us not ignore this, but let us acknowledge our great debt to Christianity.

It has been said that 'The world revolveth about the creators of new values' and the greatest tribute one can pay to Christ is that his moral code is still the basis of Western civilisation. We also owe a debt to Judaism for the Ten Commandments (of the greatest value, though inadequate now, for the attempts at creating a harmonious society), and for its valuable contribution to hygiene, science, law, poetry and ethics. Other religious systems are also worthy of praise for their moral teachings and for their attempts to solve still-unresolved problems.

From all past teachings, humanism (scientific humanism is the correct term) takes what is best for modern civilisation. The belief in man replaces the belief in God. Morality and science and moral conduct become all-important. But in some respects there is a great difference between scientific humanism and Christ. The teachings 'blessed are the meek, the humble, the weak, the lowly' are discarded. This is a doctrine that does nothing to create higher life, and is only a consolation for the meek, humble and weak. I am not attacking modesty. I just don't see why they should be blessed. I would rather say, and I believe many humanists would too, praised be the upright, the strong and the fearless. There is nothing immoral in strength. It is only the way strength is used. Humanists praise strength and physical and mental fitness because they do not venerate power or fear the misuse of that strength. Strength is the tool of the humanist. He uses it for a good purpose. A point worth mentioning here is that the 'ungodly' ought no longer to be considered as immoral. I think agnostics like Thomas Huxley and Darwin and atheists like Bradlaugh and Marx provide sufficient evidence against this grossly unfair and prejudiced assertion.

It is necessary now to show how the 'ungodly' themselves are divided. On the one hand we have the Nazis and Fascists and their immorality and evil: whilst, on the other hand, we have the Soviet Union and the Rationalists, who are moral and good. The Nazis are the descendants of the African savages and the ancient pagans. The Socialists have few historical ancestors. Their morality surpasses anything of former times.

I feel I must turn now to a thinker who has influenced me greatly in the past few months. I refer to the German philosopher Friedrich Nietzsche (1844-1900). This man was an atheist. He became a 'human metaphysician', if you grasp my meaning. He pronounced the ideal of the human race, the being who was to bring purpose to a world of chance, the Superman. Nietzsche had many of the qualities of a humanist: truthfulness, politeness and uprightness, yet he could better be termed as a 'Superhumanist'. His moral teachings revolve round his idea of the Superman he proclaimed, with what I consider an excess of pride and immodesty, his 'transvaluation of all values'. Like all other 'religions' or 'faiths' begun and finished by one fallible human being, his teaching has many contradictions. At one minute he respects honest Christians, and then he calls Christianity 'indecent'. He saw that the basis of modern civilisation was Christ's teachings, and he revelled in his discovery. About immortality and the 'Truth' he writes: 'Weariness which desireth to reach the ultimate with one leap, with one death leap.' He worships strength, he shows that the 'will to power' is the basis of all life reaction. However, there is much wisdom in his great moral story *Thus Spake Zarathustra*. At bottom he is a poet, and he utters moral truths in metaphorical language, which metaphors have been taken too literally by modern Fascists. He has greatly influenced modern thought, and on one individual at least he has shown how powerful the humanist can be, and how powerful it must be.

That is the story up to the present. That is my religion. You can call me an agnostic with regard to God and a humanist with regard to man. In any case I have tried to present my religious experiences clearly and simply. Lately I have begun to wonder about new and old ideas. I have decided to give God and Christ another chance, to investigate new trends in religion, Spiritualism and Christian Science etcetera, to consider other religions, especially Eastern ones. I have also begun to wonder about 'reality' and to ask myself more perplexing questions about it.

I do not wish to ignore anything. Each religion is a challenge to me. I must go forward to meet it. I believe in tolerance. I believe in facing the challenge of God and religion, and considering the efficacy of reason and emotion. I want to penetrate the fog of words. I want to know. Ignorance is a great disease which I desire to conquer. I don't wish to deny the value of religion. I believe it is an attempt at higher things. I will go forward unafraid and determined. I will search the truth; I will be tolerant and above all, I shall act like a man who believes intently in the future of the human race. (Next episode in at least thirty years' time.)

### 4th May 1945

*A lot of this, especially the latter part, is sheer bunk.*
*I am now eighteen-and-a-half.*

A. Rosenberg

## Author's Postscript
### (continued)

In 1945 the war ended. We all danced around Piccadilly Circus, and breathed a deep sigh of relief. Churchill and the British people had shown what they were made of.

I became an apprentice, officially an articled clerk, working in a City law office for four-and-a-half years at the princely wage of £1 per week, rising to an inflationary £1.50 in the last six months.

'Put him in an office,' said the Bank Manager. 'No point in university.' My parents hearkened. I bless that man, since the practical experience I gained, both of law and of people, could never have emanated from college halls. This enabled me to start my own practice in Fleet Street in 1952 before the age of twenty-five.

However, my apprenticeship was served in two halves, severed by the call to arms of HM Government that I buttress the needs of the nation and join the army. I must confess that my military career, apart from sport, was undistinguished. Yet I learned so much about our human kind in those two, khaki-clad years.

One lesson was the immense, intense materialism surrounding otherwise religious holidays. Christmas, the justified celebration of the birth of the inspired teacher from Nazareth, seemed to have reached a commercial peak and a spiritual low. So I sat down and wrote, for my own benefit, the following poem, inscribed in a tattered document that also emerged from the dusty realm of accumulated old papers. Here it is.

### Xmas 1949

O! Christmas! Christmas! Christmas!
The happiest time of the year,
'Tis Christmas! Friends, 'tis Christmas!
The season of joy and good cheer.

And I've come up to London for Christmas,
Forgotten the smell of the farm,
Forgotten the smell, and the cows in the dell,
And the streams, and the green, and the calm.

And Lord! How the people are busy!
A-running around all the day,
A-spending of cash on trinkets and trash,
Well, they've got to give something away!

And the postmen are bearing great burdens,
And sweating as Christmas comes near,
For Jane must wish Jim, and Till must wish Tim,
Merry Xmas! And Happy New Year!

O! 'tis a wonderful season at Xmas!
Pay your premium, your bills, and your rent,
Give the clerks a half-day, and a week's extra pay,
And say things that one never quite meant.

Spread mistletoe, holly, and bunting,
Carry whisky and turkey and stores,
And wait in a line for crackers and wine,
Then, 'Daddy, where is Santa Claus?'

In Mayfair the ladies are busy,
But not like my lass on the farm,
No carols and fun, when praying is done,
But taxis, and phone-calls and charm.

For it's a generous season, a prosperous time,
Every pocket is pregnant with gifts,
Two bob for the doorman, two pints for the foreman,
Ten cigs for the man on the lifts.

The pavements are sinking beneath a great load
Of people, brown paper, and chatter,
But the ear-drums are quaking with the hooting and braking
Of monstrous vehicular clatter.

There's kids at the door, two bars for a penny,
They've even devalued the carols,
Whilst Dad's in the cellar, with some other fellow,
Drowning himself in the barrels.

The dinner is over, they've eaten too much,
And they're all just a teeny bit tipsy,
Ma's lying, exhausted, John's stomach is worsted,
And Jill's like a Freudian gipsy.

O! It's a wonderful season at Christmas!
A wonderful season forsooth,
There's plenty of cheer, and plenty of beer,
And sometimes a little of Truth.

For it's Christmas! It's Christmas! It's Christmas!
And the riot goes on till the dawn.
But perhaps one or two thought, as one or two ought,
Of a Child, in a manger, new-born.

My world progressed, to marriage in 1954 to a wonderful wife. Three delightful children emerged. My practice of the law was stimulating, exciting, eventful, as described in *Brief Encounters of a Legal Kind*. Other demands and opportunities arose, described in the previous *Rainbow* book, but then harsh, unbending reality hit us.

David, aged almost twenty, was diagnosed with an inoperable, untreatable cancer. We were engaged in another battle that ended in his passing from us in July 1978.

Yet we learned so much from him, had been so inspired by him both before and after that date, so that I set out his story, again in a book, *Journey Into Immortality*.

Once more, an old crumpled piece of paper came to light whilst I was writing his story. On this rough sheet he had written the following:

*And lo! Man created politics and religions and social values, and traditions; many great and awesome Gods he created him. And seeing his work prospered he created many lesser Gods and these he named '-isms'.*

*And over all his work man created one all-powerful omnipresent Lord, Dogma, Lord of all. And he ruled and shone in his colours of Black and White and man saw that all was Good, for he felt safe and all was simple*

*Yet verily, a being came out of the shadow, and placed before man Grey. And he came with his disciples, reason, understanding and logic.*

*But man saw that it made him unsafe, and made him think, and so was Evil, and man cast out Grey into a void so that few could reach him.*

*So the Gods ruled and man was content. And lo, there was great destruction, but man named why he destroyed, and it was justified. And man named his causes and the destruction was righteous; and man saw that any that opposed him were evil, And so destruction was Holy.*

*And man saw that all was still not perfect, so he saw that to be truly safe he must create great organisations into which he can flee. And these he named with many names. And into them he breathed all his powers and these organisations grew, swallowing man, and man was dark and safe, and so he saw that it was good.*

*And soon man saw that if he snuffed out man altogether then he would be safe, and he did, and it was good.*

His biblical-like phrases reflect so much that has happened in the last decades, the moral decline of mankind in so many ways. My son seemed to possess a prophetic gift.

For myself, I have been truly honoured to have had such an advanced being here as part of our family and in the role of a son.

# LIST OF BOOKS

These are books I have read or used in connection with this book, together with details of publishers. The books, are, of course, but a small part of an enormous amount of relevant literature and material. Jim Ellis has referred to 836 books and several thousand tapes relating to Independent Direct Voice alone. I have one room full of books. The following list could easily be doubled but there has to be a limit, unlike the wit who commented: 'I have read part of this book all the way through.' I have in fact, read almost all the way through most of the following books:

Karen Armstrong *The Case For God* (Vintage 2010)
Joseph Ratzinger, Pope Benedict XVI *Jesus of Nazareth* (Bloomsbury 2008)
Jacob Bronowski *The Ascent of Man* (BBC Books 1973)
Deepak Chopra *How To Know God* (Harmony Books, New York, 2000)
Marcus Chown *The Universe Next Door* (Headline Books 2002)
Richard Dawkins *The God Delusion* (Black Swan 2006)
Sir Arthur Stanley Eddington *The Nature of the Physical World* (JM Dent & Sons 1928)
Susan Greenfield *ID: The Quest for Meaning in the 21st Century* (Sceptre 2009)
Stephen Hawking *A Brief History Of Time* (Bantam Books 2005)
Angela Howard *Only A Thought Away* (Quacks Books 2010)
Kit Mouat *What Humanism Is About* (Barrie & Rockliff 1963)
David Robertson *The Dawkins Letters* (Christian Focus Publications 2007)
J H Reyner *Psionic Medicine* (C.W. Daniel 2001)
Lyall Watson *Supernature* (Hodder & Stoughton Ltd 1973)
Elie Wiesel *Souls on Fire* (Weidenfeld and Nicholson 1972)
Victor Zammit & Wendy Zammit *A Lawyer Presents the Evidence for the Afterlife* (White Crow Books 2013)
Jonathan Romain (ed) *God, Doubt and Dawkins* (Reform Judaism 2008)
John Simmons *The 100 Most Influential Scientists* (Robinson 1997)
John Taylor *Superminds* (Picador 1976)
Leslie Flint *Voices In The Dark* (The Bobbs Merrill Company, USA 1971)
Raymond Smith & Oliver Lodge *Nobody Wants to Listen – And Yet!* (Con-Psy Publications 1997)
*For Those Who Are Willing To Listen...Read On* (Con-Psy Publications 1998)
*The Truth The Whole Truth And Nothing But The Truth* (Raymond Smith 2002)

Dr John S Hislop *Seeking Divinity* (Sai Books 1998)
Howard Murphet *Sai Baba: Man of Miracles* (Samuel Weiser 1973)
Judy Warner (ed) *Inspired Medicine* (Leela Press 2000)
Charles Darwin *The Origin of Species* (1858)
Alfred Russel Wallace *Miracles and Modern Spiritualism* (1886)
Ivan Cooke (ed) *The Return of Arthur Conan Doyle* (White Eagle Trust 1963)
Aubrey Rose (ed) *Vera – The Amazing Autobiography of Vera Chesno* (Queen Anne Press 2001)
Alan E Ross *The New Testament of Spiritualism* (Ross Publications 2003)
Alan E Ross *The Genuine Jesus* (Ross Publications 1998)
Ramus Branch *Harry Edwards – The Life Story of the Great Healer* (Ramus Branch 1982)
Paul Miller *Born To Heal* (Spiritualist Press 1948)
Paul Miller *The Science, Art and Future of Spirit Healing* (The Healer Publishing Co 1975)
Ruth Grant *From Bitter Came Sweet* (Message Publications 2004)
Rosalind Cattanach *Nan Mackenzie, Healer and Medium* (Psychic Press 1982)
Stephen Turoff *Seven Steps to Eternity* (Elmore-Chard)
Joseph Millard *Edgar Cayce: Man Of Miracles* (Neville Spearman 1961)
Michael Evans *Dead Rescue: Or The Techniques Of Guiding Lost Souls* (Con-Psy Publications 2007)
Lord Dowding *God's Magic* (Spiritualist Association of Great Britain 1962)
Coral Polge with Kay Hunter *The Living Image* (Regency Press 1984)
Coral Polge with Kay Hunter *Living Images* (The Spiritualist Association of Great Britain 1985)
Irene Sowter *Tails To Tell* (Irene Sowter 1992)
Elizabeh Farrell *The Unfolding Journey* (Pelegrin Trust 1990)
Gladys Hayter *Healer* (Privately published)
Douglas and Eira Conacher *There Is Life After Death* (Howard Baker 1978)
Douglas Conacher *Chapters of Experience* (Frederick Muller 1973)
Ivy Northage *Light Of The World* (Spiritualist Association of Great Britain 1999)
Michael Bentine *The Door Marked Summer* (Granada Publishing 1981)
S Jeffery & D Underdown *An Introduction to Spiritualism* (Amherst Publishing 2006)
Maurice Leonard *The Medium: Biography of Jessie Nason* (Regency Press 1974)
Rosamond Lehmann *The Swan In The Evening* (Virago Press 1982)

Linda Williamson *Mediums and Their Work* (Robert Hale 1990)
Ursula Roberts *Letters Between Healers* (Psychic Press Ltd 1976)
Ursula Roberts *Wisdom of Ramadhan* (Pyschic Press Ltd 1985)
C G Jung *C G Jung Speaking* (Thames & Hudson 1978)
Paul Brunton *A Search In Secret India* (Rider & Co)
*Healers and The Healing Process* (Theosophical Publishing House 1977)
George Chapman *Surgeon From Another World* (WH Allen 1978)
George Chapman *Extraordinary Encounter* (The Lamp Publishing Co 1973)
Raymond A Moody (with Paul Terry) *Reunited* (Rider & Co 1993)
Raymond A Moody *Reflections on Life after Life* (Bantam Books 1977)
George. F Dole & Robert M Kirven *A Scientist Explores Spirit: A Biography of Emanuel Swedenborg* (Chrysalis Books 1997)
Arthur Findlay *The Psychic Stream* (Psychic Press 1947)
Arthur Findlay *The Way of Life* (Psychic Press 1953)
Brian L Weiss *Many Lives, Many Masters* (Piatkus 1994)
Rabbi Nathan of Nemirov *Rabbi Nachman's Wisdom* (Breslov Research Institute 1973)
Doris Stokes *Innocent Voices In My Ear* (Future Publications 1980)
Sylvia Barbanell (ed) *Silver Birch Speaks...* (Spiritualist Press 1949)
Gordon Smith *Stories From The Other Side* (Hay House 2006)
Michael Newton *Journey of Souls* (Llewellyn Publications 2007)
Wilma Davidson *Spirit Rescue* (Llewellyn Publications 2007)
Betty Shine *Mind to Mind* (Bantam Press 1989)
Paul Beard *Living On: A Study of Altering Consciousness After Death* (George Allen & Unwin 1980)
Elisabeth Kubler-Ross *On Death and Dying* (Tavistock Publications 1970)
Elisabeth Kubler-Ross *On Life after Death* (Celestial Arts 1991)
Lawrence LeShan *Clairvoyant Reality* (Tavistock Press 1974)
Frederick W H Myers *Human Personality and Its Survival of Bodily Death* (Pelegrin Books 1919)
Violet Rutter *The Teachings of the Mandarin* (Violet Rutter 1981)
White Eagle *Wisdom From White Eagle* (White Eagle Publishing Trust 1967)
G Maurice Elliott *When Prophets Spoke* (Psychic Pess Ltd 1938)
Maurice Barbanell *Keep The Rome Fires Burning* (Psychic Book Club 1946)
Maurice Barbanell *He Walks in Two Worlds* (Herbert Jenkins Ltd 1964)
Rudolph Steiner *Life Beyond Death* (Rudolph Steiner Press 1995)
Alain De Botton *Religion for Atheists* (Hamish Hamilton 2012)
Dolores Cannon *They Walked With Jesus* (Gateway Books 1994)

William Stainton Moses *Spirit Teachings* (London Spiritualist Alliance 1937)
Isaac A Ezekiel (ed) *Kabir: The Great Mystic* (Radha Soami Satsang Beas 1966)
Michael Talbot *Mysticism and the New Physics* (Routledge & Kegan Paul 1981)

## ACKNOWLEDGEMENTS

A grateful word of thanks to authors and publishers who had no objection to my quoting from books written or published by them.

# Index

Absolum, Mary 48, 49–50
Albert, Prince 24
Anne (poetess/author) 53
Archimedes 91
Arthur Findlay College 27

Bach family 73
Baird, John Logie 144
Barbanell, Maurice 27, 48, 162
Beard, Paul 27
Beethoven, Ludvig van 73
Bell, Alexander Graham 42
Bentine, Michael 165
Best, Albert 28, 72
Birkett, Lord 20–21
Blackwood, Norah 53
Blake, William 8
Bohr, Niels 16, 195
Branch, Joan 9, 31, 36
Branch, Ray (Ramus) 9, 31, 36
Britten, Emma Hardinge 112
Bronowski, Dr Jacob 16
Bruno, Giordano 14
Brunton, Paul 53–54
Buddha 62, 73, 110, 165, 194, 212

Caird, Mrs 61
Carter, John 55–56
Cavell, Edith 154
Cayce, Edgar 31, 32
Chain, Ernst 29
Chang-tzu 49
Chapman, George 32
Chesno, Vera 34–35, 36, 37, 52, 177–80 (see also Noah, Irène)
Christie, Agatha 36

Churchill, Winston 23, 146
Cicero 8
Collins, Doris 48, 53
Columbia University 25
Conacher, Douglas 24–25, 173–76, 179, 198
Conacher, Eira 24, 173, 176, 179
Conan Doyle, Sir Arthur 27, 44, 60, 61–62, 64, 75, 144, 149, 161–68, 199
Confucius 49, 73, 212
Cooke, Grace 149, 162
Copernicus 73
Crick, Francis 17, 67, 195
Crookes, Sir William 44, 69, 143, 144, 150, 151
Cummins, Geraldine 148, 149

Darwin, Charles 13, 17, 42, 67, 69, 145, 147, 198
Davy, Sir Humphry 42
Dawkins, Professor Richard 13, 66–69
Dickens, Charles 73
Disraeli, Benjamin 13
Dizengoff, Meir 177
Dow Baer, Maggid 179
Dowding, Hugh (Lord) 47, 48, 146
Dunblane tragedy 140–41
Duncan, Helen 53, 152

Eddington, Sir Arthur 12, 17
Edison, Thomas Alva 143
Edwards, Harry 31–33, 36, 40, 58, 65, 69, 166, 167, 170
Einstein, Albert 16, 67, 69, 73, 74, 91, 166, 194, 195

Elijah/Elisha (Biblical characters) 31, 166
Ellis, Jim 22, 23, 53
Euclid 73
Evans, Michael 45–47, 142, 192

Faraday, Michael 42
Farrell, Elizabeth 56–58, 72
Feynman, Richard 17, 194, 195
Findlay, Arthur 27
Finestein QC, Israel 109
Fleming, Sir Alexander 29, 73, 91
Flint, Leslie 20–26, 27, 28, 31, 40, 45, 55, 69, 154–55, 173
Frank, Doctor 155
Freud, Sigmund 73
Fricker, Ted 32, 162
Fry, Colin 146

Gaia Hypothesis 150
Galileo 14
Gandhi, Mahatma 23, 40
Gell-Mann, Murray 195
Gerson, Dr Max 56
Goering, Hermann 145–46
Goff, Martyn 76
Grant, Ruth 32, 40, 171, 179
Grenfell, Joyce 58
Grossman, Professor Louis 53
Gurdjieff, George 73

Handler, Arieh 42
Harris, Bertha 146
Hart, Billie 53
Hawking, Stephen 195
Hayter, Gladys 53, 61
Heath, Ronald 53
Heisenberg, Werner 195

Higginson, Gordon 28
Hislop, Dr John 169
Hitler, Adolf 145
Horowitz, Vladimir 34
Huldai, Ron 177
Hume, Cardinal 109, 111
Huxley, Aldous 58
Huxley, Thomas Henry 18, 147

Isaiah (Biblical prophet) 73

Jack (psychologist) 53
Jacob's Ladder 46, 166
Jeans, Sir James Hopwood 12, 195
Jefferson, Thomas 15, 73
Jenner, Edward 73
Jesus of Nazareth 31, 32, 53, 60, 62, 63–65, 69, 73, 163, 164, 166, 170, 181–84
    and Christianity 12, 24, 175, 212, 213–14, 215
    and Jewishness 109–11
John XXIII, Pope 111
Johnson, Dr Raynor 148
Jung, Carl 58, 73

Kelvin, William 147
Kemp, Charlie 56
King, Martin Luther 12

Lamming, George 76
Lang, Ron 170
Lao-tzu 49
Lehmann, Rosamond 27
Levi-Strauss, Claude 17
Lincoln, Abraham 24, 73, 142–43
Lister, Joseph 73, 147
Lloyd, Marie 22

Locke, John 15
Lodge, Raymond 43, 144
Lodge, Sir Oliver 24, 27, 42–44, 53, 69, 143–44, 150, 156–60, 182, 198, 199
Luther, Martin 193–94

McKenzie, Nan 28, 72
Malthus, Thomas 147
Mandarin 49–50
Marconi, Guglielmo 144
Margulis, Lynn 17
Marshall, Brenda 27, 57
Mason, Peggy 170
Maxwell, James Clerk 42, 195
Mehalalel, Rabbi Akavya ben 68
Mendel, Gregor 195
Mesmer, Anton 31, 158, 159
Micah (Biblical prophet) 80, 121
Michelangelo 74
Milstein, Nathan 34
Mohammed 62
Moses 62, 121
Mouat, Kit 15
Mozart, Wolfgang 73, 199
Murphet, Howard 169

Nachman, Rabbi 46, 56, 67, 74–75, 86, 89, 179
Nason, Jessie 22
Newton, Dr Michael 148
Newton, Sir Isaac 42, 67, 73, 91, 195
Nietzsche, Friedrich 67, 212, 215
Nightingale, Florence 29
Noah, Irène 34, 35–37, 52, 177–80 (see also Chesno, Vera)
Northage, Ivy 57, 73

Ortzen, Tony 112

Padgett, James E. 63, 64
Paine, Thomas 15, 16, 68, 73
Paracelsus 199
Pasteur, Louis 29, 73, 91, 198
Planck, Max 67, 195
Podmore, John 48–50, 61
Polge, Coral 52–53, 61
Pratt, Ambrose 148, 149
Pratt, George 145
Price, Avril 53
Priestley, Joseph 42
the Psalmist 73, 195
Pythagoras 73

Rembrandt 73, 74, 199
Richet, Professor Charles 31, 155
Roberts, Ursula 57
Rose, Aubrey
    experience/expertise 224–25
    healing experiences 30–31, 32, 33
    personal background 11–14, 19, 59–60, 201, 216–18
    religious experiences 202–15
    speaking experiences 36–37
    spiritual healing 19, 90–99
    writings 90–99, 100–108, 121–39
Rose, David
    contacts 21–22, 28, 45
    death 20, 59
    illness 29, 51, 162, 178, 192
    poems/writing 27, 72–86, 75–86, 87–89, 218–19
Rose, Esther (daughter) 30
Rose, Jonathan (son) 32, 45, 59

Rose, Sheila (wife)  22–23, 53, 55, 56, 59
Rosenberg, Aubrey  202, 216
Ross, Alan  63–65, 181–84
Russell, Bertrand  16

Sacks, (Lord) Jonathan  66–69
Sai Baba, Sri Sathya  39–41, 163, 164, 166, 169–72, 182, 195, 198
St Francis  73
St Teresa of Avila  110
Salk, Jonas  71
Samuels, David  64
Saunders, Dame Cicely  59, 72
Schindler, Oskar  42
Schrödinger, Erwin  195
Schweitzer, Albert  15
Semmelweis, Ignaz  29
Shakespeare, William  40, 42, 199
Sheth, Pranlal  39
Silver Birch  48, 193
Sinclair, Sir Archibald  146
Smith, Gordon  28
Smith, John  24
Smith, June  43–44
Smith, Raymond  42–44, 156–60
Socrates  14, 73
Sowter, Irene  55, 56
Spinoza  14, 73
Sri Sathya Sai Baba see Sai Baba, Sri Sathya
Stein, Edith  110
Stokes, Doris  48
Swaffer, Hannen  27, 48

Tagore, Rabindranath  40
Tel-Aviv  177
Terry, Ellen  23

Tesla, Nicola  144
Thomson, J.J.  17, 42
Tolstoy, Leo  73
Turner, Gordon  57

Valentino, Rudolph  25, 154
Victoria, Queen  24
Virène (see Chesno, Vera; Noah, Irène)
Voltaire  15

Wallace, Alfred Russel  13, 42, 55, 67, 69, 150, 151, 152, 166, 198, 200
    as scientist and spiritualist 142, 146–50
Watson, James  67, 195
Weedon, Bert  82–83
White Eagle  48, 162, 192
Wood, Wilfred  12
Wordsworth, William  7

Yitzchak, Levi  179

Zalman, Shneur  179

# Index of Organisations

Arts Centre, Barnet  72
Bhaktivedanta Manor  40
Brahma Kumaris  39
British Association for the Advancement of Science  144
Cancer Relief  72
City of London School  78
College of Psychic Studies  27, 57, 72
Exeter City Library  145, 146
Hare Krishna Centre, Letchmore Heath  55
Hospice Movement  59, 72
Imperial Cancer Research Fund  29, 72, 90
Indian-Jewish Association UK  12
Jewish Association of Spiritual Healers  36
Leslie Flint Educational Trust  25
Linnaean Society  147
London Spiritual Mission  28, 53
National Book League  76
Nehru Centre, Central London  40
New Assembly of Churches  12
Rationalist Press Association  213
Royal Albert Hall  31
Royal British Nurses' Association  29
Royal College of Veterinary Surgeons  56
Society for Psychic Research  143
South Place Ethical Society  12
Spiritualist Association of Great Britain (SAGB)  28, 52